Westcountrymen

in Prince Edward's Isle

BASIL GREENHILL AND ANN GIFFARD

INTRODUCTION BY MARVEN MOORE

D1258334

*There are never wanting some persons of violent
and undertaking natures, who, so they may have power
and business, will take it at any cost.*
— Francis Bacon

FORMAC PUBLISHING COMPANY LIMITED
HALIFAX

Formac Publishing Company Limited acknowledges the support of the Cultural Affairs Section, Nova Scotia Department of Tourism and Culture. We acknowledge the financial support of the Government of Canada through the Book Publishing Industry Development Program (BPIDP) for our publishing activities.

We acknowledge the support of the Canada Council for the Arts for our publishing program.

National Library of Canada Cataloguing in Publication

Greenhill, Basil
    Westcountrymen in Prince Edward's Isle / by Basil Greenhill and Ann Giffard ; introduction by Marven Moore.

Includes index.
ISBN 0-88780-602-3

    1. Shipbuilding—Prince Edward Island—History.
2. Shipping—Prince Edward Island—History. 3. Prince Edward Island—Commerce—Great Britain—History. 4. Great Britain—Commerce—Prince Edward Island—History. I. Giffard, Ann, 1924-
II. Title.

VM299.7.C3G74 2003   382'.09717'041   C2003-904319-3

Cover image: Green Park Shipbuilding Museum and Yeo House in Port Hill, PEI

Formac Publishing Company Limited
5502 Atlantic Street
Halifax, Nova Scotia B3H 1G4
www.formac.ca

Printed and bound in Canada

FOREWORD TO THIS EDITION

When *Westcountrymen in Prince Edward's Isle* was published in 1967 the collective memory of the shipbuilding era in Prince Edward Island was tenuous at best, relying principally upon oral tradition and passing references in a few local histories. Only a handful of publications were informative about the ships themselves, and fewer still told the story of the people and the communities involved in the industry, especially in an international context.

Such was the impact of Basil Greenhill's book that the historical research facilitated the establishment of the Green Park Shipbuilding Museum at Port Hill in 1973, on the former estate of James Yeo, Jr. The author's unwavering support for the museum continued for many years thereafter.

Like many historical works that present previously under researched subjects, it stimulated others to investigate community and family connections to the shipbuilding era. Many authors in Prince Edward Island in the 1970s drew upon *Westcountrymen* for guidance and inspiration. During the same period, the National Film Board of Canada produced *Passage West*, a film based on the events in the book. Today, the book continues to foster an understanding and appreciation of the impact that shipbuilding had on the development of Prince Edward Island.

Basil Greenhill's connections to the province actually began in the fall of 1961 when, at a reception in Ottawa, he met the Honourable J. Angus MacLean, Minister of Fisheries and Member of Parliament for the Island. What ensued between the two men was a conversation about William Yeo of Appledore, Devon, who apparently had a family tie to Port Hill. For the next five years Basil Greenhill researched the trans-Atlantic connections between the two coastal communities. In addition to the discovery of the Port Hill papers, shipping registers and oral history interviews enabled him to tell the extraordinary story of James Yeo, Sr. and his family who became central figures in the timber export and shipbuilding industry. The connection between North Devon and Port Hill lasted almost 80 years and resulted in the construction of more than 350 vessels on the Island by the Yeo family interests. Whether standing on the remains of Yeo's wharf jutting into Campbell's Creek at Port Hill or lecturing to a local audience, Basil Greenhill's enthusiasm for this story reflected his assiduous research and compelling insights.

Westcountrymen in Prince Edward's Isle remains one of the most significant books in the historiography of Prince Edward Island and of Atlantic Canada generally. The most obvious reason is its subject. The shipbuilding and ship-owning industry that emerged in the second decade of the nineteenth century elevated the economic status of many small communities. During the first 75 years of the century, shipbuilding was key to the growth of towns and villages, giving them a position of international recognition and instilling a strong sense of autonomy. Small wonder many Maritimers resisted Confederation during the halcyon days of shipbuilding in the 1860s. The dramatic economic decline in the late nineteenth century was a blow from which some experts claim the region has never recovered.

This book sheds light on key personalities who shaped the Island communities during this era. This story of the Ellis and Yeo families reveals a lot about the urge to settle on the Island and about James Yeo, Sr., whose hard driving and questionable tactics earned him the sobriquet "Robber Baron of Port Hill." It is a fascinating insight into the lives and politics of the merchant class which emerged throughout the region during the "Golden Age of Sail."

As director of the Green Park Shipbuilding Museum in the late 1970s, I had the pleasure of accompanying Basil Greenhill during his visits to Prince Edward Island. My most vivid impression was his passion for seafaring history on both local and international levels. His ability to see one in the context of the other not only explains his motivation for writing *Westcountrymen* but also defined his career. Beyond the local focus of this account, the author's influence on our understanding of seafaring history is formidable. The current flourishing state of historiography on the subject owes much to his early scholarship and sustained support. A major study of the region's shipping and seafaring history undertaken by the Maritime History Group at Memorial University of Newfoundland in the late 1970s benefitted greatly from his participation in its early conferences. He researched, published and lectured on the seafaring history of Great Britain, Japan, India, Pakistan and the Baltic region of Europe.

As director of the National Maritime Museum at Greenwich, England from 1967 to 1983, he is widely credited with transforming it into a more dynamic institution with both a national and an international stature. He was instrumental in the foundation of the International Congress of Maritime Museums, and was its first president. This organization continues to actively promote cooperation among maritime museums world-wide. In these endeavours he instilled in others the idea that maritime communities are inextricably bound together by the very nature of seafaring. This fine book is just one of Basil Greenhill's many achievements to make this point.

Marven Moore
Manager of Collections
Maritime Museum of the Atalantic, Halifax
2003

CONTENTS

LIST OF ILLUSTRATIONS

8 LIST OF ILLUSTRATIONS

page

All maps drawn by Ann Giffard

DRAWING

Drawn by Vernon Boyle from a contemporary painting.

To
THE PEOPLE OF PRINCE EDWARD ISLAND

AUTHORS' NOTE

We wished to avoid footnotes, so Appendix 1 contains the numbered key to the numerous quotations and Appendix 2 deals at length with sources. Our acknowledgments to the numerous people who helped us are there also.

Because the distinction is nowhere closely relevant to the story, in order to avoid unnecessary complication in the money figures quoted we have not differentiated between sterling and the colonial currency, which was at a discount.

Prince Edward Island itself has been our main inspiration. It was impossible for us to come into the intimate contact with The Island which the writing of this book required without forming a deep and enduring affection for the Province and its people.

BASIL GREENHILL
ANN GIFFARD

PROLOGUE

THIS is the history of events which took place in the British North American Colony of Prince Edward Island, now one of the Atlantic Provinces of Canada, and in the county of Devon in Britain, and also on the North Atlantic ocean between these two places in the half-century between 1818 and 1868. These happenings had their origins and causes in Britain and North America in the eighteenth century and their effects on both sides of the Atlantic are still apparent at the present day.

Three years after the Battle of Waterloo, people from Devon settled in Prince Edward Island. The community developed as a result of their arrival and the continuing connection with Britain which they maintained. West of England merchants were able in the nineteenth century to exert in the Colony something of the influence their forbears had once had in Newfoundland. Partly as a result of the Devon settlement a minor economic miracle took place in a century in which such miracles were common. A great shipbuilding industry developed on the beaches below the Island's forests, made possible the economic development of the Colony at a critical stage in its history and then, after a generation or so, died away. Another consequence was that over half a century some ten thousand people emigrated from North Devon and North Cornwall to settle in different parts of North America.

For the rest of the nineteenth century the settlement on the Island affected events in North Devon. So the narrative goes backwards and forwards across the unquiet ocean, like the merchant sailing ships which carried alike the cargoes of timber, which were the reason for the whole enterprise, and the men and women to whom the New World gave the chance of new life.

*   *   *

11

Prince Edward Island lies along the southern shore of the Gulf of St Lawrence (Map 1). Much the smallest of the provinces of Canada, it is only one-tenth the size of Nova Scotia, visible on clear days across Northumberland Strait, and about seven-eighths that of the county of Devon.

Air liners flying to Montreal from Europe sometimes take a course which crosses the Island near its narrowest point, where Richmond or Malpeque Bay in the west cuts it to a neck measuring three miles from sea to sea. Below the aircraft the

Map 1

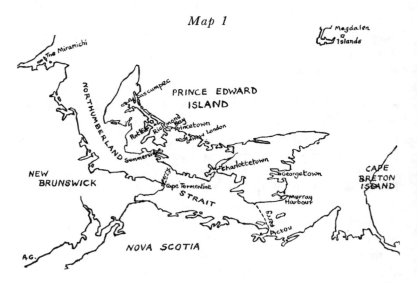

long red sandstone arc of the Island, its surface broken into thousands of small fields and woodlots, lies stretched out, a narrow wash of red all around it in the blue sea. From the air the most obvious features are the great bays and sea creeks which penetrate into the heart of the land. No part of the Island is more than ten miles from salt water.

It lies open to the sun and the sea air. The red dirt roads make the grass look greener and there is a strong tonal contrast between the grass and the dark softwoods. The sea gives to the light a peculiar clarity, and in the evenings the little white farm-houses standing on each hill, with their great wood-tiled barns, and the tall spired wooden churches become luminous, seeming to retain the light long after sunset. A few hundred wandering Micmac Indians were the Island's sole intermittent inhabitants until the beginning of the eighteenth century. When the language of their descendants was written down 200 years later it was found that their favourite name for the Island was *Abegweit*, pleasantly if liberally translated 'Cradled in the Waves'.

The pattern of small fields and sheltered inlets reflects the economy and the society of the Island. Almost half the Islanders are farming people and every spruce-lined creek has its long, narrow, white-painted lobster boats. At the beginning of the short spring season on the north shore, forty boats may lie off beaches where white banks of snow are still heaped above the red sand.

Summer visitors flow in increasing numbers by the two car-ferry routes across the Northumberland Strait and to the airports at the Island's capital, Charlottetown, and Summerside, the only other town. There is much to attract them. The sea, because of the gently-shelving sands, is warmer than any other north of Long Island Sound. A National Park covers twenty-five miles of the great sand beaches of the north shore. Charlottetown, a market town of 18,000 people, still with a little of the feeling of the frontier about it, provides the setting for a yearly summer festival.

Americans visit the Island for its rural charm and quiet. Many of them have particular reasons to make a pilgrimage; they began life there or are the children or grandchildren of Islanders. For the Province has sent its children to the great continent for 150 years, and for most of the nineteenth century it was for thousands of people a stepping stone on the long road west. The few Britons who have so far discovered the Island have found there something quite unlike any European experience; North America on their own scale. Here is the openness of the great continent, the feeling of light and air and space, the freedom on the door-step, but the distances are comprehensible, the scale of life is familiar.

So the people farm, fish and cater for visitors. There is little manufacturing industry in the Island, much as the Government would like to see it there and although considerable incentives are offered to businessmen. Like the rest of Atlantic Canada, it has been in a state of economic debility for nearly ninety years, since the world developed past the stage of using the wooden sailing ships which these lands below the Gulf of St Lawrence built so cheaply and so well.

The Islanders' way of life is dominated by the climate. The long winters are harsh, the summers Mediterranean. From January to March blizzards sweep across the Island and the creeks and all the sea around are frozen. Cattle and sheep live in the great barns. Snow drifts into banks as high as the telephone wires by the roadside. During the dreadful month of April everything is wet and red. Cars, roadside trees, houses, those who work out of doors, are caked with red mud. In May the hardwoods are still bare but the temperatures can be up in the high sixties. The colours are subtle, the grass still grey from the winter snow, the farm buildings silvery-grey wood, or painted white or yellow, the open landscape punctuated by dark green spruce under which snow still lies. Big skeins of wild geese fly across the bays. While farmers harrow and plough, pursued by the turbulent gulls, fishermen launch their great lobster boats from the high land above the creeks where they have been hauled clear of the grinding ice of winter.

In August the grass is vivid green in contrast with the red soil. Sandpipers and killdeers feed on the tide lines of the beaches, great blue herons stand like statues on the edges of the creeks and kingfishers flash over the rivers. The fields are white with potato flowers or yellowy green with ripening grain, the roadsides are bright with black-eyed Susan and golden rod, the evening breeze off the sea is welcome at the end of the long hot days. In the fall of the year it is neither too hot nor too cold. The maples turn flaming red and the birches yellow, blending with the omnipresent dark green spruce. Then, in November or early December, winter sets in again and the creeks get their first light covering of ice.

Wherever an Islander may travel he remains an Islander. He

speaks of his home as 'The Island' without explanation or qualification, and he uses the term as if less to describe a body of land surrounded by water than a state of life.

*   *   *

The Atlantic swell which dissipates its enormous energy on the north shore of Prince Edward Island beats also on the pebble ridge at Northam in Devon in Britain. Northam village straddles the crest of a peninsula between the Torridge River and the Atlantic (Map 2). A mile or two to the north of the village the

Map 2

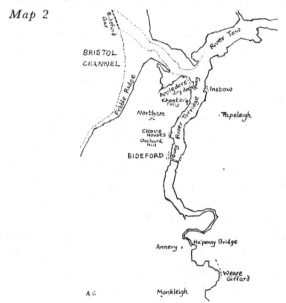

Torridge makes a right-angled turn to the west and flows out to the sea through the southern part of a great gap in the coastal range over Bideford or Appledore bar, a sandbank across the river mouth notorious for the difficulty it presents to sailing and small craft in anything but good conditions of wind and tide. Where the river Torridge turns it is joined by the Taw, a stream coming down a broad shallow valley from the east. At the meeting place of the two rivers a deep tidal pool has formed where ships can lie afloat. Over the years a community grew up here with some fine houses clustering on the northern shore of a small triangular bay which, tucked away under the hill, was completely sheltered from the open sea and the best place in the whole river for the small ships of earlier times to lie. This is the town of Appledore, technically a creek of the Port of Bideford, with old colour-washed houses, narrow streets and alleys and a broad quay along the riverside—a place of great fascination. There is a busy shipbuilding yard which, directly or indirectly, gives a living to most of the inhabitants.

From wherever it is seen, Bideford, a few miles upstream, looks what it is, a community of the right size for its position, splendidly sited. Although it has only a little over half the population of Charlottetown, it is a busy place, the market centre for a series of windswept hill-top towns and villages above the Torridge valley: Abbotsham, Littleham, Monkleigh, Great Torrington and Bradworthy.

From the first British attempts at settlement in North America, organised from the Torridge by Sir Richard Grenville in the late sixteenth century, until the American Revolution, Bideford and its neighbours had a great trade across the North Atlantic. This commerce died out in the late eighteenth century, but it revived and reached its greatest proportions in the fifty years after the Prince Edward Island venture of 1818.

Bideford and the country around share many of the problems of the Island today. The steep hillsides and narrow valleys do not lend themselves to large farms and mechanised agriculture. There is little industry. There is nothing to compare with the Island's fisheries.

So on each side of the Atlantic the two communities live on happily in slow, not obvious decline. Each owes its development in part to a great trade with the other which is now almost forgotten. Both are now quiet places in which to opt out of the strains of late twentieth-century life. The Garden of the Gulf, the Million Acre Farm, are names public relations men have dreamed up for the Island. For years North Devon has been called The Atlantic Coast Playground.

But it was not always so.

PART ONE

THE MERCHANT PRINCE
AND THE ISLAND

Who seeks the way to win renown,
Or flies with wings of high desire;
Who seeks to wear the laurel crown,
Or hath the mind that would aspire :
Tell him his native soil eschew,
Tell him go range and seek anew.

To pass the seas some think a toil,
Some think it strange abroad to roam,
Some think it grief to leave their soil,
Their parents, kinsfolk and their home;
Think so who list, I like it not,
I must abroad to try my lot.

Who list at home at cart to trudge,
And cark and care for worldly trash,
With buckled shoes let him go trudge,
Instead of lance a whip to slash :
A mind that base his kind will show :
Of carrion sweet to feed a crow.

If Jason of that mind had been,
The Grecians when they came to Troy,
Had never so the Trojans fought,
Nor never put them to such annoy :
Wherefore who list to live at home,
To purchase fame I will go roam.

Sir Richard Grenville (died 1550)

CHAPTER ONE

THE MERCHANT PRINCE

ON the last day of October 1812, the *Four Friends*, William Ramsay, Master, was entered at Bideford Custom House with a cargo of lumber from Prince Edward Island and established the first direct contact which has so far been traced between the Island and North Devon. The *Four Friends* was Danish-built, a prize of war. She belonged to her master, who had an Island name. The Ramsays were already an old family in terms of the colony's history of British settlement. Their little farms were at its western end on the shores of Richmond Bay. This cargo of timber was probably consigned to Thomas Burnard, a merchant of Northam and Bideford in whom imaginative enterprise, business acumen and accumulated wealth were combined with a gentle character, so that he fully deserved the title of merchant prince. With his rise there was to come a great change in the life of Bideford from the days at the end of the eighteenth century when, because of the American Revolution and the effects of the long wars with France and Spain, the port's traditional trade with North America had almost ceased.

Thomas Burnard was born in 1769, the son of a small merchant and brewer who, when the registration of all ships at the local custom houses became compulsory in Britain in 1786, was entered as the owner of some shares in one little vessel. By 1792 Burnard senior was prosperous enough to be made a freeman of Bideford, and at about the same time Thomas was married to Martha Elizabeth English, a strong-minded and lively woman of about his own age.

In the 1790s the name of Thomas Burnard begins to figure prominently in contemporary shipping records. Two vessels in which he had shares were trading with Lisbon and Cadiz and by the time he first became Mayor of Bideford in 1806 he had financial interest in twenty-five ships. Most of them were small coasters. But the *Venus*, which he owned in partnership with her master, James Lowther of Clovelly, was bigger. So also was the *Nautilus*. She was already in the North American trade but she sailed the Atlantic from London, never from her home port of Bideford.

When war with the United States broke out in 1812 the *Nautilus* was taken over by the Government for use as a transport and put under the command of one Lewis Grossard. Thomas Burnard was serving his second term as Mayor of Bideford and had started a timber yard on Bideford Quay. His eldest son, also Thomas, who had been born in 1793, was to be elected an alderman of Bideford for life as soon as he became twenty-one. Two other sons, Nathaniel Edward and William Henry English, were born in 1802 and 1803, and there were daughters. The rise of the family's fortunes shows itself in a characteristically British way. The two younger sons were sent to the Devonshire boarding school of Blundells, but Thomas, born before the family could aspire to this kind of education, is not recorded as having been a pupil there. The family lived on Orchard Hill, a south-facing slope in the parish of Northam, looking down across a creek to the houses of Bideford.

At the eastern end of Orchard Hill, where it slopes steeply down into the Torridge, there stood a few isolated cottages called Upper Cleave Houses; among them was Richard Chapman's shipyard. Richard was born in 1761, the son of Emanuel Chapman, also a shipbuilder. Emanuel died when his son was in his late teens, but the boy took firm charge of his father's business and became the most important shipbuilder in North Devon. He built very well. One of his ships, the *Newton*, sailed for ninety years.

The sheltered triangular bay at Appledore dried out at low tide and there was a cart road across the sands among the mooring posts to which the ships tied up. It ran on around the north shore of the bay out on to the river shore and downstream under the back gardens of the houses of Market Street and across the sands to the hamlet of Irsha, West Appledore, a cluster of poor cottages, built on the rock of the low cliffs above the river, whose owners might hope to avoid paying rent.

In the middle of the eighteenth century Thomas Benson, a great Northam merchant in the American trade, had built a new quay, a wide stone wharf 200 feet long, down the south side of the bay at Appledore, and houses had crept up the hillside above it. At the head of the bay was a little row of four small houses occupied 'rent free by poor persons placed therein by the overseers of the Parish'.[1] On the north side of the bay, behind the cobbled top of the foreshore, stood Docton House, a mansion built on the site of a religious foundation. Docton House was standing there when Sir Richard Grenville sought to settle North Carolina at the end of the sixteenth century. It must be the only feature of the scene then which remains today.

Appledore society was almost literally in three separate layers. The merchants and the gentry lived on the hill high above the little bay. The prosperous shipmasters' and small ship owners' houses led down the hillside. Lower down, in the warren of small houses, of alley-ways, called 'drangs', and of courts above the beach and above Benson's New Quay and in Irsha, lived the seamen and boatmen, the shipwrights and sawyers and the hired men of the shipbuilders. These parts of the little town were lawless, rough and poor.

Among the prosperous shipmasters lived John Williams and his wife Elizabeth. John had made his small fortune with a brig which was named the *Clevland*, the family name of the local squire. Their son, Joshua, became master of the *Clevland* in his turn. When she was lost in 1810 after adventures with French privateers in the English Channel he entered Thomas Burnard's employment and became master of one of his brigs and eventually one of the great British shipmasters of his age.

Above the local residents of Appledore, Northam and Bideford, above even Thomas Burnard himself in social esteem and authority, were the landed gentry in their great country houses. These too had their hierarchy, though they were intermarried into a complex of relationships. There were the old families, great in the sense that their lands were extensive, their rent-rolls long, and that they had, over the centuries, given many leading figures to British life. Among these were the Chichesters centred on Arlington near Barnstaple, (who were descended partly from the Giffards), the Fortescues of Filleigh and the Rolles of Sevenstone, a few miles up the Torridge from Weare Giffard. There were the descendants of the successful merchants and men of affairs of the seventeenth and eighteenth centuries, now moulded into the squirearchy; the Bucks of Daddon, the Saltren Willetts of Petticombe, the great house of the hill-top village of Monkleigh, and the Clevlands of Tapeleigh, a splendidly situated house looking west across the estuary to Appledore and Northam. There were the new squires, merchants in their own life-time, now established on old estates, like William Tardrew of Annery in the hills above the Torridge between Monkleigh and Weare Giffard.

Sir Richard Grenville's place as Lord of the Manor of Bideford was occupied in the early nineteenth century by John Clevland of Tapeleigh, who was also Lord of the Manors of Northam and of Saunton on the other side of the river Taw. He was the son of John Clevland who had been a successful Secretary of the Admiralty during the wars which had helped towards the temporary ruin of Bideford's international trade, but his line ended with him and his heir was his great-nephew, Augustus Saltren Willett, who came of a branch of that family which had built itself a discreetly proportioned small mansion on the top of a hill in Northam. This house, looking down over Bideford and over mile upon mile of the Torridge valley, was and still is called Port Hill.

In 1810 one Moses Chanter moved into Staddon, a handsome Georgian house standing above Appledore, which Richard Chapman the shipbuilder had just left. Chanter was a prosperous cloth merchant, born at Chulmleigh, twenty miles inland, in 1772. For two centuries Chulmleigh had been a rich little town, but with the shifting of the wool trade to the north of England it had gone into a slow decline. By 1797 Chanter had moved to

Great Torrington, the hill-top town above the Torridge valley. He had married Elizabeth Burnard, a sister of Thomas, by whom he had two children, a daughter Elizabeth and a son whom he tactfully christened Thomas Burnard. Thomas grew up, probably with a tutor, among the talk of the merchants and bankers and shipmasters of Bideford, where the family moved in 1805, and then at Staddon.

In his teens at Appledore, Thomas Burnard Chanter was in a special position. No ship could go up to Bideford without its being seen from Staddon. What was then the main road into Appledore passes the gates. The house conferred status upon its occupants, even though they did not own it, and Moses Chanter, a merchant who had already been Mayor of Bideford, was now a large shipowner in his own right. Tommy Chanter was in a position to learn the practical details of ships and seafaring, as well as of a merchant's business, at many points. He could learn in his uncle's parlour and from the lawless lads around the boats on the Appledore river strand. He could mingle with children who were to be the seamen of the next generation, with those of more prosperous parents who were destined to be shipmasters, and with merchants' sons and the sons of the gentlemen in the big houses.

His uncle Thomas Burnard had a special problem which was a tiny fragment of a great problem facing Britain. All except one of the few foreign cargoes which came into Bideford in the ten years after Trafalgar were cargoes of lumber from ports on the Baltic Sea. There were three timber-laden ships in 1805, three in 1806, one in July 1807. Then the timber ships suddenly stopped coming and there were no foreign entries or clearances at Bideford for two years. Thomas Burnard's timber business was in a difficult position.

Napoleon had declared a blockade against Britain in the Berlin Decree of November 1806, closing the ports of his empire and its dependencies to the ships of Britain and declaring British goods liable to seizure. A consequence of the Treaty of Tilsit of July 1807 was that Russia, Prussia and Denmark joined the blockade. Although the British Navy controlled the Baltic Sea,

Napoleon controlled the ports of all the Baltic timber-supplying countries except Sweden. The effects of this situation can be likened to the cutting off of the supplies of steel in a mid-twentieth century war. Timber was vital to the conduct of the naval war and almost equally important for the construction of the merchant ships upon which commerce depended. On the banks of the Torridge alone, one hundred and seven merchant ships and seven warships had been built between 1800 and 1808, far more than in any other eight years in the shipbuilding history of the river. To be deprived of Baltic timber meant that Britain faced the eventual loss of the war.

The price of a load—that is, an arbitrary unit of 50 cubic feet, the equivalent of 600 American board feet—of Memel fir timber in England rocketed up from 15s in 1806 to £16 in 1809. Freight rates from the port of Riga were normally about 7s 4d a load. In 1808 and 1810 a London merchant could not get offers of ships at 42s a load. In 1806 Russia sent 297 loads of timber into Britain, Prussia almost 6,000, Norway 1,400. The corresponding figures in 1808 were 19, 27, and 69. The local effect on the Torridge was equally clear and dramatic. Richard Chapman's stocks of timber enabled him to complete six ships in 1808. Next year he built only one, a fifty-foot vessel with one mast, rigged as a sloop, the *Peter & Sarah*.

The answer to this desperate problem lay 3,000 miles away, in the thick mantle of trees under which most of the north-eastern part of North America lay; trees which as far as those parts of the continent still in British possession were concerned, Upper and Lower Canada, Nova Scotia, New Brunswick and Prince Edward Island, were (except in the St Lawrence Valley), largely uncut, the land underneath them largely uninhabited. There had been the beginnings of exploitation. A timber trade had been established in New Brunswick but it had declined. An American, Philemon Wright, had begun to raft timber down the Ottawa River in 1800. A London finance house which was granted a monopoly of the naval trade had, after 1804, established a considerable base for handling timber at Quebec.

After 1807 the finance houses were able to dictate their own terms. To develop a St Lawrence timber trade on the same scale as the Baltic trade had been would require enormous investment. Freight rates across the Atlantic were roughly three times those to Britain from the Baltic. Once the crisis was over the trade would revert and the capital invested would be lost. Therefore, before they would invest, the bankers and merchants required guarantees that the trade would continue, and over several years up to 1813 they succeeded in obtaining the imposition of almost prohibitive duties on Baltic timber imported into Britain, duties which amounted at first to several times the cost of the wood at the loading port. These duties remained in full force until they were slightly reduced in 1821. Then they continued unchanged until 1842, when they were considerably lessened. Progressive reductions, made against opposition from the timber lobbies, took place in 1845, 1846 and 1851, but it was not until 1860 that the duties were totally abolished. It was these timber duties, stemming from wartime crisis, that made possible the development of the Canadian and to some extent the American lumber industries in the nineteenth century. They were of great importance in the opening up and settlement of Canada. Indirectly they played a part in the peopling of the United States.

The effect of the duties, like that of the embargo, was dramatic. Between 1809 and 1811 imports into Britain of oak timber and plank from British North America went up from 6,000 loads to 24,500. Softwood imports went up 1,000 per cent to over 150,000 loads in five years. Oak came from the Ottawa valley, from Vermont and New York State, and it flowed out through Quebec and the St Lawrence. So did some softwood, but anything up to eight or nine times as much came from New Brunswick and a substantial amount from Nova Scotia. Much New Brunswick lumber went out through St Andrews on Passamaquoddy Bay in sight of Northern Maine across the estuary, and through St John on the Bay of Fundy, but it was increasingly cut in Northumberland County, around the area of the present towns of Newcastle and Chatham, and was shipped out through the great sea creek called the Miramichi. Between 1806 and 1807 imports of New Brunswick softwoods into Britain doubled. By 1815 they had multiplied by six and a half times the 1807 figure. British ships lay at the loading places in scores and the roaring lumber camps of the Miramichi were beginning to boom.

Thomas Burnard dealt in softwoods. In June 1812 the ship *Hellen* arrived from St Andrews with lumber, the first American cargo to have come into Bideford for many years. September brought another cargo, and then a month later Captain Ramsay in his *Four Friends* arrived from Prince Edward Island.

Though there is no evidence that any of his own ships went to Prince Edward Island before 1818, Thomas Burnard soon had other ways of knowing about the Colony besides what he learned from Captain Ramsay. Sir Charles William Chalmers, Commander, Royal Navy, retired after the Napoleonic Wars to live in a house near Staddon in Appledore. In 1802 his father had been appointed a member of the Lieutenant-Governor's Council of Prince Edward Island, and within a year a controversy had arisen over the use for the private purposes of Sir Robert and his son Charles of the site of the battery at Charlottetown. So Sir Charles knew his Island and its officials and its politics at first hand and what he knew he was no doubt ready to pass on to Thomas Burnard.

In 1813 Richard Chapman built a new ship for Burnard. She was called the *Bellona*. As soon as she was ready she was armed with ten guns and sent off to Bermuda in an escorted convoy carrying troops and supplies for the war with the United States which had started the year before. Her master was the Joshua Williams who had commanded the *Clevland*. The Burnard timber business was busy. In the late summer of 1816 he sent the *Bellona* (now released from transport service) across to the Miramichi and thus Bideford resumed her historic North American trade. To shipmasters and merchants in the Miramichi trade information about what was going on in the Island was readily available, for it was the best market for the potatoes and oats of the west end of the Island which came over in schooners and were paid for with the finished goods the timber ships brought out. Joshua Williams must have gathered a lot of information for Thomas Burnard about the Island's timber resources.

In December 1817 a new Prince Edward Island built schooner, the *Despatch*, bound for Liverpool put into Appledore in distress. Her master's name was Richard Moys. The son of a Dover carpenter, born in 1792, he knew the Island well. Thomas Burnard employed him, and from him also must have heard much about conditions in the Colony.

CHAPTER TWO

THE ISLAND

BEFORE the crisis brought about by the Treaty of Tilsit Prince Edward Island had exported almost no timber to Britain. In 1807 it sent across the Atlantic just over 1,000 loads of softwood. In 1809 this increased to 10,000. John Hill, one of the two or three merchants doing business on a large scale in Prince Edward Island in the second decade of the nineteenth century was quite frank when he gave evidence before a Select Committee of the House of Lords in London in 1820. When asked 'Was not the timber trade with Prince Edward's Island created by the high duties on the Baltic timber?' he replied 'It first originated there'. The questions and John Hill's answers went on :

> Can you state the present situation of that country with respect to its agriculture and population?—The agriculture of that country is daily increasing; the population during the last seven years, I think, has nearly quadrupled, at least it has tripled.
>
> Is the timber trade carried on there to a considerable extent? —According to the size of the colony, to a considerable extent; it is the principal trade, almost the only trade upon which returns can be made; I think four-fifths of the returns are made in timber.
>
> Are the population of that colony principally employed in felling and preparing that timber for market, and bringing it down to the shipping?—The population, during the winter time, are almost wholly employed in cutting and squaring timber.
>
> Are not all agricultural operations suspended during that season?—Most assuredly; the severity of the weather is such that very little can be done in agriculture. . . .
>
> Are the exports of timber the principal means the inhabitants of Prince Edward's Island have of paying for their imports of

British manufactures?—Certainly; the import of British manufactures : these I take to be from forty to forty-five thousand
pounds annually; four-fifths of which have to be paid for in
timber, and at present they have no other means of paying
for it.

If the timber trade should be discouraged, what resource will
the population of that colony have?—In the present infant state
of the colony they have no other; if it were not for the
timber, I could not support the settlers I have upon my lands;
I have placed forty families upon my lands : those families
all require sustenance for at least two years; before they can
produce sufficient to live upon from the cultivation of their
lands. They have first to cut the trees down, clear the woods,
and afterwards to bring the land into cultivation, build a
house, and they must be supported by a proprietor or merchant,
and the timber is the only thing they can depend upon.

Is there not a considerable cultivation of grain in Prince
Edward's Island?—Very little more than supports the
inhabitants. . . .

Did you enter upon this line of business depending upon
the protection of the British Government?—I most assuredly
did; I sent out emigrants at a considerable expense; I have
eighty thousand acres of land there; I have already established
forty families; the only return for this I can receive at present
is in timber, and they can no longer have supplies from me if
the timber trade is destroyed.[1]

John Hill knew his Island better than most. Though a frequent
subject of mention in Colonial records, his career remains obscure
and he may have sought deliberately to make it so. According to
his own account he established a prosperous fishing business at
Cascumpec in the northern tip of the Island in the 1780s but
it was wrecked by the plottings of Island officials and of a rival
merchant, John Cambridge. John Hill withdrew, but he retained
ownership of many thousands of acres and years later, when the
timber trade began to boom, he returned and established a
prosperous business. Once again he became deeply immersed in
Island politics. His name is perpetuated in the Hill River, west
of the modern town of Alberton.

Basque fishermen used its creeks as a base in the seventeenth
century but it was not until 1720, after the French settlers had

been driven out of their lands around the head of the Bay of Fundy by the British, that Europeans made an attempt at permanent settlement of what French explorers had named the Ile de St Jean. It was the first permanent settlement, for the wandering groups of Micmac Indians who camped on what is now called Lennox Island in Richmond Bay never stayed there for any length of time.

The early French Islanders scraped a bare living from fishing, hunting, the tending of a few domestic animals and by growing wheat and peas on patches of land laboriously cleared of trees or on the bayside 'meadows' of forest-free land where the grass grew tall and lush. Some of them settled on the shores of the great Richmond Bay. On the tip of Low or Gillis Point there are still today traces of dykes which may be the last remote traces of these true pioneers of two centuries ago, squeezed between the sea and the wilderness and, from contemporary accounts, almost always on the verge of starvation.

In 1758 the ebb and flow of the wars between Britain and France arbitrarily gave the Island to the British. They straightway proceeded to ship all the settlers back to France. Many escaped deportation by moving to the north west of the Island and then across to the Miramichi and on to Quebec. When the evacuation was finished a few pockets, variously estimated at between two and three hundred people, were left behind. These were the stock from which has grown the French-speaking minority in Prince Edward Island today.

The British Government arranged a systematic survey of a large part of its possessions in North America. Captain Samuel Holland, a British Army officer who had helped to train James Cook in survey work, was in charge of the operation. Because of the apparent value of the fisheries, he was directed to survey the Island, now renamed the Island of St John, first, and he did so in 1764 and 1765. The results of his work, because of political decisions taken by the British Government, had such an influence on the history of the Island that they must be described in some detail.

Holland's survey parties worked on the magnetic north, which in 1764 was approximately fifteen degrees thirty minutes west. With this as his baseline he divided the Island into three counties, which he named from east to west, King's, Queen's and Prince, fifteen parishes, and sixty-six 'lots' or 'townships' which he thought were of about twenty thousand acres each, one lot of about a third that size, and three town sites with attached small pasture and garden lots for the townsfolk. He numbered the lots from one in the extreme north-west to the sixties in the extreme south-east and he named the main geographical features on them.

True to the custom of his age, he sought in these names to perpetuate those who might be in a position to help him. Thus he scattered the map with the names of the families and connections of the Lords Commissioners of Trade and Plantations and of distinguished officers of the British Army and members of the nobility who had already advanced his career and might do so again. Richmond Bay itself and Lennox Island he named after Charles Lennox, third Duke of Richmond, and Goodwood River, flowing into the Bay, after the Duke's house, Goodwood, near Chichester. The great creek off Richmond Bay he called the Ellis River after the then Secretary of State for War. Conway Inlet he named after Henry Seymour-Conway, son of the first Lord Conway and a Secretary of State in 1765. The Indians had called it Chochekchidoocheech.

Most of Holland's names have stuck, but in a few cases the French or French renderings of Indian names have crept back into use over the years. The Ellis River is now almost always called the Grand River. Holland Harbour, which he named after himself, has been called Cascumpec again for over a century. Princetown has reverted to Malpeque, and in recent years some maps have used the name Malpeque for Richmond Bay itself.

The divisions of Holland's counties, parishes and lots were all straight lines running either along the magnetic north and south or at right angles to it. As in time property was divided up and roads built, the boundaries and highways tended to follow the boundaries of the lots or to run parallel to them. So today the map is still covered with a sloping grid which is deeply impressed upon the life of the Island.

Holland reported in terms favourable to a fishery on the Gulf shore, which he thought should be conducted from a town to be called Princetown on the north-east corner of Richmond Bay. But he realised that most of the settlers would have all their time occupied in cultivating their lands and would have little time to fish. He was right. It is only since the coming of the long, lean, powered lobster boats and of trucks and aeroplanes to take the catch quickly away to well organised continental markets that the fishery has been profitable to the Islanders themselves. So, as there seemed little prospect of immediate revenue from it, the British Government decided that the Island should not be a drain on the Treasury. The long wars with France which had had such a disastrous effect on Bideford's international commerce were over, and the American Revolution had not begun. Britain was full of men seeking grants of land in any part of the Empire. The Government decided to attempt to meet some of these petitions and solve the problem of the Island of St John at the same time. All applicants who had asked for land in the Island were therefore summoned to appear before the Lords Commissioners of Trade and Plantations in 1767. Those with good claims (and the criteria would of course include family and other connections) were selected by ballot, to a total of sixty-six military and naval officers, merchants and supporters of the Government.

Thus in the course of an hour or so the Island was saddled with a social and economic situation which was to be the bane of its people for 108 years and was to set the pattern of their life and determine to a large extent their social, economic and political history. Seventy-one years later, when the evil effects of that hour had still much of their harm to do, Lord Durham, reporting on the affairs of British North America generally, wrote to Lord Glenelg from Quebec on 8 October 1838:

> . . . you desire that I will express to you my judgment on the whole subject of escheat in the Island of Prince Edward. . . . The information before me now is so ample that upon no

Bideford from East-the-Water in the late eighteenth century. Orchard Hill where Thomas Burnard and later Thomas Chanter lived is the slope beyond the creek on the extreme righthand side of the picture. Sloops, brigs and schooners are lying at the Quay. Tapleigh and Port Hill are shown in the centre and righthand vignettes respectively

Appledore from Instow, painted by G. Shepherd, 1819. Staddon stands alone on the hillside in the centre of the picture. The houses of East Appledore clustered round the sheltered triangular bay to the left and the hamlet of Irsha to the right are distinct settlements with St Mary's Chapel in between

This engraving made by G. Townsend in 1856 shows Appledore across the water from Instow. Chanter's new (broad gauge) railway to Bideford is in the foreground, his signal tower stands bold on the hill-top opposite. On the crest of the saddle in the hills the brand-new Richmond House is bare of surrounding trees

matter of facts can I entertain a doubt. Nearly the whole Island was alienated by the Crown in one day, in very large grants, chiefly to absentees, and upon conditions of settlement which have been wholly disregarded. The extreme improvidence, I might say the reckless profusion, which dictated these grants is obvious; the total neglect of the Government as to enforcing the conditions of the grants is not less so. The great bulk of the Island is still possessed by absentees, who hold it as a sort of reversionary interest, which requires no present attention, but may become valuable some day or other through the growing wants of the inhabitants. But in the meantime, the inhabitants of the Island are subjected to the greatest inconvenience, nay, to the most serious injury, from the state of property in land. The absent Proprietors neither improve the land, nor will let others improve it. They retain the land, and keep it in a state of wilderness. Your lordship can scarcely conceive the degree of injury inflicted on a new settlement, by being hemmed in by wilderness land, which has been placed out of the control of Government, and is entirely neglected by its absent Proprietors. . . . Some influence—it cannot be that of equity or reason—has steadily counteracted the measures of the colonial Legislature. I cannot imagine that it is any other influence than that of the absentee Proprietors, resident in England. . . .[2]

In return for their lots the sixty or so individuals and syndicates were to undertake to do three things.

They were to pay rent at what now seems derisory rates, 2s, 4s or 6s per hundred acres, depending on the quality of the land. Thus, since the lots were assessed as wholes, partly on the basis of Captain Holland's report of the nature of the land in different parts of the Island, the maximum annual rent payable for a lot was £60 and the minimum £20. Very few lots were originally assessed at £20, most of the Island being about equally divided between the two higher rents. Sixty pounds was, of course, a reasonable annual income in 1767 and for a long time afterwards, and experience was to show that it was far more than the proprietors could hope to make from virgin land needing heavy investment, land which could be reached only by water or on foot, covered with snow and invisible for a third of each year, and nearly 3,000 miles from its owner's base. In consequence

B

the history of Prince Edward Island under what became known as the proprietorship system is a history of unpaid rents. Secondly, the new proprietors were required to settle their lands within ten years with a hundred people on each lot and a third of each lot was to be settled in the first four years. Thirdly, they were to undertake that the settlers would be Protestants from outside the British Empire, though those who had already been in North America for two years or more were made an exception to this rule.

Twelve years later forty-nine of the lots still had not a single settler on them. At the end of the century, when the Colonial Government appointed a committee to go into the question, they found twenty-three lots still totally uninhabited; twelve more lots had an estimated population of only two hundred and sixteen persons between them, six others were reasonably well settled and the remaining twenty-five 'settled agreeably to the terms of the grants'. In fact, in direct contradiction to the terms of the grants, the great majority of the settlers had come from Britain, where they had been born, and many of them were Roman Catholics.

For the first few years of its life under British rule the Island of St John was governed, so far as it was governed at all, as part of Nova Scotia. Then in 1769, on the petition of the proprietors, a separate British colonial administration was established for the 271 Islanders, over 200 of whom were of French origin. All the trappings were set up; Governor, Lieutenant Governor, Council and Supreme Court, Chief Justice, Colonial Secretary, Attorney General, Provost Marshal and Receiver of Rents. There was to be an Assembly as soon as there was anyone to assemble. All this was expected to cost just under £1,500 a year and for the first ten years this was to come from the rents which were to be ploughed back by the Crown as a long-term investment. Afterwards the Island was expected to be developed enough to support its own administration from taxes, and the rents were to go to the British Government.

The first Governor, Walter Patterson, had to arrange to build his own log cabin on arrival in what was to become the capital,

Charlottetown. He received no salary for more than five years. There was no means of enforcing the payment of rents on the proprietors and so they did not pay.

No sooner had a sort of Government been established than it collapsed. For ten years, from 1775 to 1785, because of the absences from the Island of senior officials, the squabbles amongst them when they were there, and the effects of the American Revolution, the Government virtually did not exist. When it was effectively reconstituted, the Governor and the Lieutenant Governor became one, and subordinate to Quebec, though throughout the history of the Colony the successive Lieutenant Governors continued to report to London and the Governor in Chief of British North America came little into the Island's affairs.

Until at least 1850 the Colony's Government presented a confused picture of squabbles between its members and with London. Nepotism, corruption and profiteering from official positions ruled within a system of family compact. There was a continuous conflict between the Assembly, the Lieutenant Governors, and the Colonial Office; this eventually became one between proprietors and settlers and continued until the proprietorial system ceased in 1875.

Nevertheless settlers came and the population slowly grew. Some of the original proprietors rapidly disposed of their property for what they could get, and the history of the ownership of many of the lots soon became obscure. This obscurity became in the next century a big factor in the economic and political life of the Island. It helped the rise of the shipbuilders and lumber barons, who throve on doubts as to the ownership of the timber they took, and was the bane of the lives of the illiterate settlers who were obliged to pay tribute to any who could bully them in the name of a doubtful title and an even more doubtful right to act for its owner.

Some proprietors, both original and new, did bring out settlers in quite considerable numbers. Others arrived on their own. It has been estimated that about 900 came in between 1770 and 1785. Some dispossessed loyalists drifted to the Island during and after the American Revolution. Disbanded troops came after the Revolution and English and Scots settlers had brought the population up to nearly 4,500 when a census was taken in 1798. In the early nineteenth century the pace accelerated and by 1825 there were probably about 15,000 people.

In 1812, when the *Four Friends* brought her cargo of lumber into Bideford, Prince Edward Island, as it had been renamed after Queen Victoria's father, had only one truly nucleated settlement, its capital, Charlottetown. The town site had been laid out in 1768 with the main streets, running on Holland's magnetic north and south, one hundred feet wide, the lesser streets forty feet wide at right-angles to them. The original plan of the town is still very obvious today. Wharves had been built out over the river into the deep water channel. The town was tiny, with not more than a hundred widely-separated houses built straight out of the rough grass, where pigs and cows belonging to the townsmen grazed and rooted on lots destined one day to hold the buildings of a busy city.

Travelling from the capital to other parts of the Colony was preferably done by water and the vast ramifications of the creeks meant that in fact almost all the settled areas could be reached in small schooners and boats. There were two rough tracks cleared through the woods, one to the site of Captain Holland's Princetown on Richmond Bay, the other to a site he had proposed called Georgetown in the far east of the Island. Both were areas of settlement, but neither had or ever did remotely succeed as towns. Land travel was easiest in the winter by snowshoe or sled, impossible in the spring or in heavy rains.

Most of the inhabitants in 1812 lived, on a bare subsistence level, in crude log huts within a few dozen yards of the edge of a creek. Every winter they worried over the supplies of food to get them through the months of snow. Between January and March lumber was cut and hauled over the frozen ground and shipped in June and onwards through the summer. Though he might have an agreement with his proprietor (or more likely his proprietor's agent in the Island) which was probably oral, or even tacit, by which he was considered the tenant of a hundred

acres or so, the settler was unlikely to have cleared from high
timber more than the bare minimum he needed to live on, plus
whatever area had been roughly cleared in the process of cutting
timber for sale.

On this little patch between creek and woods he grew spring
wheat, barley, potatoes, peas and some hay for his few scrub
cattle, his sheep and the pair of small draught oxen he might
own if he was lucky. Pigs ran nearly wild in the woods. The
more prosperous settler might have a horse for riding; this was
a symbol of some status. Some settlers on the north coast fished,
salted fish being one of the settlers' winter staples, but this was
mainly a traditional occupation of the expanding French population. Other people with larger markets on their doorsteps and
better organised finance exploited the Island's fishery, and already
in these early years of the nineteenth century the north shore
settler might see glinting white against the blue of the gulf the
sails of the fleet of New England schooners, pinkies and Chebacco
boats, from Cape Ann and Newburyport, Marblehead and down
Maine, already over 600 of them, their crews fishing from the
short decks and open wells.

The forests, which were just beginning to be exploited on a
large scale, were at once the settlers' enemy and almost his
only potential source of wealth. Prince Edward Island was an
outcrop in the sea of the great forest which filled New Brunswick
(as it still fills much of that Province) and rolled away to the
Mississippi in the south, west up the St Lawrence valley and far
beyond, and north to the tree line where the snows last nine
months of the year. The settlers had to come to terms with the
forest.

The settler lived in isolation, rarely moving away from his own
farm, rarely seeing other than his immediate neighbours. His
social and recreational life was simple. He probably could neither
read nor write. When he was neither working nor eating there
was little to do except sleep. For the outside world he had both
the hospitality and the guarded insularity of the very poor. Drink,
unless he came from a social group whose customs expressly
guarded him against this menace was, when he could get it,

something which could, and all too often did, lead to utter disaster. For, apart from its effects, drink was imported. There was hardly any money in circulation, which meant that, like all other imported goods, alcohol was bought on credit at marked-up rates.

The settler was dependent on the importing merchant for everything he could not make himself and could not do without. Nails, shoeleather, rope, cloth, pots and pans, needles, thread, buttons, tools, sugar, knives, powder and shot, oil, soap, salt, bar-iron, string, fishing gear, the essential iron stove, all these things had to come from overseas. There was money in this for the merchant who created his own market by bringing in settlers, starting them up on lines of credit and taking in return a mortgage of their future agricultural surplus. But the land was not kind at first. It was too much of a wilderness for any but the best and most enterprising and physically the strongest to make an early success of it. The techniques of handling it were not properly understood. Life had to be rearranged around the winters. There was not enough capital available. People's hearts were broken. But there was no way of leaving. They were already in debt to the merchants and for many it had been even worse at home.

The merchants and the developers were in as bad a fix. They invested and got in return only a doubtful line on doubtful exportable surpluses. Not until the duties gave an assured market for timber in Britain did the economy come in sight of a take-off point, and even then for the individual merchant success required certain very special circumstances. And often the early merchants had to compete not only with the economic facts of life but with the inefficient and venal administration.

One of the first of these merchants was Robert Clark, a Londoner. He was a Quaker who had begun life as a Methodist and in his case commerce and a conception of an ideal society were mixed. Walter Patterson, the colony's first Governor, recorded that Clark told him that a vision was the occasion of his coming to the Island. In association with a partner, Robert Campbell, he bought Lot 21 and in 1774 settled more than a hundred people on the shores of the next system of creeks east of the entrance to Richmond Bay in an area they named New London. Clark set up a lumbering establishment and a water-powered sawmill, but even if there had been an economic market for North American timber in Britain at that time the investment needed to establish the business would have been beyond his resources.

Clark's adventure had an important long-term effect. One of his employees was a Bristol Quaker, John Cambridge, who stayed on after Clark's failure and eventually acquired among other property (including Lot 14 which he was said to have bought for a cask of wine) Lots 63 and 64 which surround the great creeks of Murray Harbour. References to John and his sons, Lemuel and Artemas, are scattered through the documentation of the colony in the late eighteenth century and the first half of the nineteenth. They were a highly litigious family and the complexities of John Cambridge's quarrels with his associates, his involvements with politics, his difficulties with local officials and the pattern of charge and countercharge each made against the other provide a vivid picture of the problems which faced those who sought to exploit the Island's resources. Though their scale of operation was small in comparison with what was to follow, the Cambridges were Prince Edward Island's first great merchants. They brought many settlers to Murray Harbour and they established for themselves the reputation of liberal and far-sighted landlords—a reputation which was reflected in a sprinkling of little Artemases and Lemuels among the sons of settlers, so that these uncommon names occur with improbable frequency in Island history.

The Cambridges were among the earliest to exploit the possibilities of the timber trade. They established saw-mills at Murray River and from 1811 onwards they financed the building of a series of at least twenty large ships which took timber cargoes to Bristol and brought back goods and settlers. They set an example which was to be followed by others in that they kept a close personal grip on their business affairs on both sides of the Atlantic. In later years John Cambridge and Artemas operated at their timber yard at the Sea-Banks in Bristol while Lemuel managed affairs at Murray Harbour and in Charlottetown, where the Cambridges kept the first real store.

*   *   *

When Captain Holland made his survey and division of the Island it came about that Lots 12, 13 and 14 fronted the whole of the north-western shore of Richmond Bay. Travelling from south to north, Lot 14 fronts Richmond Bay and lies along the north shore of the Grand River. Lot 13 alone stretches across the Island to have a west coast. Its east coast comprises, still travelling from south to north, first three great creeks reaching into the countryside from a common mouth (which Holland named Village Cove) in the low wooded shores of Richmond Bay. These creeks have for many years been called, in order, Mill Creek or Schooner Creek, Brown's Creek and Crooked Creek. Then, still travelling north, comes the headland of Low Point, sometimes called Gillis Point, and beyond it the coast runs westward to comprise the south side of Port Hill Harbour between the mainland and Bird or Connolly Island and Lennox Island. At the western end of the harbour two more creeks, named Ramsay and Campbell, run south into the Lot. Between them is a

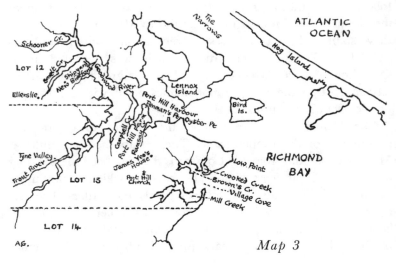

Map 3

peninsula called Penman's Point. The tideway of the Trout River cuts into the northern part of the lot. There is a narrow strip of Lot 13 on the north side of the Trout River and then Lot 12 and the creek called the Goodwood River running north and ending in the shallows of Smelt Creek and Schooner Creek (Map 3).

In 1765 Holland found that none of the French Islanders had settled in Lot 12. On Lot 13, which he reported as 'one of the best Townships on the Island', there was a church and twenty-four houses and barns and seven hundred and fifty acres of cleared land, all of it on the shores of the creeks off Richmond Bay. On Lot 14 Holland found twelve houses and three hundred and fifty acres of cleared land. Certainly the French had taken to the west side of Richmond Bay.

A year or two later the Governor of Nova Scotia, then responsible for the Island, directed his chief Surveyor, Charles Morris, to visit it and lay out the capital city and Princetown and Georgetown. Morris visited Lot 13 and made a very accurate and careful survey of the part of it which fronts Richmond Bay. In the great share-out the lot had fallen to one John Pownall, formerly Secretary to the Board of Trade and Plantations and later Secretary of State. Morris reported to Pownall's agent, John Butler :

> Mr Pownalls Lott is one of the best on the Island both for Farming and Fishing, in the Front of it is a fine capacious safe Harbour—water enough for Ships of any Burthen—The Land in general is of a red Loam will produce wheat Pease, Barley, Oats, and Vegetables of all kinds where Properly cultivated, The Cleared Upland in general is intirely worn out and produces little Else but weeds will never be of any Value or Profit till well manured/Except the Plot where the Mass House stands which is some of the best grass Land I saw any where/the Marshes what little there is produces a Coarse Salt grass that will Keep Cattle over the winter very well,—The uncleared lands in general are well Cloath'd with Timber Trees naturall to these northern Colonies, such as Beach, Black, white and Yellow Birch, Maple, some Oak, Pine, Spruce, and Fir, This Lott is better watered than any other in that part of the Island.

By the appearance of the improvements made by the French I immagine there might have been on this Lott about twenty Families settled but there is now no Houses on it worth repairing except the one Mr Hart lives in this Man came there last summer from New York with a large Family and Stock and proposes if the land is to be let upon reasonable Terms to bring ten Families from thence who understand both Farming and Fishing.

I found the remains of a small Gristmill at the Head of Good Wood River [Morris's plan shows this was just where the present settlement of Tyne Valley stands] and another at the Head of Village Cove [where the Port Hill-Grand River road crosses the head of Mill Creek] but both must have been very inconsiderable ones by the Streams good Wood River is the best stream of the two, and a Mill might be erected there that would serve that district. . . .

. . . I would further Observe that if Mr Pownall coud Obtain the two Islands in the Front of his Lott it would add double to its Value they are finely situated for turning young Cattle and Sheep upon there is Marsh enough round the Borders of them to keep One hundred Head of Cattle over Winter; and they are so surrounded with Flatts that they will never do to make Fish upon except a very small part of 'em.

I am, Sir, your Most Humble Servant,

CHARLES MORRIS jun. Halifax 12th Jan'y 1767.[3]

Morris did his job very thoroughly. The plan he enclosed with his letter, when compared with aerial survey photographs taken in the mid-twentieth century, is startlingly accurate, more accurate as to the features of the coastline than any map has been since. It shows many interesting things. All the way along from the tip of Low Point past Oyster Point around the shores of Ramsay Creek and Campbell Creek right to the shores of the Trout River the forest appears to have been cleared back from the tide line for considerable distances and all along the shores were the remains of buildings. Almost exactly half a mile from the end of Low Point, just above the shore of the sound, Morris showed a 'Chapple'—his 'Mass House'. Just over half a mile inland from Oyster Point was a windmill and about two hundred yards south-east of it, about twenty-five feet above the sea, just where the French settlement had been widest and the

houses thickest, was 'Hart's house' where the solitary American
settler (who was in fact named George Hardy) had already
established himself. Morris took very complete soundings off
the north shore of the lot and well up into Trout River and he
marked an anchorage on a three-fathom bank one and one-
eighth miles due east of the tip of Oyster Point. Hardy's house,
its occupant and the anchorage, where the American brig
Susanna lay, all feature in a diary kept by one Thomas Curtis,
who in 1775 was wrecked in Robert Clark's brig *Elizabeth* on
the sandhills to the north. Thomas Curtis' diary has been edited
in recent years by Dr D. C. Harvey and published by the
Macmillan Company of Canada in *Journeys to the Island of St
John*, but Charles Morris' letter and map with their evidence
of the origins of George Hardy and of the location of his house
and the anchorage had not been discovered at the time the book
was finished.

So good a site, already so well cleared and fronted by a great
natural harbour, would not stay empty for long. In 1770 one
Robert Stewart arrived with a party of settlers on Lot 18 on the
east side of the mouth of Richmond Bay. In the party was John
Ramsay, and by 1775 two Ramsays, Michael and Malcolm, presumably sons of John, had crossed the great bay and settled on
the north side of Low Point. In the next twenty years they were
joined by other settlers, and by 1793 the old French clearings
all along the shore of the sound from Low Point to the Trout
River were occupied again. Among the settlers were Alexander
Brown, who gave his name to Brown's Creek, Roderick Gillis, and
George Penman who had been paymaster of the Island's first
British garrison and helped to expel the French. The lot was now
in the possession of Captain Hugh Seymour-Conway, Royal
Navy, who had it from his father, the First Marquis of Hertford,
who had bought it in 1772.

George Hardy squatted successfully for at least twenty-five
years, but when the question of rent came up he moved on to
Lot 6 in the north, where his descendants still live. George
Penman's clearings were on the fertile peninsula between Ramsay
Creek and Campbell Creek. Here he died about the time of the

Battle of Trafalgar. Next year the proprietor, now Hugh Seymour-Conway's eldest son, George Francis Seymour, leased 300 acres on Penman's Point for 999 years to a merchant named Hugh Montgomery in return for the sum of £90 and an undertaking to pay 15s a year and the rent to the Crown due under the original grant. The area comprised the peninsula itself and 'the land which might be enclosed with two parallel lines to be drawn from the two several points where the said promontory connects with the mainland in a South-west direction'.[4] This in practice meant joining up what were then the heads of the two creeks with a straight line through the woods. Exactly this unit of land still exists today as Port Hill farm.

Hugh Montgomery agreed that, should he or his heirs either fail to pay the annual rents or fail to occupy the land for a period of six months or more, then the land would revert to the Seymours. But he did little or nothing with his new property. In 1810 he mortgaged it, but as he did not occupy it and certainly did not always pay the rent, the Seymours, or at least their agents, soon began to treat the lease as effectively lapsed.

A map made in 1816 shows twenty-one families settled around the shores and creeks of Lot 13. The families tended to be large, so there were at least a hundred people. Most of these families held a hundred acres, by oral agreement with the proprietor's agent. Most of them had cleared only a dozen or so acres; Malcolm and Michael Ramsay who had been settled for forty-years had cleared fifty-five acres and James Brown twenty-five.

The land on the south shore of Ramsay Creek was occupied by John Ramsay and George Jacques, who had cleared about twenty acres between them. Some of this was on the shore of the creek near its mouth, and here the map shows a shipyard. The site of this shipyard, as also the sites of the houses around, and of George Penman's clearing on the north side of the creek, are still clearly visible in aerial photographs, pale variations in the tones of grass and crops, shadowy traces of human life and endeavour, of pioneers clinging to the edge of a wilderness that ought to have been free, but here in the Island was not; traces of where, perhaps, the *Four Friends* loaded a timber cargo for

Thomas Burnard in Bideford three years before the Battle of Waterloo.

*   *   *

The Island timber trade was beginning to develop. At the only Custom House 10,680 loads were cleared in 1818, 17,335 in the following year. John Hill loaded no less than seven ships at Cascumpec in 1818. Things were going on in the creeks, some of them beyond the strict margins of an unadministered law. In August 1818 the Collector of Customs at Charlottetown, Charles Townsend, wrote to the Commissioners of His Majesty's Customs in London :

> It is needless to remind Your Honours that in conformity to the Navigation laws the Masters of all Vessels arriving in the Colonies must come to the Custom [House] and Report before unloading Cargoes, they must also have [a] permit to load Outwardly when the Cargoes are compleated and the Masters must come and clear with a Regular Manifest.[5]

A month earlier the Lieutenant Governor had explained certain difficulties which faced him.

> Charlottetown 14 July 1818—My Lords, I feel it incumbent upon me to apprize Your Lordships that under some circumstances which have existed in this Colony it has been no easy matter to obtain the due enforcing the Navigation & Custom Laws and when even that difficulty has been surmounted, the Parties effected by them hardly ever fail to apply to the Board of Customs for a Stay of Proceedings which is most usually granted That such a Discretionary Power should be vested in that Honourable Board is not meant to be controverted by me, but that it should be so unsparingly excerted has the effect of rendering the important Laws alluded to almost Nugatory here, and has also the effect of actually deterring—seizing officers from the execution of their Duty from the apprehension of incurring expenses in a Seizure which they thus become liable to answer for.
>
> The heavy responsibility which attaches to a Governor on the subject of enforcement of the Navigation Laws etc. arising out of the Oath he takes and the positive Royal Instructions he acts under compels me to make this representation to your Lordships.
>
> I am, etc. D. SMITH, Lieutenant Governor of P.E.I.[6]

The temptation to be one of those who sought to evade the 'Navigation and Custom Laws', despite the hundred-pound fine which could be imposed on those finally found guilty of violation, was considerable. John Hill described the conditions in a letter addressed to the Board of Customs from his headquarters in Rotherhithe on 25 March 1820 :

> . . . Every time a vessel arrives at our port (Cascumpec) we have to despatch the Captain & Papers to Charlotte town to enter and obtain the necessary documents for discharging and again when we enter and clear the vessel outwards there is no other means of communication with Charlotte town than by sending a boat from the above port to Prince town, Richmond bay, and then by land to Charlotte town—There is no other way of communicating, the shortest time in which it is usually done is not less than a week, and it is frequently more than double that time, and besides the delay and expense stated in our former memorial it is frequently attended with considerable danger in crossing Richmond bay in boats such as we are under the necessity of sending on acct. of the shallow water in a place called Cascumpec Narrows or Cavendish channel, Cascumpec bay and Richmond bay as Layn down in the charts submitted to your Honors inspection.[7]

One who had not observed the Customs Law, David Crighton, master of the brig *David* of North Shields, in a Memorial to the Lords of His Majesty's Treasury dated 20 February 1818, gave an account of the way the trade was being conducted :

> That in the month of April last the said Brig was chartered in Shields by the House of Simon Dodd & Co. of Newcastle Timber Merchants to proceed to Prince Edward Island with a quantity of British Manufactured goods for the Purchase of a Cargo of Timber and that on the 7th of July he arrived in the Harbour of Crappeaux in the above-mentioned Island, where he had loaded in the proceeding year and at which time he made some conditional arrangement for a cargo for the ensuing season—that on his arrival there finding a cargo had not been provided agreeably to his expectations he made immediately application to the inhabitants in the vicinity of the above-mentioned port to know at what time a cargo of timber would be provided for shipping the payment for which

was to be made in the goods he had on board—The Settlers who usually provide Timber being scattered over a considerable part of the country it was found necessary to give notice that if they would meet on board on the seventh of the same month and ascertain what quantity of timber each could furnish should it be thought sufficient to complete the cargo the ship would remain and load. The Custom House being at a distance of thirty miles or upwards through intricate woods and difficult roads your Memorialist thought it more prudent to defer going to make his report until he could ascertain whether a cargo could be provided or not and when the inhabitants met on board they desired to know in what description of goods payment would be made and in consequence thereof he found it necessary to open several packages to show what articles would be exchanged for timber—[8]

As for the conditions on the shores of Lots 12, 13 and 14 in Richmond Bay, the Collector and the Acting Controller of Customs in Charlottetown wrote to the Commissioners in London in September 1819 :

Your requisition of 10th May, 1819, No. 57 directing us to transmit forthwith an account of the Number of Vessels which have loaded and discharged at Three Rivers and Prince Town for the Years 1817 & 1818 distinguishing the trade in which the vessels were employed and the nature of their cargoes for each year respectively—I am unable to comply with—

& I respectfully state that this inability arises from the several Bays, Harbours & Rivers on the Island having always been considered as comprehended in the term—'Port of Prince Edward Island' so that all vessels arriving at the Island; no matter to what part have always been entered in the Custom House books as arriving at the 'Port of Prince Edward Island' without distinguishing the creek or Inlet—

I also respectfully state that the places on the southern coast of this Island where it is practical for vessels to discharge & take on board their cargoes are so numerous that that side of the Island may be considered as one continuous port.

The only Merchant residing at Three Rivers is a Mr McDonald—George Town [the name of the town at Three Rivers] consists of about three Huts—& Prince Town is in the same state of progression—but there is no merchant residing at Prince Town to my knowledge.

This Town is situated near the Mouth of a spacious bay

called Richmond Bay—to various parts of the shores of which timber is in the winter time hauled—*Many* Vessels repair thither for timber after discharging their cargoes at other parts of the Island—but there are no depots of Timber, formed at Prince Town in the winter, to be ready for shipping in the summer consequently there is *no* trade carried on with Prince Town—but the Vessels go into parts of the Bay where Lumber has been prepared for them in the winter time—to load—precisely as they do at all the other Creeks and Inlets of the Island where Lumber can be procured—The impossibility of conveying to your Honors by report the state of the places that are here *dignified* by the name of Town is puzzling—

*But wherever a speculative Merchant finds a quantity of Timber, & a creek or bay to ship it from—there he builds four or five huts & calls it a Town—& feels surprised that as the Lord of his own Territory he may not enter & clear the four or five Vessels he loads throughout the season—**

I have only to add that the Trade of this Island must be some years yet before it can support a more numerous Custom House establishment—the duties at present collected do not defray the salary of the only Waiter & Searcher on the Island—for the truth of which I refer your Honors to the former Accts. from this Office.

FREDK B. BARWELL, Collector.[9]

In these conditions, interest in the possibilities of the Island for the enterprising and adventurous was stirring among West of England merchants. It was, after all, the end of a long period when what could be taken at sea was largely free for all. The background of such men as Thomas Burnard and Thomas Chanter was one in which privateering and near-piracy were everyday risks. Their approach to their business was conditioned by the centuries, only now coming to an end, in which law and order at sea did not exist.

There were timber cargoes waiting to be purchased very cheaply in informal barter with the settlers, and not too many questions about who the timber really belonged to were ever asked. The imaginative enterprise of West of England merchants was quick to take the business one stage further and build ships in the Island with the same cheap and readily available timber,

* Authors' italics.

load them up with more lumber, and sail them home to Britain where some of the ships could be sold, some of the better ones kept and put into trade.

It took only a few skilled men, a few simple tools, a lot of knowhow, and a sheltered sloping beach with deep water close inshore to build a wooden ship of 200 or 300 tons, perhaps 100 or 120 feet long. Ships were being built all round the coasts of Britain in these simple conditions and were to continue to be built in this way until the end of the century. Shipyards were less shipyards in the modern sense than sites where a master builder could put a vessel together and rig her, working slowly with the aid of a few men less skilled than himself.

The decisions taken around 1815 by several merchants to risk capital and put men ashore on Prince Edward Island with the simple equipment used to build wooden ships and enough stores and gear to get themselves established and survive the winter were to prove very important in the Island's history. At the time this great step forward passed almost unnoticed. The Cambridges were first, in 1811. John Hill was soon active in the same field. The Pope family, Plymouth shipbuilders and timber merchants had established two of their number, John and William, at Charlottetown by 1817 when they built the schooner *Brothers* there. Soon afterwards with a third brother, Thomas, they set up a shipbuilding business on the shores of the Northumberland Strait, at Turn Chapel Yard, Bedeque, immediately south of Richmond Bay.

Besides what he heard from Sir Charles Chalmers, Joshua Williams and Richard Moys, Thomas Burnard knew of all these merchants' activities and had dealings with some of those concerned. In 1818 he decided to risk a small venture himself at a shipbuilding settlement in the Island.

CHAPTER THREE

THE VOYAGE OF THE
PETER & SARAH

T HE *Peter & Sarah* was the solitary little sloop-rigged
vessel Richard Chapman had built in the timber famine
year of 1809. Thomas Husbands, her first owner, employed
her in trade about the ports of the Bristol Channel. When she
was two years old she was rigged as a special kind of brigantine
developed on the Torridge and locally called a polacca, with
sails and rigging more simply and efficiently arranged than was
usual in very small square-rigged sailing ships. It was a little absurd
to rig square sails on a fifty foot ship at all. If the *Peter & Sarah*
had been North American she would have been a schooner.

In 1816 the *Peter & Sarah* became the sole property of Thomas
Burnard. In July 1818, with other local sloops and brigantines,
she was sent to collect the 7th Dragoon Guards on transfer from
duty in Ireland to Devon. When she arrived in Bideford on 25
July she must have stunk of human excrement and bile.

The process of cleaning her up and loading her for the
transatlantic voyage was quickly completed. She was handled by
three or four men including the master. She had a small cabin
under the deck aft where the master lived and a smaller space
which was called the forecastle under the deck right in the
bows. Here the crew existed. There was nothing on deck except
a scuttle and a skylight for the master's cabin, a hatchway and a
winch for winding the cargo in and out of the hold by manpower,
another hatch to get in and out of the forecastle and a crude
hand windlass for working the anchors. She was steered with
a tiller. The food was cooked on an open fire on deck when it
was fine, in the almost unventilated forecastle or not at all when
it was not. There was nowhere for the crew to relieve themselves
and nothing to wash in except a wooden tub.

Even though she was a very full-bodied little ship she cannot have carried many pioneers among the stores and equipment in her hold. The evidence of old people recently alive in Prince Edward Island who could just remember the youngest of them agrees on three who stayed on in the Island and founded families there—William Ellis, a master shipwright, and his two apprentices Edward Williams and John England. Tradition suggests that William Ellis may have had with him one or two of his six sons. It was very much a lumbering and shipbuilding gang got together by William Ellis from his own native village of Monkleigh, high above the Torridge valley, where he was born in 1774.

William Ellis was a most competent master shipwright. He worked for Richard Chapman at the building of the *Peter & Sarah* and the *Bellona*. Richard Chapman's health began to fail after his fiftieth year and in the end he went mad. Ellis gradually took more and more responsibility for the work at Cleave Houses and moved into a kind of partnership with Chapman. Of the two last ships built at Chapman's yard, both for Thomas Burnard in 1818, one had her builder's certificate signed by both men. On 4 July 1818, Ellis alone recorded himself as the builder of the other, the *Susan*, and thereafter the certificates were signed by another hand.

The *Peter & Sarah* was in charge of her regular coasting master, John Eastridge. In the hold, along with the temporary accommodation for the six or seven men, were the tools, iron-work, rope and fittings needed to equip and rig a 200-ton three masted ship. According to a strong tradition in the Island there was some food and cooking equipment, blankets, boots and spare clothes enough for two years, just the time John Hill considered a settler needed to be supported before he could become independent.

At three miles an hour the *Peter & Sarah* fought her way to the westward, towards Richmond Bay, and those on board her lived on intimate terms with the North Atlantic, two feet below the deck. There was nowhere for them to go except the deck and the hold. But these were men who had been born and had lived in dark, damp, two-roomed hovels, who had worked with hand-tools on wooden ships all their lives and knew nothing except this appalling simplicity. Forty-four year old Ellis led the young gang of landsmen, Eastridge and the crew were professionals, brought up in a world in which people looked for nothing at sea except survival and, with luck, profit. And the *Peter & Sarah* was a dry, safe little ship with a relatively easy motion, riding like a cork on the water.

She was entered at Charlottetown Custom House on 13 September 1818. There was one site on Richmond Bay which had everything to commend it as the place where Thomas Burnard's four or five huts could be built and called a town. Whereas the coasts of Lots 13 and 14 were by now fully taken up and settled (except for the vacant three hundred acres of Penman's Point) Lot 12 was almost uninhabited and a census of 1814 had shown only three families there. Right up the Goodwood River, where Smelt Creek joins it, a long spit of red sand juts far out into the water. Behind it is a deep sheltered pool. The deepest water, fourteen feet when the first survey was made in 1845, is right under the narrow beach, covered with purple sea lavender, on the west side of the river. It is an ideal site for building small ships of local timber.

By water or across the ice (there was no land communication) the place was only a few miles from the settled shores of Lot 13, where food was grown, where there was already a surplus of labour experienced in the problems of living and working in the Island, and where there were the ship- and boat-building skills of the Ramsays and others. There was timber, and the arrival of the *Peter & Sarah* meant that there would for the first time be a regular market for it. There were settlers only too ready to cut and haul it in return for store goods. It is indicative of the relationship between the newcomers on Lot 12 and the established settlers on Lot 13 that the earliest of the many surviving documents concerning the Bideford men in Prince Edward Island should be a small piece of torn and yellowing paper with writing as follows :

> Wm. Ellis to Neel McArthur Dr
> To One Man and two Oxen
> 4 Days at 10/ pr Day—£2. 0. 0.
> Octr. 29th 1818 Settled the above Neele Mcarthur.[1]

On the 1816 map the only settler shown on Lot 13 on the north bank of the Trout River, and therefore much the nearest to the new shipbuilding site, was N. McArthur. Thomas Burnard's men paid Neil McArthur more for two days' work than a Devon labourer earned in a month. But winter was coming and so they had to hurry.

While the men went ashore each day and cleared enough land to begin to lay down a vessel and to build the huts they would live in during the winter, the *Peter & Sarah* lay in sheltered safety in the deep pool behind the long sandspit. The land off which she lay, the eastern half of Lot 12, belonged to Sir James Montgomery and members of his family. On 20 October 1818 an agreement of lease was made between James Curtis, agent for the Montgomerys, on the one hand, and Richard Moys, shipbuilder of Richmond Bay, on the other. Under it Richard Moys was granted for 999 years 313 acres bounded by the Goodwood River to the east. This was the wooded hinterland of the little bay in which the *Peter & Sarah* was lying and almost all of it was easily accessible from Smelt Creek. For it Richard Moys contracted to pay the rent due to the Crown on the original grant and also 1s per acre per year to the Montgomerys. Although it was entered into in the second half of October, the agreement was dated to run from 14 September, the day after the *Peter & Sarah* had been entered at Charlottetown Custom House.

Richard Moys had the knowledge of Island conditions which the party needed to establish itself and survive the first winter. The evidence suggests that he was one of the party in the *Peter & Sarah*, or that he crossed in another vessel and was waiting for them when they arrived. He took charge of the first ship William Ellis built on the Island and sailed her across the Atlantic to arrive in Bideford early in 1820.

In late November or early December the *Peter & Sarah* sailed away with John Eastridge and her crew of three and probably with timber in the hold where William Ellis and his gang had lived in stinking discomfort for five and a half weeks. She was reported as reaching Bideford on 23 December and was put straight back into the coasting trade around western Britain. There she stayed for the rest of her fifty years of hard-worked life.

In the Island the creeks froze over, the snow came and the lumbering season began. The settlers of Lot 13 had not had a new colony landed on their doorstep; they had received an injection of capital and knowhow and they had for the first time a regular market for their labour and lumber, a market where the buyer's currency was finished goods and rum. All winter they worked at the gathering of timber for a 200-ton ship and lumber cargoes while William Ellis and his men began to build her in working conditions that were totally unfamiliar and in appalling cold. But Moys knew the techniques of working in the Island and so did the settlers, and by the spring great progress must have been made towards the completion of the *Mars*, as the new ship was called.

Three of Thomas Burnard's ships visited the Island during the summer of 1819, one of them twice. In one of these ships came Burnard's nephew, Thomas Burnard Chanter, and for the next ten years this young man became a transatlantic commuter, spending his summers (with one exception) in the Island and most of his winters in Bideford and London.

He was now twenty-two years of age, and intelligent, determined and physically active, able to take charge of a ship at sea, to conduct his uncle's business—and his own—in the Island and to enter into the complex warfare of colonial politics. He had a personal charm which was to serve him well all his life and enable him to deal on terms of equality with anyone in Charlottetown. Quick-tempered on occasion, he was enterprising and adventurous in his approach to business. He was also a man of gentle and cultivated tastes. He provided the continuity and the driving force for much of what happened to Thomas Burnard's venture at New Bideford—the name given by Burnard's men to the group of huts at the creek's edge. But he was also always ready to take opportunities to found his own fortune.

George Seymour's agent on Lot 13 at this time was J. B. Palmer, a bankrupt Irish lawyer who had come to the Island to mend his fortunes as an employee of John Hill. In the eight years after Trafalgar he became the right-hand man of the Lieutenant Governor, then J. F. W. Des Barres, the great cartographer and author of the 'Atlantic Neptune' turned proconsul in his old age, who came into conflict with the all-powerful proprietors, represented by a London committee in which John Hill was the main protagonist; so Palmer, once Hill's creature, came to be on the opposite side in the shifting pattern of Island politics. At the end of the struggle Des Barres was replaced by Charles Smith and Palmer lost his public offices. But the first political society in British North America, the 'Loyal Electors', which he had founded in Charlottetown during the years of his opposition to the Establishment, marked the very beginning of the long fight for the political emancipation of the Islanders, first towards a government responsible to the people and then to the freeing of the people from the incubus of the landlords.

Palmer stayed on in the Island practising as a lawyer as well as acting as agent on Lot 13. He wrote long letters to George Seymour painting a glowing picture of prospects for development. At first he concentrated his enthusiasm on the neglected west coast of the lot where there were no settlers. Here in 1816 he envisaged the setting up of an import/export business under a resident ('B') who would do extensive trade with an agent ('A') in the West Indies. Palmer went into great detail as to how this business would be run. But meanwhile his real preoccupation was naturally with lumber and with the depredations of the merchant lumber pirates from Britain and the settlers acting on their behalf, so that he saw lumber from which he might himself have profited disappearing before his eyes.

> A Sawmill upon Lot 13 is now to be considered in a different point of view from that it bore some years ago—or even months—Lots 15, 13, 10, 9, 6, and even part of Lot 7 are at present subject to depredations nearly at the pleasure of the public on the south coast, for it is impossible to prevent them unless by actual settlement—there are some saw mills already at work at Bedeque and others are erecting, and there is one lately erected at Cascumpec on Holland Bay by Mr Hill,

which although on the north side of the Island, lies at an easy
approach for timber from the south side by means of the roads
originally made by myself—one across Lot 10 from Percival
River to Foxley River (only one mile and three quarters apart)—
the other across Lot 9, also leading from Egmont Bay to a
branch of Foxley River : and other mills still more contiguous
will soon be established—there is not any great quantity of
timber on Lot 13, but there is too much to lose—and experience
shows us all here that it is unprofitable to preserve it—it
therefor becomes a consideration whether a Proprietor should
not, by erecting or encouraging a saw mill, endeavour to turn
to present profit that which he would in all probability otherwise
lose three fourths part of.[2]

In 1819 Penman's Point lay empty. On each side were the
small clearings of the settlers, James Campbell to the west, Neil
Ramsay and George Jacques with the shipbuilding place to the
east. This was a commanding site and there was good timber
on it. There was also a point just behind the site of George
Penman's house and barns where a roofwalk on a two storey
building might command a view, not only of all the 300 acres
Hugh Montgomery had leased, but of the sound north of Lot
13 and of the entrance to the Goodwood River, so that no ship
could sail on these waters without being seen.

Many of the tenants of Lot 13 were settled under informal
agreements with the agent. Under some such arrangement in
1819 Thomas Chanter took squatter's rights on the vacant site
at Penman's Point. Although the site offered no good shipbuilding
facility, it had better timber than Lot 12 and reasonably sheltered
deep water at its north-western edge. It was easily accessible to
all the settlers of Lot 13. Lot 12 was the place for the marine
stores, but to do business with the settlers by selling them imported
goods in exchange for labour and timber meant having the stores
where they, and their wives, could get at them, and Penman's
Point provided a good location.

The *Mars* was completed and loaded with lumber. At the
end of the fall there was a sudden flurry of legal activity in
Charlottetown. As Richard Moys was to deliver the *Mars* to
Britain and then take charge of her in the Atlantic trade, he would

be away from the Island, Thomas Chanter was going to England
in the *Mars* and so somebody else had to be left in charge at
New Bideford during the winter. The obvious person was the
master craftsman William Ellis. This had been foreseen, and a
power of attorney creating him Thomas Burnard's agent had
been brought out. This was now registered at the Land Office
at Charlottetown, and with it a document transferring the rights
at New Bideford from Richard Moys to Thomas Burnard, a
necessary precaution, for had Richard Moys and the *Mars* been
lost while the land was still in his name there would have been
a considerable legal tangle. Next day the *Mars* cleared for
Bideford.

Charlottetown was still no great city. There were three shops
and no proper school. In a large square in the middle of the
town stood the church, the courthouse and the market house.
The houses were built entirely of wood. There was still only one
brickmaker in the Island and no bricks had yet been imported.
Though there were carts there were no wagons and no passenger
gigs. But soon the Cambridges would import a cariole, a light
passenger vehicle made in Quebec. Travellers over long distances
went either by boat or on horses, usually riding bareback. There
was no hotel in Charlottetown, but there was an amateur theatre
which, a month after the *Mars* sailed, began a two-month season
with a comedy in five acts entitled 'John Bull or the Englishman's
Fireside' and followed it next month and in February with a
farce, a melodrama, a comedy and the 'Burlesque Tragi-Comic
Opera' called 'Bombastes Furioso'.

The *Mars,* still under Richard Moys, was the relief ship for
New Bideford in 1820 and she was out very early, probably in
June, with Thomas Chanter and with sails, gear and crews for
three new ships which had been built for Thomas Burnard.
These vessels, which were registered in Charlottetown Custom
House as the sole property of Thomas Burnard by Thomas
Chanter as his 'known agent', were sailed across the Atlantic
with lumber cargoes and registered again at Bideford. One of
them, the brig *Bacchus*, had a bad crossing, losing her deckload
of lumber and her boats. Chanter did not waste his summer on

the Island. Apart from the developments at New Bideford and on Penman's Point, he purchased some land on Lot 15 and petitioned the Lieutenant Governor for an outright grant of 500 acres. He also got himself appointed a Justice of the Peace for Prince County, an appointment which was to be useful to him in later years.

He spent the winter of 1820-21 in New Bideford. In April 1821 he wrote a letter to Lieutenant Governor Smith's Private Secretary renewing his application for a grant of a part of Lot 15.

> Sir, In obedience to His Excellencys Commands and in reply to your Letter of the 12th instant, I beg leave to state that I have been in possession of 313 Acres of Wood Land, under Lease from the Proprietor, for Two years, of which I have brought about Twenty Acres in a State of Cultivation, exclusive of Building Nine Hundred Tons of Shipping, I have also Settled Five of my Domestics, who came with me from England, on these Farms, and my Prayer for a Grant of Five Hundred Acres on Lot 15, arose from a desire of forming a small Establishment there, and of carrying on Agricultural, Fishing and other Pursuits for which the situation (hitherto unattended to) appears to me Eligible.
>
> I have the Honor to Remain, Sir, Your most Obedient, Very humble Servant, THOS B. CHANTER.[3]

Thomas Chanter was not above slanting the facts a little to give a favourable air to his case. The 313 acres on the banks of Schooner Creek were not in his name as his letter might be taken to imply. On the other hand the ships already built for Thomas Burnard totalled exactly 918 tons. But the real importance of the letter is its report on what had happened at New Bideford in the three years since the *Peter & Sarah* arrived, an account of Chanter's stewardship of what he evidently regarded as very much his own little show. They had brought over very few people. Those five 'domestics' who had settled on the twenty cleared acres were William Ellis, now joined by his wife and three daughters, Sarah, Agnes and Mary Ann, and some of the rest of his six sons, the two apprentices, John England, who married Sarah Ellis, and Edward Williams, who, similarly restricted in his choice, married Agnes, and two others. One of these may have been

Richard Moys who married Miss Craswell, a daughter of a family which had recently settled on Lot 13. Thomas Chanter made no mention of his squatter's holding on Penman's Point. But the evidence suggests that the fifth family was settled there.

When at the beginning of the present century fragments of oral traditions of these events were set down in a delightful book of local lore called 'Past and Present of Prince Edward Island' it was there recorded that Ellis and his party built a clapboard house in a slight sheltering depression a little to the south of the building slip at New Bideford. In this house lived Thomas Chanter with the marine stores in the same building all around him. From this point of vantage he managed the affairs of the little business. William and his two apprentices drove, cajoled, persuaded and guided the men who felled and hauled the timber, sawed it and built the ships. Nearly all these men must have rowed or sailed over from Lot 13 each day, or walked across the ice in winter. In the early winter and the spring, when the ice was thin or broken and they could do neither, all work must have stopped. Work outside must have stopped also in snow storms and in periods of windy cold. It was a pretty erratic business, and a very slow one, but the ships got built somehow.

Chanter not only managed his uncle's business and pressed the Lieutenant Governor for lands on Lot 15. In partnership with one Gilbert Ormsby he established a fishing station and a store on Fish Island, so called in those days because it was shaped like a fish. It is a high dune of yellow sand covered with coarse grass and it marks the north side of the entrance to Richmond Bay. Now it has joined with the rest of the offshore dunes and it is called Bill-hook. Here a thriving barter trade, codfish for finished goods, was done with the expanding settlements along the lovely downland coast between Richmond Bay and New London.

Chanter went back to England for the winter of 1821-22. While he was away Lieutenant Governor Smith reported to the Secretary of State on his application for land on Lot 15 saying:

> Mr Chanter is at present absent but will probably return to the Island among the earliest arrivals. He is a settler every

way deserving of encouragement. He is in the Commission of
the Peace and I see no reason whatever to doubt his statement
which I forwarded in my despatch No. 259 of April 30th
last year.[4]

And Chanter himself petitioned again from Cheapside in London.
Ellis stayed in the Island over that winter, supplying rum from
the stores to help John Hill's men at Cascumpec to keep out
the cold.

By now the pattern of North Atlantic passages in the timber
trade was beginning to establish itself; for ordinary merchant
vessels it was not to change much until the end of the history of
sailing ships. Six weeks was a good average passage west, twenty
to thirty days east. But in 1821 the *Bellona*, under Joshua
Williams, left Bideford on 12 June, and was back from the
Miramichi on 22 July, six weeks for the round trip. The *Mars*
did four crossings of the North Atlantic during the season, returning from St Andrews on her last passage in twenty-five days.

In the spring of 1822 the relief ships brought with them not
only sails and rigging and replenishments for the stores, but also
more shipbuilders. An Exeter newspaper reported at the end of
April:

> A number of mechanics have embarked this week for Prince
> Edward's in the employ of Thomas Burnard, Esq., a Bideford
> merchant, who has fitted out two very large brigs for that
> Island. A number of young apple trees have been sent out in
> them.[5]

The large brigs were the *Alert* and the *Bacchus*, both of which
made two crossings to the Island in 1822, while the *Bellona* went
twice to the Miramichi and the *Mars* at least once. The
'mechanics' were probably on contract for work for a season or
two, as William Ellis himself had once been.

That winter (1822-23) Tommy Chanter stayed in the Island
again. At Penman's Point a wharf was built jutting out into
Campbell Creek, and beside it the Devon mechanics built a
Devon limekiln, a form of architecture with which they were
very familiar because there were then nineteen kilns working on
the shores of the Torridge Estuary. These Torridge kilns burned

limestone brought from the north coast of the Bristol Channel
in the *Peter & Sarah* and many other small ships, but the stones
for the kiln at Penman's Point were brought out as ballast in the
timber ships, half empty as they were with their cargoes of sails,
rigging, stores and passengers. The lime was valuable fertiliser
for the sandy soil. From the wharf a road was driven up through
the woods to the clearing where George Penman had lived. Here
more trees were being felled, a store was already set up and a
house was under construction which was to be the finest in the
whole western half of the Island. A farm and trading establishment
worthy of the site were being cut out of the wilderness.

In the spring of 1823 the *Bacchus* came with Leicester rams and
ewes, two Devon bulls—one named Tommy Chanter—and a
Devon cow, for the new farm at Penman's Point. These animals
were the subject of very favourable comment because the sheep
gave a nine-pound fleece in contrast to the two-and-a-half pounds
usually obtained from the scrubby Island breed. A fifty-foot
schooner was built for Thomas Chanter and named the *Gleaner*.
He was entered as the master of this first shipowning venture and
there is a record of at least one voyage he made in charge of her
across to the Miramichi. But her main use was as a fishing
schooner to work from the fishing station on Bill-hook Island.

Until now Thomas Burnard's venture, nearly 3,000 miles from
home, had largely been Chanter's little kingdom. There is no
record to indicate that either Burnard or his eldest son had crossed
the Atlantic to see what was going on. The other two sons had
been too young, Nathaniel at fifteen had left Blundell's School
just over a month before the *Peter & Sarah* sailed and William
was a year younger. But in 1823 Nathaniel was twenty, Tommy
Chanter was to go home again for the winter, and the enterprise,
now on an increasing scale, was a big one for Ellis to manage.
Nathaniel therefore came to the Island and in the autumn
was armed with a legal document, sent out from England, which
empowered him to take complete charge of the whole enterprise.
To help him he had with him Thomas Chappell, a member of
an Appledore family who had been merchants and seafarers
since the seventeenth century.

The season was late when the *Bacchus* came to the Island on her second voyage and she loaded her lumber as fast as it could be put into her. With Chanter on board she went out from Richmond Bay into the unsettled weather of late November and off New London fell in with the *Commerce*, a large ship belonging to John Cambridge which had developed a leak on her way from Quebec to Liverpool with timber. Her crew were exhausted and some of them frost-bitten, and she was so full of water that only her cargo kept her afloat. The wind was blowing from the west with repeated threats of snow-squalls in it. On board the *Commerce*, besides her master and her near-mutinous crew, was Alexander Anderson, a fisherman farmer from New London who with four companions had pulled seven miles out from the land in his own boat to see what he could do. They were set on running her ashore, ostensibly to save the cargo and as much equipment as possible. The master of the *Bacchus,* William Chappell, another member of the Appledore family, and Chanter were intent on a profitable salvage claim. The inhabitants of New London were deprived of the pickings of the wreck and Anderson was pushed off with a lantern, a compass and a vague promise of five pounds next summer. The weather closed down, an attempt to tow the *Commerce* to Nova Scotia failed, and the master and ten of her men abandoned her for the *Bacchus*. They were landed at the Gut of Canso and their vessel ended piled up on the coast of Cape Breton. There was no salvage money for anyone. Chanter's voyage home began badly. It ended worse, for when the *Bacchus* arrived in Bideford he learned that the great Thomas Burnard was dead.

Nearly 150 years later there remains something strangely attractive about the shadowy figure of Thomas Burnard. Almost certainly of poor beginnings, he died in the words of a contemporary press report: 'owner or shareholder of nearly sixty sail of vessels in the coast and foreign trades.'[6] He was a banker, a merchant, owner of a great timber business and a colonial merchant adventurer in the classic tradition. Four times Mayor of Bideford, he had relinked North Devon and North America after the connection of two-and-a-half centuries had been completely broken. He had turned the eyes of North Devon men westward again, beyond the limits of European seas, and westward-looking they were to remain for more than half a century. In the long run he had perhaps done more than anyone else firmly to establish the shipbuilding industry in Prince Edward Island, and this was to have a great effect on the Island's prosperity. But he was more than all these achievements indicate. Although both discretion and convention demanded praise of the powerful from the Devon press, the contemporary references to his charity and gentle way of life ring true. His funeral, when the whole town of Bideford closed down, was more numerously attended by all sorts of men and women than any that could be remembered.

There remains a faint atmosphere of mystery about his end. He appears to have died at the height of his power and wealth. His will, a concise, lucid document, was signed confidently and strongly on the day of his death, and having made due provision for his daughters it left everything he possessed to his wife and his eldest son. Nathaniel, managing affairs over in the Island, got no mention and neither did William. Thomas Burnard Chanter was not mentioned either, though without his enterprise and drive and readiness to endure pioneer life the business in Prince Edward Island would have been no more than just another merchant's group of huts abandoned on the edge of the forest.

Perhaps because he died while still in the prime of life, Thomas Burnard made no attempt to build a great house and become assimilated into the lives of the gentry of the Devon countryside, as the forbears of many of them had been assimilated in the century before. Though his eldest son, Thomas, seems to have inherited some of his father's qualities, neither he nor Nathaniel were to prove proper heirs to a merchant prince, while William English, who was to be the most successful of them, carved out a professional career for himself. What Thomas Burnard had started was exploited to its logical conclusion by somebody in every way quite different.

He would have been very surprised to know who his real heir was.

CHAPTER FOUR

THE HEIR TO THOMAS
BURNARD

THE immediate problem which faced Thomas Burnard's widow and his eldest son was what they should do with the Prince Edward Island venture. For a year they went on as if nothing had happened. On 3 June 1824 Thomas Chanter arrived at Richmond Bay in the brigantine *Rover*, only four weeks and two days out from Bideford, and with him came twenty 'shipwrights and mariners'. A few days later a notice appeared in the Island's first regular newspaper, the *Prince Edward Island Register*, announcing that the 'mercantile establishment of the late Thomas Burnard Esq. on this Island' would in future be carried on under the name of Thomas Burnard & Co. This notice was signed by Nathaniel and by Thomas Chanter and it was issued from 'Port Hill, Prince County'. This was the first use of the name of the home of the Saltren Willetts at Northam for the new house and the farm on Penman's Point. In 1817 Augustus Saltren Willett had changed his name to Clevland and had inherited Tapeleigh, becoming Lord of the Manor of Northam and of Bideford, and shortly after of Instow, and thus he was a useful person to flatter. There was some similarity between the two Port Hills, each raised high on a peninsula overlooking the shipping channel to Bideford.

The new house called Port Hill stood surrounded by a low earth bank inside which was a smooth lawn. It was a clapboard house two storeys high with a flat top to the roof which commanded a view over miles of creeks and forests. This roof was caulked with oakum like a ship. The house was decorated with carved corner pilasters of softwood. Inside was an entrance hall with a staircase rising through it. In the rooms the

This photograph of shipping clustered alongside the 1845 Quay at East Appledore was taken circa 1875. Besides ketches and schooners it shows two of the distinctive local polacca brigantines, the Newton *built by Richard Chapman at Cleave Houses in 1788 alongside the Quay and another vessel heeled over behind the schooner in the right foreground*

Seven square-rigged ships lie in the Torridge off Appledore and the masts of an eighth large vessel show that she is lying in the Richmond Dry Dock. This photograph taken from near the base of Chanter's signal tower, must have been made in the 1860s

A brig discharging timber in Appledore Pool

wainscoting stood as high as the bottom of the windows and above them the walls were of lath and plaster. The lime for the plaster was made in the kiln by the wharf below the house. The mantels were carved in unsophisticated imitation of classical styles, as were also the mouldings of the doors and the sash windows. Altogether it was a magnificent structure to put in the wilderness of Lot 13, more like the homes that were being built by prosperous ship owners in the long-settled districts of contemporary New England and Nova Scotia than the crude, squared log, moss-caulked houses of the Islanders. Because of Thomas Burnard's sudden death it was never finished and it stood incomplete for a hundred and ten years.

Thomas Chanter dabbled a little in Island politics. As a Justice of the Peace and Captain of the Fifth Battalion of the Island Militia he defended a group who met at Princetown in March 1823 to declare their opposition to the Lieutenant Governor, Charles Douglas Smith, an interesting and complex character who made himself unpopular with all the warring groups in the Island's political scene. For the last four years of his term of office Governor Smith dispensed with the services of a Parliamentary Assembly altogether. The breakdown in administration in these last years of his Governorship established that the Assembly had a fundamental part to play in the government of the colony.

Smith's successor was John Ready, one of the most successful Governors Prince Edward Island ever had. Accepting the reality of the situation, he summoned a new Assembly as soon as he arrived. Thomas Chanter joined with John Hill's son and other prominent citizens of the western third of the Island in an address of welcome to the new Lieutenant Governor and at the same time offered himself as a candidate at the election for the new Assembly, though he was aware of certain difficulties.

> 'There are two great obstacles which may operate materially to my disadvantage', he wrote, 'viz. My short residence among you, and the imperious necessity which now calls me for a short time to England; with regard to the first, Gentlemen, allow me to say, that were my public conduct during that period

to pass in review before you, intimately connected as it ever has been with the prosperity of Prince Edward Island in general, and of Prince County in particular, I have little doubt of your liberality removing that objection, and as temporary absence is incidental to us all, the greater assiduity will be expected in the interests committed to our care when we have the power to exert it.'[1]

By the time the election was held in the fall Chanter was on his way back to Bideford and he was not even nominated. Perhaps it was just as well for, as the *Prince Edward Island Register* put it :

Time would fail us were we to attempt giving even a part of the speeches delivered on this occasion, in which however it may be stated that invective formed the chief if not the sole figure. The panoramic effect produced by the hoisting and pulling down of the flags and banners of the rival parties as their strength or numbers alternately rose or fell, with the concomitant consequences, knocking off hats, bloody noses, bruised bones, &c. of the combatants is described as forming a curious *coup d'œil*.[2]

Although he had been Governor Smith's principal opponent, the ageing J. B. Palmer was unsuccessful in the election for the new Assembly. Not only did he fail to gain a seat in the house, he had also lost the agency of Lot 13. In April 1824 Sir George Seymour signed a Power of Attorney appointing as his agent Thomas Heath Haviland 'now Naval Officer and Provost Marshal at Charlottetown in Prince Edward Island in America'.[3]

T. H. Haviland was then a few days short of twenty-eight years old. Born in the country town of Cirencester, he had come to the Island ten years previously to take up a minor appointment which patronage had found for him. An exceedingly clear-minded, dispassionate and discreet man who handled his colleagues with tact and studied courtesy and avoided involvement in the continuous warring of groups and personalities, his talents had already by 1823 brought him to membership of the Lieutenant Governor's Executive Council and he had great influence, mostly behind the scenes.

To him the agency of Lot 13 was just another of many

preoccupations. His first act was to list the tenants and the nature of their tenancies for Sir George. He found over forty families, perhaps two hundred people, settled on the eastern shore of Lot 13. The Ramsays, the Browns, James Campbell, Neil McArthur were all still there, as was J. B. Palmer himself at Seymour Lodge—'a log house built on this ground worth about £40'.⁴ There were some newcomers, but few if any Devon men were among them except for William Ellis, noted by Haviland as 'a good tenant' who already had a hundred acres on lease. Ellis also had an unspecified amount of land on the site of the old French grist mill at the head of the Trout River. Here he proposed to build a new mill. Chanter, presumably acting as agent for the Burnards, was listed as about to become by formal agreement the lessee for 999 years of 'the 118 acre farm'. There was no such farm on the maps and the 118 acres must have been the actual area of cleared land out of the 300 at Penman's Point on which he had been paying the rent due to the Crown.

It is difficult to estimate how many permanent settlers had come as a result of Thomas Burnard's venture. It did not take many skilled men to build a 100-foot wooden ship, given time, and William Ellis' ships took a year or more each to build. In October 1823 Chanter and five other leading citizens on the shores of Richmond Bay had petitioned the Society for the Propagation of the Gospel for the stationing among them of a clergyman of the Church of England. It was a long time before there was a resident at Port Hill (as the whole eastern end of Lot 13 increasingly became known), but a visiting missionary, the Rev L. C. Jenkin, in later years a famous figure in the Island, reported to the Society in 1825 that 'At Bideford, where I occasionally officiate, the hearers were seldom fewer than eighty'.⁵ By Bideford he must have meant the whole area of eastern Lots 12 and 13, and it is not surprising that a visiting preacher would get a large congregation among a people starved of all diversions.

Thomas Burnard's widow and eldest son had a prosperous merchant's business with a big timber yard in England, a fleet of ships including a number in the North American trade, the lease of land at New Bideford and a good shipyard site and marine stores there. They also had a farm and a licensed stores with a fine house at Port Hill, held on squatters' rights which were about to be partly legalised. There was a formidable body of debts due to the Burnards. Great quantities of goods had been sold from the stores and not paid for in money, labour or timber. The inevitable process by which the settlers passed into the thrall of the storekeeper had not only begun but had gathered momentum, and the Burnards had become the creditors of settlers from all over Prince County.

But in an economy largely without money debts were of value only to a person on the spot who was in a position to collect in kind or service. A farm with a fine house and stores was of use only to a man who was going to live there. A shipbuilding site and marine stores were for a master shipbuilder who could use them to build ships for sale. Martha Elizabeth and Thomas Burnard had enough to do in Britain. The managerial responsibilities and financial risks of developing a project 3,000 miles away, on land covered with snow for four months of the year, was too much for them. Chanter was not going to act as their agent and manager indefinitely. In 1825, for the first time in six years, there is no record that he spent the summer in the Island (in spite of what he had said to the electors of Prince County). Nathaniel Burnard and Thomas Chappell were left at Port Hill on their own. The *Gleaner* was transferred to the Burnards and put in charge of Richard Moys.

First the Burnards sub-let the shipbuilding site to the only man who could use it, William Ellis. Then they advertised that :

> The trade and business heretofore carried on at Port Hill and Bideford, Prince County, in this Island, by Thomas Burnard, or under the firm of Thomas Burnard & Co will from henceforth be discontinued and all persons indebted to the Estate of the said Thomas Burnard are hereby required forthwith to pay and satisfy the same to Mr Nathaniel Edward Burnard, or Mr Thomas Chappell at Port Hill aforesaid, and not to any other person or persons, the said Nathaniel Edward Burnard, and Thomas Chappell, being the only persons who are authorised to receive and give discharges for the same. . . . Notice is hereby also given that the Estate of Port Hill aforesaid, and also a

genteel and newly built Dwelling House and Stores thereon, will be immediately sold by the said Nathaniel Edward Burnard by private contract. . . .[6]

This advertisement, which appeared in the *Prince Edward Island Register* in late May 1825, was written in Devon seven weeks before and sent to the Island by post, that is through Halifax, by coach across Nova Scotia and then in the ferry schooner across to Charlottetown. Nathaniel remained in charge throughout the summer.

The advertisement suggests that the debts owed to the Burnards were reckoned among the more valuable assets accruing from the Island venture. It is clear that Thomas and his mother were afraid that somebody else might collect in their name. They had good reason for this.

Nobody bought the lease of Port Hill farm or 'estate'. Ellis farmed on Lot 13 and worked on at New Bideford. There seemed very little chance that the Burnards would ever realise their investment in the Island. There was only one man in Britain with the local knowledge needed to make something out of New Bideford and Port Hill and he was Tommy Chanter. At the end of March 1826 Mrs Burnard and her son, in exchange for £430 and an undertaking to pay certain of their own debts, made over to Thomas Chanter in a formal assignment 'all and every the debt and debts, sums and sums of money balance of capital accounts and dues and demands whatsoever which were due and owing to them', the shipbuilding yard at New Bideford and 'all the Farming Stock Stores, Furniture and other goods, chattels and effects in Prince Edward Island aforesaid which were the property of them'.[7] There were a few exceptions made: one of the new ships building at New Bideford, to be named *Superb* (H.M.S. *Superb* had just paid a visit to Appledore), and 'such part of the marine stores in the shipbuilding yard as will be required for completing the said ship *Superb*', and a debt of forty-five pounds owed to them by Ellis for the rent of the shipyard and farms on Lot 12.

Armed with this document, Chanter returned to the Island in the *Bellona*, arriving on 10 June. He was sworn in as a Justice of the Peace again on 24 June. On 26 July he entered into a contract with William Ellis by which he transferred to him (subject to the master shipwright fulfilling his part of the bargain) his :

> Right, Title, Interest and Property in the concern now carried on at Port Hill and Bideford in Prince County aforesaid from the day of the date hereof. . . . The Shipbuilding Yard, Farms & Marine Stores . . . and also all and every the Debt and Debts Sum and Sums of Money—Balances of Accounts—Dues and Demands whatsoever, which may be at this day due and owing the said concern from person or persons in Prince Edward Island aforesaid, to and for the absolute use and benefit of the said William Ellis.

In return,

> William Ellis hereby agrees to pay unto the said Thomas Burnard Chanter the Sum of Fourteen Hundred and Seventy five Pounds in consideration of the above, in manner following viz. one hundred Pounds Sterling in Cash to be paid into the Hands of Thomas Chappell Esquir on Account of the said Thomas Burnard Chanter One Hundred and Twenty five Pounds in full Payment of a Cargo of Timber to be shipp'd in the first Vessel built for the said Thos B. Chanter and Twelve Hundred and Fifty Pounds in Two Vessels—The Contracts for which Vessels are hereunto annexed. . . .[8]

Unfortunately the contracts are missing from the record.

William Ellis also took on all the debts Chanter had contracted to pay for the Burnards. Chanter kept back the equipment for a brig of one hundred and fifty tons Ellis was building for him, The 'Beds Bedding, Table Linen, Glass, etc.', the 'Ullage of Port & White Wine', the bell of the house, the Devon Bull called Tommy Chanter and a ewe and a lamb. Altogether, if Ellis fulfilled his contract, Chanter had cleared a profit of at least 300 per cent on the deal.

In the spring the press spoke of a year of depression in the timber trade and quoted round-voyage freights of £2 sterling per ton from Britain to the Miramichi as great reductions on what had gone before. Island-built vessels were expected to fetch £8 10s to £9 per ton on delivery in Britain, which was claimed as low.

Quebec was reported to have 'as much timber in the yards of that city as would supply it for a year'.[9] Yet, despite these prophesies of gloom, by 29 June 154 ships had entered at the Custom House at the Miramichi to load timber, a greater tonnage than the year before, and by 1 October 202 vessels had cleared at Charlottetown, twice as many as in 1825. Fifty-four ships were built in the Island in 1826 and they totalled more than 9,250 tons. The general depression in the shipping industry did not affect North Devon, where costs and overheads were low, so much as other parts of Britain.

Tommy Chanter was not discouraged. In September, near Georgetown, at the other end of the Island from Port Hill, Arthur Owen launched for him the *Bolivar*, of which the local press said :

> Never were science, strength and beauty, those three requirements of a well built ship, more happily blended, and it is to be hoped her enterprising owners may meet with such a market as her merits entitle her to.[10]

Tommy Chanter sailed in her for Britain on 21 October. Two days earlier he had achieved a long-pursued ambition by being granted as a proprietor 500 acres of land on the Egmont Bay coast of Lot 15. In charge of the *Bolivar* was James Lowther, son of that Lowther of Clovelly with whom Thomas Burnard had once shared ownership of the *Venus*. Lowther had lost the *Mars* a year before, but this misfortune was not to deter him from a long working relationship with Chanter which proved profitable to both. It began with the sale of the *Bolivar* and part of her cargo in Bideford in January of the following year.

* * *

At Port Hill and New Bideford William Ellis was potentially master of all he saw around him, the fine house, the stores, the shipyard, the little clearings called farms. He had paid his debt to Nathaniel Burnard and had been issued with a receipt. He had signed an undertaking to pay to William Chappell of Appledore 'before Christmas next' £100 'on account of Mr Thos B. Chanter of Bideford Value Received' and next year Chanter

was to write across this document 'Charged in Acct. Settled'.[11]
The first of the ships he had undertaken to build was already
a skeleton over the snow heaped on the beach by the ice that
covered the deep pool where the *Peter & Sarah* had lain eight
years before. Ellis was on his way to being the lawful master in
the place of Thomas Burnard. He might have been excused for
thinking that he was his heir.

But to profit from his acquisition he needed capital. The capital
of the venture was largely locked up in the unpaid accounts.
When he had fulfilled his contract with Chanter the right to
collect would all be in his hands. But somebody else was already
collecting them, bullying, driving, bargaining for settlements in
kind and cash, servicing processes, riding the sixty miles to
Charlottetown across the ice and through the snow filled woods
to swear affidavits of debt before Thomas Haviland, conducting
legal actions through Charlottetown lawyers, somebody who
described himself in numerous Affidavits of Debt as 'Clerk to
Thomas Burnard and Martha Elisabeth Burnard'.

The heir of Thomas Burnard was becoming apparent. It was
not his widow, nor any of his three sons. It was not old William
Ellis. It was not even Thomas Burnard Chanter, though one day
his Island connections were going to make him one of the greatest
merchants in England west of Bristol.

It was James Yeo, a rough, tough little man who spoke softly
in the broad dialect of the country around Kilkhampton, a village
in North Cornwall twenty miles west of Bideford. He was of the
great European poor who had no inheritance. He lived on the
farm at Port Hill and he was not over-pleasant to meet. He had
been brought over to the Island by Thomas Burnard to look after
his interests, in the words of the earliest account, written in
Devon twenty years after, 'in the superintendence of the men
clearing the woods and preparing the timber for exportation'[12]
and to manage the horses hired to haul the timber. He was a
progressor, a man of all trades, a man to get things done, a
driver.

PART TWO

THE SMALL ROBBER BARON

The members of this new ruling class were generally, and quite aptly, called 'barons', 'kings', 'empire-builders', or even 'emperors'. They were aggressive men, as were the first feudal barons; sometimes they were lawless; in important crises, nearly all of them tended to act without those established moral principles which fixed more or less the conduct of the common people of the community. At the same time, it has been noted, many of them showed volcanic energy and qualities of courage which, under another economic clime, might have fitted them for immensely useful social constructions, and rendered them glorious rather than hateful to their people. These men were robber barons as were their medieval counterparts, the dominating figures of an aggressive economic age.

Matthew Josephson, '*The Robber Barons*'

Near Port Hill is the residence of James Yeo, Esq., who is engaged in agriculture, lumbering, ship-building, fishing, merchandise and other pursuits. He employs a number of mills, and, at the time of my visit, he had nine ships upon the stocks. Every kind of business is followed by this persevering individual without any apparent confusion whatever.

Abraham Gesner, *Report of the Geological Survey of Prince Edward Island, Journal of the House of Assembly, 1847*

Port Hill is owned and occupied by James Yeo, Esq., M.P.P.—another of the many instances of what industry, prudence and determination will effect. Mr Yeo is a native of Bideford, in England, and came to this country in a subordinate capacity, some 25 or 30 years since, and he has to his credit been the architect of his own fortune—and a very pretty one, by all accounts, it is.

John Lawson, '*Letters on Prince Edward Island*', Charlottetown, 1851

CHAPTER FIVE

THE KILKHAMPTON CARRIER

EVEN today the country between Kilkhampton and Bideford is thinly populated, with few settlements and in places desolate. Summer tourists use the main road which runs near Hartland, round two sides of a triangle, mostly in sight of the sea. The country in between, with the ancient village of Bradworthy at its centre, has few visitors. The roads are narrow, winding, steep where they dive into the narrow valleys, and the more confusing to the stranger because they are sunk below the level of the surrounding countryside. Some of them are still unpaved.

They were very much worse at the beginning of the last century. Then a visitor, the Rev Richard Warner, wrote :

> . . . I departed from Biddeford, and took the Kilkhampton road. Fortunately it happened to be market day at the former place otherwise I must inevitably have been again lost in the abominable and intricate roads of North Devon. From those who were going to attend this weekly day of public barter, who frequently ride eighteen or twenty miles for that purpose, I obtained directions through a country wild, desolate, and unpicturesque to Kilkhampton; without a single object to interest or amuse for the distance of two or three and twenty miles.[1]

The whole area was backward. The people were very poor and were to remain so for much of the century. It was part of a West Devon of which William Marshall had written ten years before that,

> Twenty years ago there was not a 'pair of wheels' in the country; at least not upon a farm; and nearly the same may be said at present. Hay, corn, straw, fuel, stones, dung, lime, etc., are in the ordinary practice of that district still carried on horseback.[2]

Some people lived and died without leaving the parish in which they were born. Enclosure had taken place several centuries before. The farms were small and isolated, each at the end of a rutted mud track which ran with water like a stream for much of the year. Day labourers employed on them were lucky if they made 7s a week.

James Yeo junior (the suffix is common in North Devon and Cornish Parish records of the time and current American usage may have sprung from this part of Britain) lived by labouring in the parish of Kilkhampton. He was the son of a local shoemaker, James Yeo senior, who married Ann Orsborn late in 1788. There were three other children of the marriage, John, Elizabeth and Mary. Then Ann Yeo died and in 1807 James Yeo senior was married again to Grace Francis. Five years later, when his stepmother had one child, Samuel, James Yeo junior married her eighteen-year-old sister Mary with the interesting result that when his second half-brother Thomas and his own first son William were born in 1813 it was possible for his stepmother to have uncle and nephew, who were also cousins, one at each breast, a feat which was still part of the family tradition exactly 150 years later.

James Yeo senior was literate and his eldest son learned to write an excellent hand and to express himself very well, if colloquially, on paper. James junior was a small man with short powerful arms and stubby fingers to his small hands. At some stage he suffered an injury or disease, most likely *ankylosing spondylitis*, poker spine, which tends to strike in youth. In consequence his back was held rigid and he could flex his body only from the hips. Despite this disability he had immense powers of physical endurance. He also had mental gifts which would have marked him out as an altogether exceptional man had he been born into a more prosperous social stratum. But as it was he had almost no chance of breaking out of an existence which in its roughness and poverty would be regarded as altogether sub-human in North America and Britain today. The facts of his life were such as to produce a ruthless and acquisitive personality, detached from much sense of obligation to his fellow men.

In 1814 or 1815 James Yeo somehow obtained the capital to make a first attempt to break out from this level of existence. There are shadowy traditions of something to do with scouring the tideline. The sea and a singularly inhospitable coast are ever present facts in the life of Kilkhampton. The village stands at the head of the great steep-sided cleft called Combe, which sweeps down to the sandy beach below Duckpool. A hundred and fifty years ago there was almost no control of the rockbound coast on either side of the mouth of Combe, and with an impoverished and wild people living on it there was little hope of underwriters ever receiving much of the value of what was washed in from wrecks. And there were a lot of wrecks.

James Yeo acquired a horse and a carrier's van and set up a once-weekly service from Kilkhampton and nearby Stratton over the awful roads to Bideford and back. It was a way of life which made him well known over a wide stretch of countryside, but it was not likely to soften a hard character. In 1815 the unusual relationship in which he stood to his stepmother was marked by the births of a little uncle and niece, Lawrence and Jane, and in 1817 by an aunt, Barbara, and another niece, Nancy. Early in 1818 his wife died. James took to drinking heavily and soon the horse died and the van had to be sold. He slipped back into poverty.

But his carrier business had brought him into contact with men in Bideford. He appealed to Thomas Burnard, and the great merchant, who was a good judge of men, performed one of his acts of far-sighted charity and paid James Yeo's debts and took him on a contract to go to the Island as a progresser and go-getter in collecting lumber. James Yeo had been married again to Damaris Sargent, a cross-eyed girl from Kilkhampton. She was a born shopkeeper and housekeeper.

Just when they arrived in the Island is not certain. The earliest documentary evidence of Yeo's presence in North America is an indictment for larceny of one William Stewart who is accused of robbing Nathaniel Burnard in January 1824 on board the schooner *Lady of the Lake* lying in Egmont Bay. Yeo is quoted as a witness. But in fact he was there much earlier. In

1846 he wrote in a letter that he had paid a visit to Britain in 1822. Perhaps this was at the end of his contract. In the same year he returned to the Island, according to tradition at Thomas Chanter's persuasion. All record of him in Britain ceases after his second marriage in May 1819. There are strong and persistent traditions among the descendants of the Devon settlers in Prince Edward Island that Yeo and Chanter came, both for the first time, on the same ship in 1819 and that Yeo was employed from the start in the business at Penman's Point.

As was inevitable, he did a variety of jobs in those earliest pioneer days. From obtaining timber and bringing it in for loading in the ships it was only natural that, when so few others were available to run the business, he should lend a hand in the stores where the goods were exchanged for lumber, labour and credit. In timber extraction he discovered a gift for quantity surveying, for driving men, and for rapidly mastering pioneer skills. In the stores he revealed himself as a walking calculating machine, able to add up three columns of figures at the same time as quickly as three fingers could be drawn steadily down the page. His memory was phenomenal and he soon acquired a detailed knowledge of the Burnards' affairs and of the affairs of those with whom they dealt, and also of the technicalities of shipbuilding. Yeo's gifts were suited exactly to a pioneering venture. They made him an ideal employee, as long as his interests coincided with those of his employer. Chanter thought highly of him and their relationship proved mutually beneficial for many years.

William Ellis was an entirely different personality. He was an honest master craftsman, inclined to take things slowly and seriously, apt to bemoan his own misfortunes and the wickedness of his fellow men. Once settled in a pioneer farming community he reverted to his agricultural roots and became a farmer too. He was respectable and respected, reasonably prosperous at this time, a good citizen, content to stay as he was.

Both men drank heavily at times, but Yeo's bouts were calculated affairs and his mind went on working when his body seemed helpless. As long as the Burnards and Chanter ran the business at New Bideford and Port Hill, Ellis and Yeo were employees in a British concern, each with his place in a British society which at their levels was almost static. Yeo and all his kind were condemned to the treadmill of their labouring life for ever. Ellis was likely to remain the respected senior employee. But when the employers withdrew, those who stayed behind became North American colonists. Mr Ellis the master builder and Jimmy Yeo the labourer turned factotum, whose results were appreciated and whose methods were not too closely inquired into, were on their own. Inevitably in due course there would be adjustments in the social order.

There is a story in the Island, first written in Yeo's obituary a century ago, that when Chanter sold his interests in New Bideford and Port Hill he assigned the uncollected accounts to Yeo in settlement of a debt he owed him, described in some sources as accumulated wages. It is said that with this small beginning Yeo made his start as a merchant and timber dealer. This story does not appear in the earliest accounts of Yeo's success which circulated in Devon and Cornwall in the early 1840s (with his encouragement) and were the occasion for a great outflow of emigrants (in his ships). There was no need in Britain to have an answer to the great question—how did he get so much money in such a short time? This was something that could happen to energetic people in America. Moreover Chanter was there to put the record straight. Certainly the documents already quoted show that the debts owing to the business, which was so valuable a part of it, were never assigned to Yeo. Providing he fulfilled his contract with Chanter they belonged to Ellis and represented much of his working capital.

During the five years after Thomas Burnard's business was put up for sale in 1825, there was a flurry of legal activity over these debts. In the attics of the Provincial Assembly building in Charlottetown there are dozens of papers, dating from this period, affidavits of service of processes, affidavits of debt, documents of prolonged cases in which Thomas and Martha Elizabeth Burnard ostensibly proceeded through Island lawyers towards the recovery of money owed to them by various settlers. At the beginning of this period the debts were still legally Chanter's, but Ellis had an interest in them pending the completion of what he had undertaken to do under his contract.

Nevertheless Ellis's name does not appear in any of the documents which have been examined. Notes on some of them, on the other hand, show that Yeo collected sums in settlement of certain cases, and in others he issued affidavits, describing himself as 'clerk' to the Burnards or occasionally and with cynical humour simply as 'yeoman', in which he swore that certain sums were owed to the Burnards by named individuals. Whether in the cases in which he was not named he was a beneficiary, taking or sharing in what was collected, it is not now possible to say. The fact that he is noted as the collector in some cases when his name does not appear in the formal legal record suggests that he may have received money or value in others as well. All that can be said with certainty now is that a massive campaign of debt collection, nominally on behalf of the Burnards, using the legal methods open in the Island, took place between 1826 and 1830 and that Yeo was deeply involved in it. And behind this campaign of collection by legal process there must have been a much bigger campaign of direct collection from the simpler and poorer and more easily intimidated, a campaign in which Yeo's intimate knowledge of the settlers and their business and his energy and formidable personality must have been of particular use.

It may be asked why, once he had acquired full legal title to the debts and found that some of them had already been collected by someone else, Ellis did not take action against Chanter or Yeo. But such a series of actions would have been complex and vastly expensive and out of character for Ellis to undertake. He was dependent upon Chanter for the chief market for timber and ships and as the chief source of store goods in return. As for Yeo, there may even have been some sort of partnership between him and Ellis at this early stage; there is evidence that they were working in close association until the early 1830s. While Ellis had the squatter's rights at Penman's Point, and was paying 15s a year for the property to the Seymour's agent, Yeo lived in the fine house and had his stores there.

The strand at Appledore with barefoot boys playing, a bark discharging cargo into sailing barges in the Pool and the ketches Nouvelle Marie, Harmony *and* Jane Ann & Elizabeth, *and the fishing smack* Rhoda. *The photograph was taken in the late nineteenth century but apart from details in the dress of the children and the rigging of the ships the scene had changed little in the preceding 75 years*

Appledore in the early 1920s. In the foreground is the triangular bay with the remains of Benson's New Quay and the Richmond Dry Dock filling up most of it. Around the Dry Dock are foundries, mast houses and sail lofts. The schooner with sails set is the Haldon. *Staddon stands among the trees above the houses of East Appledore. West Appledore, once Irsha, is still a distinct settlement straggling round the headland*

Bideford Quay as it was for much of the nineteenth century. Appledore is down river behind the hill on which stands Thomas Chanter's signal tower, later known as Chanter's Folly, equally visible from both places

The peninsula at Penman's Point (now Port Hill Farm) shaped like a floppy boot lying between Campbell Creek in the foreground and Ramsay Creek under the distant trees at the righthand side of the picture. The great sound of Port Hill harbour lies beyond the peninsula and beyond again is Lennox Island. The ruins of the wharf built by Thomas Chanter jut out into Campbell Creek immediately beyond the hut in the foreground of the picture. Thomas Chanter's splendid house stood on the cleared land just beyond the middle of the nearer trees to the right. The photograph was taken from the cupola on top of Green Park, the house built by James Yeo's second son, James, in the early 1860s

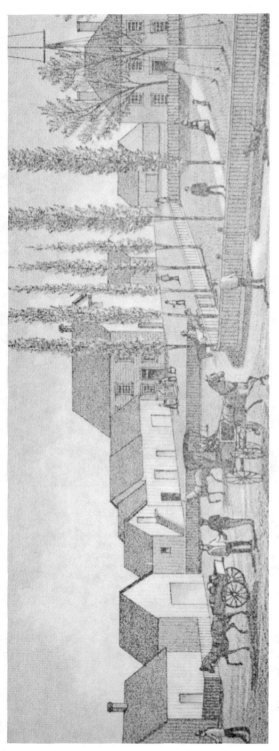

James Yeo's keep at the crossroads, the new Port Hill house built in the early 1830s with the stores, barns and carriage houses around it

For by the end of the campaign of debt collection he was a storekeeper in his own right, and Ellis was buying goods from him on a considerable scale. Perhaps the best summing up of what happened is that which was given in Yeo's son William's obituary, written in Bideford in 1872, probably after consultation with the then aged Thomas Chanter. There it was said of James Yeo as William's father that 'He was a shrewd man, and capable of any amount of work. When the firm which he served declined business, he managed to succeed to a portion of it'.[3] In fourteen years he had succeeded to it all.

The processes by which James Yeo, having acquired his initial capital from the Burnard estate, took his first steps forward are indicated in a rather shadowy way in a number of surviving documents. He began to do business on his own. Some of his deals resulted in legal action being taken against him by those who claimed he was in their debt. In other cases he himself proceeded. Usually the sums involved were small, but not perhaps to a man dragging himself up by the laces of his tattered boots.

Sometimes the stake was greater, dangerously so for a man in Yeo's position, and it is evident that he sold what he had not got and bought what he had not the present means of paying for; this was all perfectly legitimate, providing his hunches and assessments proved right, which they mostly did.

Two records of cases and a legend show his early methods. One William Wallace claimed in 1828 that Yeo had sold him Grover Island in Richmond Bay for £60, some of which he had paid over before (he said) he discovered that Grover Island was not Yeo's to sell. He added that Yeo owed him in addition £400 for other considerations received. The upshot of this case is not in the surviving records, but it cannot have been in Wallace's favour. Local juries, some members of which were perhaps already in debt to an up and coming man noted for his ungentle methods, were likely to decide for him, especially when his opponents were landlords' agents. Such was the case when in 1828 the proprietors of Lot 12, Sir James Montgomery and his brothers, sued Yeo on the grounds that, while they had formally and legally conveyed Lennox Island to him, he had paid only a quarter of the £400 he had undertaken to give for it. After three years of proceedings a jury of Prince County men found in his favour. That verdict was quashed as 'bad and erroneous', but a second jury repeated the performance.

The legend is more complimentary to him. It shows him apparently befuddled in a Charlottetown liquor store when a ship's captain came in and loudly bewailed the failure of settlers to deliver a timber cargo. The bartender told the captain that if he wanted a cargo the disreputable figure snoring at a table could provide one quicker than any other man on the Island. 'What, that fellow?' said the shipmaster, whereupon James Yeo came to life and undertook to have a cargo ready to begin loading by the time the vessel reached Richmond Bay. He rode to Port Hill through the night, and in the morning began driving his debtors to bring timber down to the creeks. The cargo was ready for the ship to load as he had undertaken. A note of authenticity is provided by the story that he had to sue the shipowners before he obtained payment. It is an interesting fact that the brig *Ebenezer* under William Marshall, owned by John How of Bideford, loaded a timber cargo in 1834 for which Yeo was paid by Marshall with bills on How which were not honoured, so that Yeo had to proceed against Marshall in 1835.

With the capital he had acquired he took over the stores at Port Hill from Ellis. He made the settled area on the east coast of Lot 13 his headquarters. Not only was there better timber here than around New Bideford, there were far more farms and people. In 1830 the liquor licence for the Port Hill stores, previously issued to Ellis, was registered in the name of Yeo, who had already attained the minor public position of a fence viewer and constable for his area. He left the stores to Damaris to run while he busied himself elsewhere. She had already borne him two daughters, Susannah in 1824 and Mary Jane in 1825, and a son, James, in 1827. Now in 1830 she gave him another daughter, Isabella.

Soon Damaris was even more on her own, for this remarkable Cornish village labourer had attained the status of master of his own ship. She was a very small one, the thirty-five foot schooner

Mary Ann, built and first owned and sailed by Lauchlan McInnes of Seven Mile Bay on the south coast of the Island. For three years from 1829 Yeo sailed her intermittently with cargoes that it paid him to carry, some of them on his own account. In the fall of 1829 one James MacArthur alleged he had found out the hard way the dangers of paying Yeo in advance. He claimed he had given him 'a certain pair of Oxen rising five years' in consideration of which the *Mary Ann* was to take a cargo to Richibucto in New Brunswick from Lot 13. She never even loaded the cargo, Yeo having other and more lucrative preoccupations which prevented him from going to Richibucto before the close of navigation that year. The case was still going on in 1842, by which time Yeo could have handed over to the luckless MacArthur a small herd of oxen and the *Mary Ann* as well without noticing that he had given anything away.

*   *   *

The five years from 1826 to 1830 were formative years in the Island's history. They covered the greater part of the Lieutenant Governorship of John Ready. The Assembly met annually. Four members were elected for each of the counties, and two for each of Captain Holland's towns, two of which, Princetown and Georgetown, were rotten boroughs indeed. The franchise went to housekeepers, lessees of land in possession, and to Protestant proprietors of lots. The voting was open and oral and the election of the county members took place at one county poll. Elections were, of course, rough affairs. There were not many proprietors in the Island, but the absentees' agents found their way into Parliament and the distribution of the franchise helped the development of a party structure, a conservative-proprietor-and-agent 'government', a liberal-tenant opposition. Gradually the feuding cliques of officials gave way to political parties with consistent principles of some sort behind them, even though these principles were even more blatantly the distillation of the group self-interest of the members than is usually the case. The movement at this stage was from the early opposition to the proprietors and the family compact of officials, which J. B. Palmer had started with his Loyal Electors, towards the establishment of formal responsible government in the Colony. In Governor Ready's time it was still largely a struggle for the raising of the status and power of the elected Assembly against the Governor's Executive Council, who were not members of the Assembly or constitutionally responsible to it. And behind all this activity all the time there loomed the dark shadow of the land question with all the harm and misery the system of tenancy to absentee proprietors brought with it.

The Island was still a tiny community. In 1826 a census showed a population of 23,250. But after 1827 the first great wave of migration began and six years later the population was almost exactly 10,000 more. Charlottetown was growing, but the development of a second big nucleated settlement was still thirty years away. The arrival of new settlers meant a push inland from the tide water of the creeks. It was as easy or as difficult to build roads as anywhere in north-eastern America because the sandy soil dried so quickly that it was as good as gravel. All men from sixteen to sixty were supposed to put in four days' work a year at road-building and the government had the right to push roads through proprietors' lands as they wished. Some enlightened proprietors built roads themselves, but most did not. Soon the government road was to be driven west to Cascumpec and on to North Cape and it became possible for the first time to ride on a road of sorts from Port Hill to Charlottetown. With the roads came wheeled vehicles, and by 1832 wagons and gigs were becoming quite common. With the increase of settlement, minute as it still was, the older cultivation began to be fenced and tiny pieces of the growing clearings acquired a more civilised appearance. Log houses began more generally to be replaced by clapboard and shingles, but the ordinary family was still dependent for survival during the awful winter cold on huddling together round a log fire in the smallest possible room.

By the early 1830's about one-fifteenth of the total area of the Island was clear of timber and cultivated after a fashion. Potatoes were still the main crop, but oats were now second to them. Oats were exported to the United States and to the neighbouring

British colonies, but in 1829 a letter appeared in the *Prince Edward Island Register* urging the export of oats to Britain as a means of acquiring more overseas currency. In 1827 Governor Ready encouraged the formation of an Agricultural Society and among its earliest acquisitions of livestock was the Devon bull Tommy Chanter which its namesake had reserved in the sale to William Ellis. The bull was six years old and its services were advertised at 5s per cow or 'half a dollar' to members of the Society, 'to be paid before covering'.

International trade was expanding, though some of it was of a peculiar kind. In 1826 rum was, in value, by far the largest single item of consumer goods imported, over £8,500 worth, almost exactly three gallons per head for the whole population including children. It is no wonder that there were said to be thirty unlicensed and illegal liquor stores in Prince County alone. In June 1828 Thomas Chanter's *Collina* brought 404 gallons of brandy and 252 gallons of gin to Richmond Bay in one cargo. These figures mean that the shipbuilders and lumber buyers were paying for labour and timber in rum and other spirits, and that the subsistence farmers who demanded this currency were going to stay subsistence farmers or even drop below subsistence level.

The imported materials necessary for the finishing and equipping of the nearly 10,000 tons of sailing ships built in 1826 cost more than three times as much as the rum. These ships were by far the most valuable export of the colony. They were worth at the very least £66,000 delivered in Britain. Lumber and lumber products were worth about £7,500, potatoes about £4,500 and oats about £1,500. By 1830 the export of oats had more than trebled, that of timber had increased, but not greatly, and, although this was a depression year in world shipping and ship-building figures were down, the ships were still the biggest source of overseas currency and gave the Island the favourable balance of trade needed for its development.

The tiny fragment of red earth on which all this was happening lay in the great Gulf of St Lawrence, off a North American continent now beginning to be settled west of the Mississippi. By

1830 the frontier ran south from Illinois around the western parts of Missouri, Arkansas and Louisiana. The first Americans were pouring into Texas and thoughts were beginning to turn towards the Oregon Trail. But much the greater part of the United States was uninhabited and largely unknown. In Canada there was a thin line of settlements along the St Lawrence and along the north shores of Lake Ontario and Lake Erie and on to Georgian Bay.

In 1828 the last survivor of those who signed the Declaration of Independence laid the first stone of the track of the Baltimore and Ohio, the first modern railroad in North America. The same year has been said to have been decisive in the redistribution of power in New England from merchant to manufacturer. The face of America had turned away from Europe towards a west where an 'empire such as man had never seen' was opening up. The steam boats were multiplying on the Mississippi and the great days of the river were just beginning. The agricultural west and the manufacturing north-east needed each other as markets. By 1825 the 363 miles of the Erie Canal, driven largely through raw wilderness, were opened and the cost of moving a ton of cargo from Buffalo to New York City was reduced from a hundred dollars to five. The west and the north-east were linked, and the effect on the modern world was to be profound. New York City was the seaward end of the waterway. In the ten years before 1830 property values there rose by about eighty per cent. Even timber from the west could be shipped out of New York at a profit and the lumber ships began to come in :

> I've got a mule, her name is Sal,
> Fifteen miles on the Erie Canal,
> She's a good old worker and a good old pal,
> Fifteen miles on the Erie Canal.[4]

CHAPTER SIX

THOMAS CHANTER AND
THE FIRST EXODUS

IN two years William Ellis fulfilled the contract under which
he had bought Thomas Burnard's Island enterprise in 1826.
He built the ships he had undertaken for Thomas Chanter.
They were a brig in 1827 which was named the *Collina* and a
bark registered as the *Calypso* next year. Both were loaded with
lumber on Chanter's account and sent off to Britain. In 1829
Ellis launched another ship for Chanter, the brig *Sappho*. In these
four years also he built four ships for other people. The brig
Jessie of 1827 he financed as to one-third himself, while Joshua
Williams of the *Bellona* took a third share and Thomas Chappell
the rest. The big *Breeze* of the same year was Chappell's and he
had not finished paying for her when he left the Island in her as
her master, for Ellis had to proceed against him as 'an Absent
or Absconding Debtor, justly and truly indebted to William
Ellis for one hundred and ninety-one pounds'.[1] In 1829, besides
Chanter's *Sappho*, Ellis built the schooner *Irene* for Samuel Smith
Hill, who was one of John Hill's sons, now running the business
as Cascumpec. Next year he built another brig, the *Bollina*,
for William Grigg of Appledore, who later settled on the
Island.

In 1829 Ellis entered into a contract with T. H. Haviland for
the construction of a large bark of over 300 tons. This vessel was
registered in 1831 as the *Jane* owned by Chanter. The contract
has survived and is unique, ten years older than the earliest
previously known contract to build a ship in what became the
Canadian Maritimes. The vessel was intended to be able to rest
upon the gravel of the tidal Torridge. Because vessels were being
delivered incomplete, it was necessary to specify how fully the

95

ship should be finished. Chanter gave detailed instructions about two pieces of juniper for the pumps in a letter which has been preserved:

> You had better send home by the *Calypso*—The New Vessels Pumps that is the Two pieces Juniper saw'd to their proper shape and coated with Paint or Tar and then we can get them completed whilst the Vessel is discharging & send them out again by her but if you send them rough I shall have to pay duty on them.[2]

The vessel was to be paid for partly in goods for the marine stores and in retail goods the prices of which are specified.

Each summer Chanter came to the Island. In 1827 the *Bellona* dropped him on her way to the Miramichi and put ashore also four and a half tons of cordage, fifteen tons of salt, twenty barrels of tar, five of pitch, two of resin, five casks of white lead, ten sails and three anchors, the raw materials for shipbuilding and for the preservation of the winter's food. Next spring he came through Miramichi and returned in his own new *Calypso*, James Lowther master. Lowther had come out in charge of Chanter's *Collina* which had brought from London among many other things 6,250 pounds of soap, nearly 6,000 pounds of candles, 9 puncheons of rum, 2 puncheons and 2 hogsheads of brandy, 4 hogsheads of Geneva, 600 pounds of coffee, 37 tons of cordage, dry goods, paints, groceries, hardware, 'and etc.', for the stores at Port Hill and New Bideford. In 1829 Chanter shipped not only stores but skill in the person of a shipwright, William Bure, who bound himself in a paper evidently written by Ellis to work on the *Sappho* for a summer in the Island, to which he was no stranger:

> I hereby engage and bind myself to William Ellis ship builder of Prince Edwards Island that I will return to his yard as on before the firs day of June 1829 if possible and to work with him as a shipwright or any other legall occupation I may be directed untill the brig Hiss building for Thos B Chanter Esq is Launched and compleated and the said William Ellis agrees to pay or cause to be paid four pounds for every calendar month that I shall actively work in withness our hands this twenty third of Octr 1828.
>
> WM BURE'S X MARK.[3] In presence of THOS B. CHANTER.

On her first voyage that year, from Liverpool to Richmond Bay, the *Calypso* brought £549 worth of stores for William Ellis and loaded from him 300 tons of pine and 9½ tons of lathwood in return. The total value of the return cargo he supplied was only £184 and it left Ellis owing Chanter a round £400, to be worked off in timber at 12s 6d per ton. On the same voyage the *Calypso* brought goods to the value of £2,000, subsequently advertised as 'British Merchandise, consisting principally of dry goods' for sale by Alexander Davidson in Charlottetown.

Thus Chanter's assets in the Island grew. He had a very flexible approach to business, readily extending or reducing his commitments as circumstances dictated. The size of the joint enterprise he had built up with Gilbert Ormsby on Bill-hook Island in the mouth of Richmond Bay became apparent when the partnership was broken up and the business sold in order that Chanter might realise a debt Ormsby owed him. Besides the schooner *Gleaner* there was a large store, a curing shed, herring nets, a large quantity of herrings, two boats and fifty or sixty 'puncheons well seasoned to cure Herrings in'. Richard Moys, who had been involved in the Bill-hook Island business, bought a new schooner in partnership with his brother Thomas. But soon afterwards he left the Island, his wife and child and this story, for Australia, so the tradition has it, and some other adventure.

Chanter's business involved legal action for the collection of debts which in two cases alone totalled more than £3,000. In one of these, against Alexander Campbell, he took the new bark *Alchymist* in part settlement. In 1829 he had the brig *Euphemia* built at Bedeque. With his small fleet of Island-built ships his fortune was on its way to being properly established and he began to advertise his ships in the British press as loading, with room for passengers, for North American ports at Falmouth, Plymouth, Cardiff and Bideford, and in the Island press as regular traders, with agents in London and Liverpool. The fare for an ordinary passage was £3, for cabin passengers £25. The response was good. The *Collina* and the *Calypso* became ships in which leading citizens of the Island preferred to travel, and the demand from

North Devon and North Cornwall for passages in the hold soon became almost overwhelming.

Chanter became closely associated with Haviland, and that powerful man acted as an overseer of his interests in the Island and sometimes as his banker. It was not surprising that Chanter was reappointed year after year a Justice of the Peace and made foreman of the Island's Grand Jury in 1828. The dignity of this role, however, was somewhat diminished by the fact that there was no business before the court.

But for all the position he had made for himself by enterprise, a vast amount of hard work, and discretion in his dealings with his fellow men in the Island, Chanter had no public position in his native Northam. For all his great charm and his liberal tastes he was still only a rising young merchant intent solely on his business, known as the nephew of the great Thomas Burnard and also of a well-known and slightly controversial cleric, the vicar of Hartland. In February 1829 he married Isabella Scott, step-daughter of Sir Charles Chalmers, the Nova Scotia Baronet of Appledore whose intimate first-hand knowledge of the Island and its politics may have been one of the factors influencing Thomas Burnard to send the *Peter & Sarah* to Richmond Bay eleven years before.

The couple arrived in Charlottetown from Liverpool in the *Calypso* on 9 June 1829. They spent a part of the long, hot summer in the house on Port Hill farm where Ellis exercised squatter's rights and Damaris Yeo was running the stores and cooking for all the men. Isabella Chanter wore a red velvet dress which made such an impression on the children of settlers accustomed to coarser fabrics that it was still remembered (and at only third-hand from one who saw it) 135 years later.

During a visit to Charlottetown the couple joined Haviland on a trip of a fortnight or so over to Nova Scotia. On 11 August 1829 the *Prince Edward Island Register* had a number of announcements concerning local comings and goings :

> The *Vestal*, Taylor, from Tobermory, with 301 passengers arrived here on Friday. Seventy of the number have since sailed for Cape Breton; the remainder settle in this country.

Departures—In the Packet for Pictou last week—Hon. T.
H. Haviland, Mr and Mrs Chanter, Mr Billing, Mr Mann of
Philadelphia.
Arrivals—at Cascumpec from England, John Hill, Esq.
Cleared—Aug. 5, schooner, *Mary Ann*, Yeo, Halifax, 1050 bus.
Oats.

Of these announcements, in terms of the Island's history in
the nineteenth century, the last was much the most important.

*   *   *

In 1824 Lord Rolle, later to become famous as the man who
tripped and, appropriately enough, rolled down the steps of the
throne when paying his homage at Queen Victoria's Coronation,
began the building of a canal from Weare Giffard to the foot
of the hill below Torrington in North Devon. It was finished at
the beginning of 1827 and soon trade began to flow up the
Torridge again as it had in medieval times. When Martha
Burnard's *Bacchus*, *Bellona*, and *Hero*, and the *John* of Sunder-
land, all from the Miramichi, the *Saltern's Rock*, a Bideford ship
from St John, New Brunswick, and Joshua William's new *Jessie*
from the Island, all lay together discharging American timber at
Bideford in December of that year, part of their cargo was rafted
up to Torrington. Soon there were lime kilns, a brick factory,
storage caves and a timber yard by the canal, and William
Tardrew, the merchant squire of Annery, started a shipyard just
where the Halfpenny Bridge at Weare Giffard crosses the river.
Here, late in March 1827, the brig *Louisa*, probably the last ship
to be built under Richard Chapman's direction, was launched
in the presence of a great crowd of people gathered from all the
villages for miles around. Many more ships were built in the
next half century.

The Burnard ships and later the Chanter and the other Island-
built vessels made their two round voyages to the Miramichi,
Quebec or the Island each summer. Though Chanter's ships
delivered some of their cargoes at other ports, these vessels brought
in great quantities of timber which was sold, to the profit of
Bideford, all over Devon. Thomas Burnard the younger was

Mayor of Bideford in 1826 as his father had been four times before him. He shared the mayorship with five merchants and gentlemen in a sort of six-year cycle. He had inherited some of his father's influence, but the real power in the land still rested with the Lord of the Manors of Bideford and Northam, Instow and Saunton and lord of the rolling acres of Tapeleigh, Augustus Clevland, commonly known as Saltren Willett. When in June 1830 he was married to Margaret Chichester, eldest daughter of the principal branch of that great Devon family, the Bideford bells rang and the Bideford guns fired all the long summer day.

Bideford was becoming solidly re-established as a port in the American trade and a small but regular business with Spain, the Azores and the Mediterranean was growing again. Its population and wealth, like that of Northam, were steadily increasing. Over 100 ships were owned in Northam and Bideford, with over 400 men in their crews, and they provided employment for many more ashore. There were seven active shipyards between Appledore and Annery. Here, because of the low prices they could offer, even in the shipping depression of 1827 eight ships were under construction at the same time.

But the cheapness of the ships came partly from the low wages the shipyard workers were paid and there was another side to the prosperity of the Torridge Estuary in the late 1820s. The North Devon paper lamented the 'insubordination of the lower classes in the town of East and West Appledore for the want of Judicial Authority' and reported a meeting of the 'major part of the inhabitants of this town' to devise the most efficient means of protecting the property of the inhabitants 'from the nightly depredations to which it has latterly been subjected'.[4] In the fall of 1827 within a few weeks accidents in the shipyards and on the water made seven widows and forty fatherless children in Appledore. When the *Queen of Cardigan* struck on Appledore bar a year later, with the loss of four out of her crew of seven, 'a dreadful scene of plunder was witnessed but which might have been prevented had the more respectable part of the inhabitants interspersed their authority'.[5] No arrests were made though search warrants were issued. In the spring of 1828 Martha

Burnard's *Superb*, less than two years old, was damaged through collision with ice on the Grand Bank. The master and some of her crew were rescued by another ship, but seven men had gone off in one of the boats. They were picked up eleven days later by a ship bound for the Miramichi. Only two of them were still alive and one of these died a day later. The survivor lost his feet from frostbite. He had lived by eating the bodies of the dead.

On the night of 9 November 1829, the *James*, belonging to James Peake of Plymouth, sailed from Charlottetown for Bristol, with Mr and Mrs Thomas Burnard Chanter on board. The tradition is that Isabella Chanter did not like the Atlantic crossing, did not much care for the pioneer society of the Island, and did not want her husband away for six months of every year. Be that as it may, Chanter was making his last departure from Charlottetown and from the Island. Fourteen years later his Island connections made his fortune, but in the meantime he had to operate at long range. Haviland looked after his affairs and acted as his banker and agent. Ellis built ships for him and, with Yeo, obtained the lumber cargoes to fill them.

*   *   *

Contemporary reports of departures from the port of Bideford, of arrivals in North American ports, and the annual Returns of Persons Emigrating agree in general that in the eleven years from 1830 to 1841 roughly 2,250 people sailed over Appledore bar bound for the New World as settlers. Despite William Cobbett, who in *Rural Rides* in 1830 described it as 'a rascally heap of sand and rock and swamp . . . in the horrible gulf of St Lawrence (which) . . . bears nothing but potatoes' of these at least 850 were landed on Prince Edward Island. The total number of those who emigrated was equal to half the population of Bideford at the period. A hundred people of the town itself went out together in the spring of 1841, but the majority of the migrants were labourers, craftsmen and small farmers from parishes all over North Devon and North Cornwall.

The area they came from was poor and backward economically and socially. The wages were low, the housing appalling. The labouring man worked twelve hours a day for six days a week and lived in one or two rooms of a mud- or stone-floored hovel. If he broke the law, however trivially, he exposed himself to penalties of the kind reflected in a sentence passed in June 1837 by Thomas Chanter, as a magistrate of Bideford, on sixteen-year-old Mary Ann Burnard (who can have had no connection whatsoever with the merchant prince) of seven years transportation for stealing 5s 6d. For all the respectable and conscientious savagery against those who challenged the sanctity of property, law and order was poor. In the countryside the power still rested mainly with the squires.

But these conditions existed through a great deal of rural Britain, and yet emigration on the scale which took place from North Devon was by no means universal. There were parts of Britain from which extreme poverty and the policy of the landlords were forcing migration. Poor though the area was, this was not the situation in North Devon and North Cornwall. Here the forces at work were those which had operated in the migrations from North Devon to North America of two centuries before. Then Devon had been third among the English shires in contributing emigrants to the early New England settlements because the great Devon fishery off the North American coast meant that people were familiar with the idea of an Atlantic crossing and had some knowledge of what lay beyond, and because there were empty ships outward bound; merchants with empty ships will carry passengers cheaply. Now the timber ships of Thomas Chanter and Martha Burnard were sailing regularly across the North Atlantic two or three times each summer. Some of those bound for the Island carried store goods for the shops of Charlottetown and the stores of Lots 12 and 13 and Cascumpec, but these were not fully laden and the rest were empty. These ships were not manned by the sweepings of the brothels of great seaports; that sort of recruitment had scarcely begun. Surviving crew lists show that they were sailed by local men, and for every one from the drangs of lawless Appledore, with its back turned to the land, suspicious of strangers, there was a lad from Bradworthy, Abbotsham or Torrington, Georgeham or (soon to out number the other inland places) Kilkhampton. Perhaps a third of the crews came from further away, Bristol, Plymouth, Milford and Ireland.

These local men from farming communities which did not make their living from the sea came back again and again to tell their families and neighbours of what a passage to the westward in one of Mr Chanter's ships was like. They were able to tell of how earlier settlers were doing, of how a former neighbour was his own master on a farm, for all that it was only a wooden cabin and a few acres of smallholding hacked out of the spruce forest. An Atlantic voyage could be made for £3 in one of Mr Chanter's ships which could be seen at Bideford quay on almost any market day in the early months of the year. So about one person in every hundred, more in some areas, less in others, in the Taw and Torridge valley countries and the wild country over into Cornwall went to the Island or to New York or Boston or St Andrews or Quebec.

This first exodus began in the spring and early summer of 1830, when Thomas Chanter started to advertise the *Collina*, the *Calypso*, the *Sappho* and the *Euphemia* as 'conveniently fitted up for Families and will take out passengers on moderate terms to Prince Edward Island, Cape Breton, Nova Scotia or New Brunswick'.[6] The *Collina* arrived at the Island in late May, bringing the London papers up to 25 April, the news in which was duly incorporated in the Charlottetown *Royal Gazette*, and:

> seventy four passengers, men, women, and children . . . a good many of whom seem in comfortable circumstances. The men consist of Farmers, Labourers and Mechanics, and are chiefly from the Counties of Devon and Cornwall.[7]

Next January direct sailings to New York and Quebec were advertised, and on 12 April the *Apollo*, the *Calypso* under the veteran master, Lewis Grossard, and the *Bacchus* left Bideford together, bound with passengers respectively for New York, St Andrews and Montreal. The *North Devon Journal* described the scene:

> Numerous friends of the emigrants were in attendance to witness their departure, and to take their last leave; on the firing of a signal gun, the ships all got under weigh, and were

cheered by not less than 5000 persons who lined the quay and bridge. Many of those persons who had thus expatriated themselves are respectable farmers and their families who carry with them very considerable property, thus transferring their property, their talents and their influence to another land. Many more would have accompanied them had the vessels afforded accommodation. And such is the prevailing rage for emigration, that a female who had given birth to a child but three days before, would not be persuaded by the most urgent entreaties of her friends to remain behind for another season.[8]

The *Calypso* was in Passamaquoddy Bay in twenty-two days and safely landed her hundred-odd passengers at Eastport on the American side as well as at St Andrews on the British. She was back at Bideford in time to make a second voyage in the late summer.

Bows of the *Lord Ramsay*.

So it continued for a decade. Thomas Chanter bought new ships built for the business at New Bideford and elsewhere—twenty-three of them between 1832 and 1840. Among them was a brig, the *Lord Ramsay*, built at Quebec and commanded by a

The Legislative Assembly building at Charlottetown in 1843 showing the circular covered market which was a feature of the mid-century capital, mud roads, board sidewalks, and no trees. Copy of a contemporary painting by Mrs Bayfield, wife of Captain Bayfield who made the first charts of the Island's shores

The Pictou ferry paddle steamer discharging passengers and cargo at a Charlottetown wharf of the 1870s. The Legislative Assembly building is at the head of the street

Ice-boats in the Northumberland Strait. They were the only means of leaving Prince Edward Island in winter until the end of the nineteenth century

veteran named Richard England. She was the first of several Bideford ships in which it became the tradition for the emigrants to present the master with a letter of appreciation and a token of silver on their safe arrival in the New World. A correspondent wrote of her in 1836 :

> Among the many vessels which have been prepared for the reception of emigrants there have been none fitted in such superior style and in so comfortable a manner as the fine brig *Lord Ramsay*, R. England, Master, now lying at Appledore bound to New York. The stanchions dividing the separate berths are elegantly turned and coloured and the whole has more the appearance of a comfortable hotel than a passenger ship. On deck there is a spacious cookhouse entirely for the use of passengers, and from the well known abilities and kind disposition of the Commander she will doubtless become a favourite vessel. We hear almost all the places in her are engaged.[9]

Despite the vicissitudes of the shipping trade the North American lumber business went on steadily. In June 1830 there were 103 ships loading together in the Miramichi, 200 at Quebec. Next year no less than 344 ships had entered at Quebec by early June. It was not surprising that other Bideford merchants sought to enter the business. The shipping records show that they obtained some of the necessary financial accommodation from Haviland, who was ready to underwrite the capital to cover building costs against the mortgage of the vessel on completion. A complex pattern of mortgages and shared ownerships grew up, with vessels changing hands frequently, either in whole or in part, especially on their completion and on arrival and re-registration in Britain. In the winter of 1833-34 Haviland visited Britain; he returned to the Island from Bideford in the *Calypso* on her early spring voyage. Next year Chanter made him formally and legally his 'attorney for the purpose of managing his affairs generally in British America'[10] and Haviland's appointment as Secretary of the Colonial Government in 1839 must have made him even more valuable as a friend.

The jigsaw puzzle of interlocking ownerships of ships was further complicated by the fact that, as he became more

D

prosperous, Chanter himself began to speculate in ships, to buy and sell and build in anticipation of capital appreciation rather than of the earning of freight money and passenger fares. He had access to and partial control of a source of cheap tonnage and, after 1835, when shipping surveyors were first appointed in Bideford, a means of presenting it on the market graded and branded with the marks of high respectability.

Among those who used the financial accommodation provided by Haviland was George Hooper of Bideford. He was the first customer to buy the first ship to be built under the supervision and financial backing of James Yeo. This was the *Cordelia*, a brigantine built at Indian River in 1836. Early in the 1830s Richard Heard, a builder and auctioneer in Bideford, began to dabble in shares in ships. Later he entered the emigrant and lumber trade with the *Em. B. Heard* and *Civility*, both built at the eastern end of the Island. He set up a timber yard at Bideford and the two barks soon established reputations as passenger ships. In 1840 he sent his son William to set up as his agent in Charlottetown and there William Heard spent the rest of his long life. John How also built up a small lumber business in Bideford and became an owner of timber and emigrant ships.

In the spring of 1832, before he became a ship owner himself, John How chartered the *Calypso* from Chanter and sent her to the Island with 197 passengers 'chiefly mechanics and labourers'. Lewis Grossard was her master, and she made the passage in forty-one days, arriving on 27 May at which time the last snow must still have been lying in low, rotting, dirty banks under the trees. Something went wrong with the arrangements for the *Calypso's* arrival. The most likely explanation is that How chartered the vessel on terms which envisaged releasing her in time to make a second voyage in the late summer. This meant that the *Calypso* had no time to go to Charlottetown to land her passengers, although How had entered into agreements with them to land them there. Chanter gave Grossard instructions to put the emigrants ashore near the site of stillborn Princetown, and this he did, on what was described by George Beer, the ringleader in the subsequent 'mutiny', as the 'wild shores of farmer Hacker's farm in Richmond Bay'. The emigrants rebelled and, by one means or another, forced Grossard to transport them and some of their baggage to Charlottetown at the ship's expense.

George Beer's description of conditions in the 100-foot *Calypso* with almost 200 people on board is indicative of what was normally taken for granted :

> . . . was there a proper space between decks?—Was not a considerable part of our luggage stowed between decks, so that we could scarcely stand or sit, and were almost compelled either to keep in our miserable berths, or stand shivering with wet and cold on the upper decks? was this legal? . . . Was there a correct and legal list of the passengers presented at the Custom House?[11]

But the stranding of the passengers was really nothing very out of the ordinary. The early nineteenth century view was that the ship owner contracted to carry the emigrants to the New World but was not responsible for what happened thereafter. And the requirements of the Passenger Act of 1828, with which Beer appears to have been familiar, were neither observed nor enforced.

For all its relatively large scale and profitableness (and at least eighteen ships were built at New Bideford and Port Hill alone, by William Ellis, John Brooks, William Grigg and James Yeo, all Westcountrymen, between 1830 and 1840), to the late twentieth-century observer the way this transatlantic shipping-lumbering-emigration business was run seems strangely casual. There exists a series of letters, accounts, bills of exchange and so forth which passed between Chanter, Ellis and Haviland during these years of the first great migration. Chanter complained of the way in which Ellis's vessels were finished and of their design :

> . . . in preventing any of those expenses to which I have been subjected after the Vessels reach England in Completing them—for it is commonly remark'd in England—I will have nothing to do with American Vessels for they are always sent home half finish'd—in the Sappho round her Bows the Plank was so shook one side that everybody at Bideford Quay noticed it, and at length I told Day [the Master] to turn her round In the Collina people say—what a pity to put such a bad Plank

in her Decks where Timber is so abundant—The Top-gallant Quarter boards of the Sappho were obliged to be taken down, just temporary put up no framing or anything inside—no opening or Hinges in the Bulwarks & Waist—and such numerous little unnecessary expenses fell on me that I was quite annoy'd—If therefore you have underlet the other Vessel do act as an Inspector for me & and see everything properly done—

. . . I am going to send out a Topsawyer and hire him for you for Three Months, as the Calypso carrys so poor a cargo it is necessary to have some Deals as well as Lath-wood to assist her stowage, and I have directed Captain Lowther to fill her cabin with Deals and completely fill the Stateroom—the Deals should be 12 feet long Nine inches wide & 3 inches thick on account of the Duty—and I think you could get some clean saw logs very cheap of black spruce to cut that dimensions.

. . . when you write me next let me know if it would answer & the expense of raising on the Calypso about Eighteen Inches, and whether it could be done whilst she is loading next voyage for really her burthen last Voyage did not exceed her Tonnage.[12]

He complained continuously of business conditions and of the quality of the lumber Ellis supplied, but nevertheless in the same letters he commissioned the building of new vessels.

Bideford, October 31 1831—My dear Sir, I am very sorry to have to inform you that the Bark Jane which sailed from Plymouth on the 8th September bound to Richmond Bay, and having on board a Crew and the remaining stores for the new Brig—together with a Crate Earthenware and a Bale of Cloths & other goods for you—returned to Plymouth on 28th—having been out as far as Long 38—and had split his sails, & otherwise damage from constant & very heavy Gales of Wind,—on his way back she sprung a Leak—and on his arrival at Plymouth both Pumps could not keep her free.

The Bacchus returned the same day here & had split her sails & been out the same distance.

The Sappho sailed on 2nd Sept from Bristol & put back here on the 11th sailed again on 13th with the Bacchus—and I have no account of her—she will I hope safely reach you, & has on board Iron Pumps & other necessaries for the Brig 'Ianthe' also 3 Puncheons Rum, 3 Crates Earthenware & a

Bale Canvas etc for sale I suppose there will be no chance if the Sappho should get out of sending the new Brig home and if that is the case I shall endeavour to run a Vessel out very early in the Spring with a few hands to get her home & make three voyages if possible—You will have a large Gang this Winter and unless you have any better employ for them you may if you think proper build me a sightly Schooner of about 65 Tons for the Fruit Trade not too full nor too lean—or any size vessel you prefer not exceeding 300 Tons on the same lines as the Jane—but this is only for your consideration—as respects the Brig if you can agree with anyone to build her a Cabin small but neat to go down aftside—I wish you to do so that no hindrance on finishing may be necessary in the Spring to delay her with you or her—and I will certainly despatch a Vessel about 15th March for the Island, on her account Tawton's Wife who is with you is getting monthly from me 30/ and Bures Wife 40/ Halfpay therefore however they may be employ'd keep back the amount Sterling from them. If you have no employment for them I will take all the Deals they can cut this Winter as Bures is a good Workman— If you can build a small Vessel this Winter I would take a Cargo of Grain home in her—The Janes last Cargo was a very good one except the lathwood which is the most profitable part if good—but what she brought is not worth the Duty—I think it would answer very well to keep a gang making lathwood & giving them a good price for Triangular pieces or only what is good & free from Knot & large but really what comes from the Island is worse than ever—I sold three Cords for 10 Guineas & they would not pay me anything for it & the Lathmaker says he cannot make Laths of it—and what came from St. Andrews at 15/ a Cord fetches 6 Guineas a Fathom and there is not a bad piece in it—but I know the difficulty you have to get any there & therefore endeavour to make the best of it—The Jane will now lay up at Plymouth & start early in the Spring for Richmond Bay—but it is a sad loss to me, for I have not sold her & now I really do not expect I shall—the extent of the damage I do not know—but I told Lowther to write you from Plymouth all particulars—and having a Master & Crew for the Brig on board makes it worse—I wish you would write me a Letter on receipt of this with an account of proceedings—This Country is in a very disturbed state and very little Business doing—Riots have prevaild lately in Bristol & on Sunday last The Mob burnt down the Mansion

House in Queen Square & 30 Houses also The Bishops Palace—
The Gaol & Bridewell & the Treadmill & a great many people
were Burnt and Kill'd—but I hope we shall hear no more of
such direful mischief—I have just heard of the Calypso's arrival
at Miramichi in 39 days & daily expect her back I am very
anxious for the Sappho and Collina—both of which I have
insur'd out It is very strange but do what we will the Sappho
cannot sail at all and you have so placed the Beams that her
Masts cannot be altered—pray avoid this in the Brig—and I
shall be glad to hear from you what sort of a looking Vessel
she is finished—what she will Register & what you expect she
will carry—

If you want anything in the Spring you must let me know as
soon as you can & I hope next year will be more fortunate
than the present.

I Remain Yours Truly, Thos B. Chanter.

I have sent out to Mr Haviland a Draft for the small Vessel
if you wish to Build her this Winter to be Built exactly on this
plan which you can send for as I send it by this Mail.[13]

In 1835, in one of the periodic business depressions, Martha
Burnard went bankrupt and the remaining ships registered in her
name were sold. Two of the ships to which Chanter refers in the
letter which follows were hers.

Bideford 28 April 1835—Mr William Ellis, I write you a few
lines by the Sarah & Eliza bound to Charlotte Town Capt
James Marshall—to inform you the Sappho will sail in Ten
days for the Island—and I have sent or shall send by her a
stock of Iron—and other things to be supply'd you for building
the new Barque—I have no answer to my enquiry whether
you could not finish this Vessel to send home this autumn
which I much wish if possible—I received your letter ordering
Iron & etc.—and I observed what you say about the Vessel
being narrow,—she is 10 Inches wider than the Lord Ramsay
and Two feet only longer—and if you like I am sure it is in
your power to make a very good and a very handsome Vessel
of her, by avoiding the unshapely *Tuck* & hollow runs.——I
trust you will give her a good long floor for laying on the
ground—I do not know who modell'd the City of Gloucester—
but she was the ugliest Beast you ever built—without the
advantages of burthen for she carried no great Cargo—I was
obliged to put her into Dock in Bristol and caulk her all over—
and after stripping her and fresh rigging her—fitting up a

Cabin & painting her throughout I sold her for L.6 per Ton—
I also put a new Chain Cable on board her besides what she
had—and she did not Register by many Tons what you made
of her on the Island—the Vessel you are now building is for
my own Trade in this Port and I do not intend to sell her—
I have therefore to claim your consideration to my interest
in making her thoroughly good. If there are any old Iron Knees
to be got I would put them in her tween decks whilst she is
building to strengthen her, or if I can pick up any here I will
send them out—the Marina saild last Evening for New York
with 220 Tons Iron & about 50 passengers but I much fear
she will lose her two voyages by the accident—for she sailed
early & off Ireland sprang a leak—and but for the number
of Passengers she would have gone down with them
[which means that the passengers did the pumping while
the crew sailed the ship]—she fortunately got back here & the
leak was found in her Garboard—Shipping are gone to nothing
in England now—The Jessie sold for about L 400 last week—
and I could not get L 300 for the Collina—I sold the Calypso
completely fitted out for America for L 925 I sent her to
Newcastle this Winter and she sank on the voyage L 30—the
Vessel by which I send this is an English Brig called the Sarah
& Eliza & I own a Sixteenth of her & never received a sixpence
in my life—Mr. How I hear has just bought the greater part
of her at the rate of L 600 for the Vessel 165 Tons Register
& in very good order The Rover was sold last week in Swansea
for L 200—Lowther complains that he cannot make anything
in the Marina what he expects—and the Bellona after going
into the Carpenters hands & being made new aloft sold for
L 1540—I bought a quarter of her—and I fully intend if the
new Vessel is built by you according to my wishes to keep her
in the Timber Trade regular to this Port and I do not wish to
own more than one or two Vessels at a time for the Captains
get their Bread when the owners are going to ruin—

I will write you more fully by the Sappho.

Yours truly THOS B. CHANTER.[14]

Less than a month later on 23 May Thomas Chanter wrote to
William Ellis again :

I have received two letters from you ordering Iron for the
New Vessel & in the Sappho bound to Cascumpeck I have
sent out a supply of Goods—and I have also sent out Capt
Day—in hopes you may get off the Barque this autumn at all

events—he will be there to see you supplied with whatever you want from Cascumpeck from the Goods sent in Sappho— I daresay you have received before this my letter to you by the Bellona—& that you are informed of my being in possession of Mr Hill's property where I intend if possible getting a large English settlement next year & doing a little business— and I hope the connexion with Richmond Bay will not be an unprofitable feature in the undertaking. . . .

. . . I should think you might get your masts from Cascumpeck and I have particularly requested Capt Day to facilitate you in every way he possibly can do so and on the other hand I do intreat you to give your best judgement in the building of the Barque—for I tend to Keep her certainly, and exclusively for this Port,—where she must lay aground with a heavy cargo particularly she should have extraordinary Bilges in thickness six outside and Four inside and I trust you will get some better Joiner to do the work aloft—for of late the Joiners work has been infamous—and I have determined on building her Cabin on the Island unless she comes home this year—any assistance or facility you need from Cascumpeck in any way Capt Day has orders to give through Mr Coady—who I have impowered to act until other arrangements are matur'd.—I lost L 600 by the Gloucester! Some of her upper deck *hemlock* Beams were shook to pieces—and she required caulking all over Docking in Bristol, & near Sixty Pounds labour to complete her—no Topg Quarter Boards— nor in fact anything about her *finish'd*—which I had to do— & after fitting her out afresh with New Chain & Anchor she was sold for L 6 per ton and a difference in the Tonnage English Measurement & Island—but the Vessel you are now building I have no idea of parting with expecting she will be a fair sailor a good carrier & a handsome Vessel. . . .

. . . and if you want any Provisions send up & order it from Cascumpeck & if to be got you will have it—Poor old Mr Chapman died a few days since—Robert Ellis your son will not go out again to the Island I understand, I gave him your message. . . .

. . . The principal thing I want to write about is the new Vessel contracted to be launched in September 1836 I believe now if it is impossible to get her away this autumn *surely* by some little exertion you can get her completed against the opening of the Navigation in the Spring instead of September—so as to insure Two Voyages—if you get her decks in this

Autumn—there would be plenty of work to do in the Winter—
the cabin can be fitted & all the Spars made in her Hold
and a great deal of joiner works Quarter Boards—Bulwarks—
Tops Caps & Crosstrees making—& I have sent you out an
extra Sawyer (Pow)—to forward you—there was one or two
bad deck Plank [?in] the quarter deck of the Gloster which
injur'd her very much to the Eye which please prevent in the
new [?barque]. . . .

  . . . I suppose the Jabez will be soon here & that I shall
hear from you by her & I will write you by the Jane & I
remain

  Yours faithfully, THOS B. CHANTER.[15]

In fact the *Jabez* did not sail until November 1835. She was
a brig built at New Bideford and owned and commanded by
William Grigg. Three days out from Richmond Bay she was
smashed to pieces on Cape Breton, fortunately with the loss of
only two lives.

The new ship about which Thomas Chanter was so very
preoccupied was called the *Atlanta*. Her completion was delayed,
although apparently she was still finished before the contract
time, and she was frozen in the ice in Richmond Bay for the
winter of 1835-36. William Ellis built her at a second ship-building
place he had established on Port Hill farm. He wrote, in his own
inimitable style, to Chanter about conditions at the time :

  Dear Sir, I Expect the Barque Atlanta will sail in a few
  days After the Unfortunate Detentions She had met with
  through the Severaty of Last fall the Winter setting in at least
  one fortnight Eariler than Usell I have no doubt but the
  disappointment to You has been Very grat Respecting her
  Cargo—But on the Other Hand perhaps is all fors the Best
  as She might have Shared the Same fate as Griggs and
  Naumbers of Other Good Vessels—the Attempt in getting her
  off has praved a Verry Serius last to me One Hundred and
  Fivty Pounds will not meet the last I have sustained by
  Lanching her Bef the Time of Cantrack In the first place
  I had to let the half of her by Cantrack And then had to send
  and get a Gang of Men from Charlottetown And pay them
  an Extravacant price for their work all in Cash—I also had
  to pay Thirty Six pound for Joiners work which aught have
  been done for three fourths of the Amount which was Also

Cash [and] not One Shillings worth of progress of any kind could be got without paying Cash for it. . . .

. . . But After Calculating all last you have Sustained you will make a Considerable gain by her Making one Voyage more if not two more than She would if Lancht according to Contrack And as you have often Talked of Making Three Voyages I think She has a Verry fair Apportunite I trust you will find her as Good a Vessel has ever You received from the Island in Every Respect—I fear she will not have a fair Trial of Her Sailing This Voyage as She has not got Suffcant Ballast by at Least Thirty Tons wich prevents her from Taking a fair Deck Load—I hope and Trust you will take it into Consideration that it has been Greatly to my Dessadvantage in Every Respect in Lanching the Vessel so many Months before Time although She did not get away I Defy Capt Day or any other person to say that I did not use Every means in my power & Spared no Expences to get her away I need not point out to you the Dissposissions of the People in this Cantry in particular them of my own Family. . . .[16]

Chanter's references to Cascumpec refer to the situation following an agreement he entered into in 1835 for a twenty-one year lease at £400 a year on most of the land and assets of John Hill, now finally retired, including the stores and shipbuilding places at Cascumpec and 'the liberty to cut, fall and carry away timber'. It is clear from the fragments of accounts surviving that William Ellis drew heavily on the Cascumpec stores in 1835, purchasing from Thomas Chanter goods worth between £200 and £300 which were moved down the narrows to Richmond Bay in boats and on timber rafts. These goods included many tools and fittings for the building of the *Atlanta*, iron, oakum, quantities of rope and a 'ship's head' at £5, and such disparate items as '18 small yellow handkerchieves at 3d each, 69¾ yards of print at 10d per yard and 21 pairs of women's shoes at 2s 9d per pair'. Ellis complained that he was overcharged on these goods to a total of over £27; he said that the advance he had been paid for the *Atlanta* had been wrongly calculated. On the other hand Haviland wrote to him at the end of 1835 saying that, apart from anything recently come down from the stores at Cascumpec, he was in debt to Thomas Chanter to the extent of over £1,500, of which nearly £700 represented the value of goods supplied and the rest cash advances :

> . . . the cash part of your advances considerably exceeds the amount of goods notwithstanding the agreement . . . and how I shall get over the excess of cash which I have paid with Mr Chanter I dont know, . . . as the whole amount will exceed your claim upon Mr Chanter for the bark I trust you will see the propriety of abstaining from drawing any more orders on me or upon Mr Chanter's account, I cannot make any further payments whatever personal arrangements I might be induced at any future period to make with you for that purpose.[17]

When the *Atlanta* had been delivered Chanter wrote Ellis a terse letter :

> Bideford 10 August 1836—Mr Ellis—I rec.d yr letter by the Atlanta & I am sorry to find you are so uncomfortable & as you say badly off but what astonishes me most is—that you are disappointed at my not building another Vessel—when you have over & over again written me you would build no more— and it is no pleasure doing business with so much grumbling— for I have always given you full value for what you have done & I understand you have a great friend in Mr Green of St Eleanors I hope you will be more comfortable & better satis- fied under his patronage—I wish no business with any Man unless it is satisfactory on both sides and I confess I thought when I had Cascumpeck that you would arrange with Mr Cambridge and still build for me. . . .
>
> You have plenty of time to overcome all your difficulties if you like to set about it & in any way I can benefit or assist you I will do it.
>
> I am, Yrs Try, THOS B. CHANTER.
>
> The Atlantas Keelson is only fit for a Vessel Ninety Tons and she is 10 feet too short I have sent her to Quebec & to have a Oak Keelson put in—[18]

Henceforth Chanter's ships were built elsewhere in the Island. For all his complaints at the state of business, he steadily increased in wealth and influence from 1830 into the early forties. And though he complained to the ageing Ellis of the poor quality of the ships, those same ships, when they were surveyed for classification by the surveyors appointed by Lloyd's on arrival at Bideford, were very favourably reported on. Of the *Atlanta*, the occasion of so much of Ellis' misfortune, the surveyor wrote :

> . . . as good as the country built in can produce. . . . This vessel was built by William Ellis a person who ere he left this had the building of several ships for H.M. Navy—& since he has been on the Island he has sent home all his Vessels, highly approved of—& this deserves to be classed with the highest of them.[19]

Chanter's rise as a public figure in Bideford took just ten years. For all his hard-headedness over deals in ships, lumber and store goods it was characteristic that he first came to prominence as the principal sponsor of an imaginative and unprofitable venture for the public good. The small sailing ships which ran between Bideford and Bristol provided a service which was irregular and unreliable and particularly unsatisfactory for passengers. Chanter instigated the formation of a company to build and run a steamer. In September 1834 she was christened *The Torridge*. About 5,000 people saw her launched, among them directors and shareholders who returned indoors after the ceremony to drink no less than fifteen toasts.

Early next year Chanter, who had been one of the assignees at Martha Burnard's bankruptcy, acquired her timber yard on Bideford Quay. After the passing of the Municipal Reform Act in the same year the Bideford Borough Council was expanded and an election held for the first time. The new council was composed with one exception entirely of reformers, among them Thomas Burnard, Thomas Chanter and John How. In 1837 Chanter became Mayor and took to London his fellow citizens' address of congratulation to Queen Victoria on her Accession. In his speeches, which were usually punctuated with cheers, he revealed himself as a staunch liberal and by the end of the year he was one of the most popular men in the neighbourhood. He developed a style of oratory which charmed his hearers into acceptance of him personally, if not always of what he had to say. He used this gift to excellent effect on more than a generation of his fellow townsmen.

With Isabella and a growing family, the eldest boy christened Heath Haviland after his North American agent, he established himself at Glenburnie, a gracious, well-proportioned house which stood alone in a large garden on the side of Orchard Hill overlooking the creek which here separated Northam from Bideford. He busied himself with all the affairs of the district. From Augustus Saltren Willett he leased in 1837 the rights of the Lord of the Manor of Northam with which went certain traditional shipping dues at Appledore and rights over the Pebble Ridge at Northam, then regarded as a vast quarry for road stone and fill. He took his duties seriously and held Manorial Court and, what was more important, a celebration dinner every winter. He became a landed proprietor, buying and renting properties down the west bank of the Torridge below Bideford. He laid heavy moorings in the Pool at Appledore at which the timber ships could lie to discharge their cargoes without the risk of taking the ground on each tide. In 1841 he built a signal tower, in appearance like a Gothic church tower, on the hillside above the beach upstream of Benson's New Quay. Placed at a focal point in the landscape, it could be seen from Bideford Quay and from every limekiln below Bideford Bridge. Here signal flags were hoisted when a watchman identified vessels in local trade, the *Swan*, the *Harmony*, the *Newton*, and the *Peter & Sarah*, still going strong, coming in over the bar, so that gangs of casual labourers called 'limestone porters', many of them women, could be collected ready to discharge them.

The local shipping trade flourished. Sometimes sixty ships lay massed at Appledore. Forty-four went out over the bar on one tide in May 1840. In July 1841 twelve were being built on the Torridge at the same time. In February of that year the wharves and quay at Bideford had presented a 'very animated appearance', as the *North Devon Journal* put it, 'from the outfit of several large ships in the North American trade, and the curiosity and application of parties from all parts of the county intending to emigrate'. The *Lord Ramsay* was there with the new barks

Falcon and *Em. B. Heard*, the old *Bellona* and the brigs *Isabella* and *Florida*, 'all expected to be filled with passengers for New York, Quebec and Prince Edward's Isle'. At the end of the year four large barks, one brig and three schooners lay together at Bideford Quay all discharging timber from the Island. The Quay was narrower and shorter and barer than the present one, with no line of fully-grown trees on it.

But for all the prosperity and wealth of these first years of the 1840's there was still the undertone of abject and squalid poverty which had been there fifteen years before. Death and disaster on the water were regularly reported and each incident left its trail of destitution. Appledore remained a poor and lawless place. Attempts were made by some inhabitants to establish a police station in the hope of reducing the frequent robberies and checking the goings-on in the beer shops 'where nightly dances are held and children and apprentices harboured',[20] but it was to be a long time before a policeman was installed and even then there was not much improvement. The local seamen were unionised at a very early date and in the spring of 1839 the general poverty was increased by a strike which prevented the seasonal re-opening of the limestone trade. The men wanted an increase of 2s a voyage on the 8s they normally received, a wage which must have given them an average income of about 32s a month during the eight or nine months of the sailing season, but the owners would offer only an extra shilling. The limestone masters tried three months later to reduce the wages paid to the limestone porters, but the porters also struck and after a week, while vessels full of stone collected inside the bar, all the owners except one gave way.

It was no wonder that when, in the same year, the bark *John Lilly*, bound from Liverpool to Calabar, was wrecked north of the bar, she was stripped by wreckers. A letter read out at Lloyd's in London asserted :

> . . . the shore was thronged with wreckers, hardened as the rock which surrounded them, wholly intent on plunder. Farmers from this and the adjoining parishes continued through the day to cart off whatever they could put their hands on . . .

and I cannot conceive a more useful lesson than the condign punishment of some of the more wealthy offenders, some of whom have been more prominent and certainly infinitely more wholesale in their proceedings than the numerous poor wretches who might plead their 14 pence a day the amount of a husbandman's wages in this parish.[21]

Early in 1842 Chanter obtained a very big contract for the supply of timber for the railway from London which was now to be extended westwards from Bristol towards Exeter. The archives of the British Railways Board show that in 1842 and 1843 he supplied rather more than one-fifth by value of all the timber used in the construction of the railway, a total of 12,136 loads, more than all the timber exported from Prince Edward Island in the early peak year of 1810. Roughly half the timber was provided at 65s per load, the rest at 59s, and the total payments made to Chanter, who operated without partners, were over £36,000—at present day values perhaps £350,000, well over a million dollars. No other merchant supplied timber for the project on this scale and the contract must have marked Chanter as one of the greatest merchants in Britain south-west of Bristol. His fellow citizens celebrated that fact by making him Mayor again, this time for two years in succession.

He deserved this kind of success. He knew more about his business than any of his local contemporaries and rivals. He had served a long and hard apprenticeship in the sea creeks of the Island and on the North Atlantic. He had commuted across that ocean in small sailing ships for most of ten successive years, returning each time in the frigid gales of early winter. There was nothing he did not know of the mechanics of the North Atlantic trade, of the problems of lumbering in the Island, of the lives of the settlers, of the Colony's politics and administration, of shipbuilding and ship management, of the marketing of timber and ships in Britain and of the personalities and parish pump politics of the Northam peninsula. And for all this he was no robber baron either, but a man most liberal in his politics for his time and place, always ready to seize upon technical advance and see how it could be applied to the greater prosperity of his native North Devon. His tastes were gentle. Glenburnie, which still stands, was a proper house for a merchant prince to live in and there remain fragmentary records of his life there, of guests invited to listen to the nightingales in the woods of Orchard Hill and of summer parties on the lawns against the music of an orchestra brought in a wagonette from Barnstaple.

But in October 1843, when Thomas Chanter was pouring lumber from Quebec and the Island into Bridgwater, partly in James Yeo's ships and partly in his own (the *Glenburnie* on 18 April 1843 was, it was reported, the earliest arrival save one ever known at Quebec) for transport down to the railhead creeping south-west towards Exeter, a man who had come back to Britain from the Island after twenty years away was married in Northam Parish church to Elizabeth Allen Williams, daughter of a candle-maker in Appledore. The couple rented a house in Market Street and settled there and the man opened business as James Yeo's agent in Britain. This man knew more about lumber and ships and the North Atlantic than even Chanter did and he also knew about other and less legitimate forms of trade. He was William, eldest son of James Yeo.

CHAPTER SEVEN

THE HONOURABLE MEMBER

I N 1838 George Goodman, the Collector of Customs at Charlottetown, in a letter to the Colonial Secretary in London, provided a detailed breakdown of imports and exports for the seven years from 1830. His figures show that imports were exactly doubled during that period. The rate of growth of exports other than ships lagged far behind with an increase of only twenty-five per cent. Had it not been for the shipbuilding industry the Island would have had an adverse balance of trade in 1837, in which year nearly twice as much in value was imported (£91,000) as was sent out (£47,000). But the 6,500 tons or so of shipping built in that year must have just about restored the balance. Though quantities varied from year to year, alcohol in various consumable forms remained a conspicuously large import. But the amount brought in did not increase as rapidly as the population and there were much greater increases in the purchase of other consumable goods. It is evident that a change towards a more stable society was beginning.

The list of merchants who handled this expanding Island trade contains many Westcountry names. William Way and William Curtis of Brixham and Charlottetown had recently dropped out of business but, besides the Bideford merchants, Thomas Billing of Plymouth and New London was still busy, as were the sons of John Hill. John Cambridge died in Bristol in 1833, at that time the proprietor of Lots 14, 21, 27, 32, 46, 48, 49 and his original Lots 63 and 64 around the Murray River. Artemus went to live in Liverpool but Lemuel remained prominent in the Island, settled first at Cascumpec where he worked in partnership with Thomas Chanter, and then on the south bank of the Grand River on Lot 16. James Peake of Plymouth was conducting a steady trade with Charlottetown. Joseph Pope, youngest of the brothers of Plymouth who had set up a shipbuilding business at Bedeque, was becoming an important man. He was a Member of the Legislative Assembly for Prince County in 1830 and of the Lieutenant Governor's Executive Council in 1839. But the phenomenal change of the period from 1830 until the early 1840s was the rise of James Yeo.

He sailed the *Mary Ann*, clearing, for instance, for the Miramichi in October 1832 with a cargo comprising 350 bushels of oats, 200 bushels of potatoes and 8 sheep. He collected debts and was already buying and selling land, or the leases of land, while Damaris ran the store at Port Hill. In 1831 he shipped his first timber cargo to Plymouth in Thomas Chanter's new bark *Jane* and next summer he sent a cargo to Penzance. At the end of 1833 William Ellis settled a stores account with him which had been accumulating since 1830 by paying him nearly £800. Thirty years later it was said of him at this period that he was already the only man in Prince County from whom the settlers could obtain cash (which would of course be paid against a sale or mortgage).

In 1833 Yeo added to his fleet the schooner *Catherine O'Flannagan* purchased from a firm of merchants on the Miramichi called Joseph, Samuel, Edward and Henry Cunard, whose name is still commemorated in the North Atlantic trade. He also financed one-third of the shares in the bark *Marina*, built by Ellis at New Bideford and owned by him and by James Lowther who sailed as her master and manager. But Ellis did not hold his shares in the *Marina* for very long.

For all his growing indebtedness, Ellis was able to do one thing in 1833 which was to have important consequences. He had been paying the rent due to the Crown on the 300 acres of Penman's Point, and with it the 15s a year due under Hugh Montgomery's agreement with Sir George Seymour, ever since he took over squatter's rights from Thomas Chanter in 1826. Because Montgomery had failed to pay off the mortgage the lease had become the legal property of the mortgagee. In June Ellis bought the remainder of it for £300.

From the sequence of events it looks as if this development caused Yeo to leave Port Hill farm, for very shortly afterwards he built a house, stores and barn a mile away by the side of the track through the woods to Lot 14 and the shores of Grand River. James and Damaris had three more children after Isabella, Caroline who died in childhood (after which Damaris is said to have refused to sleep with James for a year), John and Caroline Alice. John was born in July 1834 and when they moved to the new house Damaris had to carry him because he was still not big enough to walk.

The new house was square with a low-pitched roof. It was in a commanding position and the stores were conveniently situated for all the settlers on the west shore of Richmond Bay. It stood by a road and not by the side of navigable water, and that in itself is an indication of the change which was beginning to take place in the life of the Island.

The man who built it was set on the single-minded pursuit of money and power. Yeo seems to have been much aided in this by the awesome impression he made upon many of his contemporaries, so that forty years after his death people who had known him in their youth still shuddered when his name was mentioned. There are numerous stories of his drive to success during these crucial years of the 1830s and '40s. A version of one has been recorded by an American writer :

> And do you know that . . . from Summerside here to Tignish he run six shipbuilders. . . . And as I was going to tell you, for six months he's never go to bed. He'd go into a tavern or halfway house and have a few drinks and get a lunch and lay down in a chair and sleep for a couple of hours and then he'd go out in the saddle again—rode always in the saddle. And I've heard my poor old father say that he's seen him go past Cascumpec (that's where the road used to go then—there was no Western Road then) and he'd be sound asleep in the saddle going by the horse walking along. Yeah, he was quite a bird.[1]

He was indeed what he himself termed 'an active man'. The pace of life was still by late-twentieth-century standards incredibly slow, set as it was by manual labour without machinery, the trotting horse, the sailing ship, the rowing boat, and in the home the open fire to cook by. The struggles of the pioneering life and the social conditions in the Island tended through sheer physical labour to produce apathy and resignation among the settlers. Into this world James Yeo, his powers developing with the growth of his confidence and his capital, brought, within the technical limits imposed upon him by the achievements of the age, a thoroughly modern hustle.

His concentration on business was such that he appeared to care little for family life, and it was said of him that he did not know the birthdays of his children. The daughters in the store, the sons acting as agents at home or abroad, were part of the money-making machine. Yet his tribal loyalty to his family in the wider sense was strong. His brother John and his sister Mary Hopgood, his half-brothers Lawrence, Samuel and Thomas and his half-sisters Barbara Adams and Grace Maynard and all their families were brought over from Kilkhampton and settled on farms or in businesses in different parts of the Island. At heart he was a sentimental man. To judge from Mary Jane Yeo's Commonplace Book—a book of verses written by friends and illustrated by herself, begun when she was staying with her brother William at Appledore in 1847 and continued on her return to Port Hill— she and her sisters and brothers were brought up to be sentimental to a degree we should now consider maudlin. Living against a background of the uncertainty of sailing ships, they seem to have been obsessed with partings, farewells and death, though in fact they all lived to great ages. It was typical of Yeo that he continually commemorated his wife and children and even Mrs Chanter in the names he gave to his ships. Besides at least one ship named after his wife and each daughter there were no less than five *Isabellas* and a *Five Sisters* and a *Three Brothers*. In all this, as in his retention of the extreme roughness of manner which went with his origins and history, he was typical of the first Robber Barons.

In 1833 he stood ready for his first great leap forward. He had the capital, but, much more important, he was of the place where the money was to be made and he knew it from the roots of the trees up. And from his position as banker, storekeeper, everybody's creditor, a literate man in a largely illiterate society, intimately familiar with the business and private affairs of all his neighbours, he already had great and diverse power in Prince County. He was probably in a stronger position than any merchant in the Colony's history, even the Cambridges, even John Hill, had ever been.

The titles of those who claimed ownership of many of the lots in Prince County (as elsewhere in the Island) were already uncertain. In some of them no real landlord's authority had been established for years. Non-fulfilment of the terms of the original grants, failure to pay the rents due to the Crown, mortgages, the uncertain results of contested inheritance, all these and other factors had sapped away the pattern of ownership and responsibility. Added to this, increasing areas of land were settled by squatters who had little or no title, most of whom were illiterate and incapable of understanding their legal position. And among the settlers on some lots moved so-called agents, whose claim to act with legal authority was itself doubtful, seeking to make what they could out of rents and services they could bamboozle, bully or frighten settlers into paying.

In such a social and economic situation there was plenty of opportunity for a ruthless man supported by a little organised force and with the means of disposing of what he took, to take now, argue later, if argument arose. Some men who claimed to be agents challenged the campaign of large-scale timber rustling on which Yeo now embarked :

A PUBLIC NOTICE

Messieurs, the French of Egmont Village and Cascumpec, Mr James Yeo of Lot 13, and others.
HAVING received information from various respectable persons, during my recent inspection of Lot 10, of your having been in the practice of cutting and drawing away Timber and Hay, to a very serious extent, from this tract of Land, and applying the same to your own private uses, to the great and manifest detriment of David and Robert Stewart, of the City of London, Esquires, to whom the Estate in question doth belong, unless ye come forward and compensate these gentlemen to the utmost extent of the trespasses committed on them, law proceedings

will be instituted against ye without any loss of time, as there is abundant proof to enable me to do so. . . .
> JOHN PRENDERGAST, Prenderville, Sept. 13, 1834.

Yeo responded with a letter to the Editor of the *Royal Gazette* (in which the 'public notice' had appeared):

> *To the Editor of the Royal Gazette*
>
> (ADVERTISEMENT.)—Sir—I observe in your last paper, that one John Prendergast had made use of my name, cautioning me, unless I came forward and paid him for hay and stumpage of timber cut on Lot 10, that I was to be prosecuted for the same. I have only this to say, that I defy any person to shew that I have ever cut, or ordered to be cut, any hay or timber on said Lot without authority so to do; and I am perfectly ready at any time I may be called on, to account with the Proprietor or Proprietors of Lot 10, and half of Lot 12, or their authorised agents, for any arrears that may be due them, or may hereafter become due, for any rent or stumpage. As for Mr Prendergast, I know nothing of him, otherwise than this, that I inquired of him if he had any power from the Proprietor to act for Lot 10—he told me he had not. I rather suspected he had not, as I should suppose that the Proprietors of so much land would have sent some respectable person to act as agent for the same.
>
> I am, Sir, Your most obdt. humble servt. JAMES YEO, Port Hill, 22d Sept, 1834.

Nevertheless Prendergast made one further public attempt.

> . . . And whereas I have been credibly informed that a man, commonly known by the name of 'Jemmy Yeo', has told certain Frenchmen of Lot 6, and others also, to go into the woods of Lots 10 and 12, and cut down, square, and haul away Pine and other valuable Timber therefrom, as usual, without *now* or *ever* having the smallest shadow of authority from the proprietors, D. & R. Stewart, Esquires, *or any one deputed by them,* to do so;

Sir George Seymour's agent was now one Sidney Dealey who appears to have been both ineffective and unfortunate. The same Jemmy Yeo who was engaged in timber piracy wrote some years later of the situation which arose in the mid thirties:

> I have been the active person for the Lot these many years past Such get Roads made getting Tenants on the Lot taking

of payments from Tenants in produce and handing over the proceeds to the agent in money paid the Land Tax I may say almost Everything that was to be done I done it except to Sign Leases the Leases was most times made out in my office. I say all the business hath been done by me Except to spend the proceeds—[2]

Thus he usurped the agent's position and took the agent's perquisites.

By 1836 he was already issuing the receipts on the official forms for the rent due to the Crown from William Ellis on his holding at Penman's Point. In November of the same year the bark *British Lady* was built at New Bideford by Ellis, but Yeo, the owner, signed the builder's certificate. Poor Ellis! Two years later ships he built were described in the press as launched 'from the shipyard of Mr James Yeo, New Bideford'.

From now on, though the old building place at New Bideford remained for much of the time the principal building site, ships for Yeo were built on slips all around the western part of the Island at Miminigash, Tignish, Campbelltown, Bedeque, Grand River and on the shores of Egmont Bay, in numbers which went on increasing for two decades. The first *British Lady* was very successful. She sailed from Richmond Bay on November 29 1836 and was back again with twenty-six emigrants on 2 June next year. On 24 September she was in the Island once more, having made the round voyage in two months and fourteen days. At the beginning of December she was back in Appledore. Next year she had completed her first round voyage by 8 July.

Her master throughout this brilliant series of voyages was William Yeo, son of Ann who had died long ago, perhaps partly of starvation. It must have been when he was master in the Atlantic trade that William Yeo, describing himself simply as 'Mariner of P.E. Island', erected in Kilkhampton churchyard a plain slate gravestone to his mother inscribed with compass points and cherubs and the words :

> Think not that youth will set you free
> Just in my bloom death called for me
> God took me hence as He thought best
> To dwell I hope with Christ in rest.

William had been left behind with his aunt and his sister Nancy when his father and his stepmother went to the Island. What he did for the next fifteen years is a mystery and one which he intended should never be solved. The account he gave of the first ten years of his life at sea when he came to claim a Master's Certificate was a piece of cynical falsification and the clerk who issued the certificate in Bristol in 1851 should never have done so. William inherited almost all his father's ruthless strength and many of his mental gifts, though his vices were different. He was the last man to confuse the record from lapse of memory, yet in some cases the vessels he claimed to have served in were not even built at the time he said he was at sea in them. All that is certain is that he was at sea in square-rigged ships, for he learned the techniques which enabled him successfully to take command of the new *British Lady* on the winter passage across the North Atlantic. A reasonable supposition is that he was employed in slavers, an illegal occupation for British seamen at this period, but financially sometimes more rewarding than other forms of sea service.

While his ships sailed backwards and forwards across the Atlantic, James Yeo was busy at home in the Island. In 1840 Sir George Seymour was able to visit Prince Edward Island and to stay on Lot 13. He took a great interest in local affairs and his notes and correspondence show his concern with the position of the settlers as well as with the rights of the landlords. He

> failed . . . to find any plan more just to the settlers or more reasonable in itself than that on which it [Lot 13] has been managed for several years.[3]

It might have been supposed that Yeo would be embarrassed by a visit from a landlord whom he was systematically robbing. But he was strictly a realist and, fortunately for Prince County, Sir George Seymour was a realist too and he rapidly appreciated Yeo's special position and peculiar merits. The evidence suggests that a relationship of mutual respect grew up between the aristocrat and the former carrier. Among Seymour's papers is a series of very rough notes telling the tale of a crossing of the Island at Lot 13 with his younger son George Henry Seymour, Sidney

Dealey the agent and, of course, Yeo, on whom the whole party was clearly very dependent. Although the area was still heavily wooded it was worth taking horses. They had a rough crossing among the woods, creeks and hay marshes. At one creek Seymour recorded, showing knowledge of contemporary American popular song :

> Yeo, who would beat a Kentucky Man in resource being more than half hosse half alligator that is with rather a bit of English cartership sculled us over in a bit of a canoe towing the hosses.
>
> They found a spring and watered the hosses in doing which Cantilo's bridle got around his hind fetlock. He backed into the canoe. The grey stallion took the opportunity of biting him, the brown that of kicking the stallion and we had as fine a scene of equestinate excitement as Lady Dunne could be asked to define. Yeo and I paddled on and found Henry and Dealey again in a fix at the sheep river where a small passage was out of their depth. A boat attending a raft of Yeo's ferried them across Henry riding in the water with girths unbuckled and Yeo and I next up and landed on a promontory between the Ox and Sheep Rivers. . . . This is the spot at which Palmer fixed my paradise, or that rather of A and B but B would be badly off for a harbour, there is no such depth of water as he described and though only a quarter ebb there was little more water than our canoe required and the whole sea seems an extensive flat drawing off at low water a long way out. It seems to be a rendezvous for the timber Yeo bags or cribs.

Later they visited an area on Sheep River where Yeo and one Joseph Higgins were collecting material for building a saw-mill. There were then thousands of trees visible all around, but, they soon came to places 'where there were a few good pines and evident signs of the plunder of others going on'. They reached the Western road to Cascumpec again and went up it and

> back then on in less than an hour to Yeo's where we dined and went to bed tired. I stood my long day's work much better than I anticipated in the morning.

Sir George went on to note :

> The young men are as fine a set of men as I ever saw but are said to be little disposed to work more than is absolutely

necessary for subsistence—They unfortunately prefer lumbering to agriculture.[4]

In another place he wrote :

> I am by no means inclined to wish a Man should enter the forest without a reasonable prospect of enjoying the fruits of his labour, and my lands are let on Lot 13 on leases of 999 or 99 years with an option of purchase for 20 years at a fixed rate. Farms in new clearances rent free for 4 years, in all afterwards 1s. an acre annually. . . . Young men would enter a Forest Farm under more favourable circumstances if they would by the produce of their labour for a couple of years commence with a little Capital to buy some stock, & the necessaries requisite for this mode of Life. They more usually commence without that advantage, and only the hardy & most industrious overcome the first difficulties—a large proportion trying to cancel an always recurring debt to the next Storekeeper by lumbering (cutting timber); their lands are little and frequently their habits become irregular.[5]

Then, later among the notes,

> Yeo—Charge high have no competition get every body in their Books and employ them as they please I must send him or Mrs out a present as he was personally active and obliging.[4]

This was a state of affairs which suited James Yeo very well.

Though the greater part of it was still forest and remained so for many years, the Island was steadily increasing in population and the settled areas were growing. Life was becoming more comfortable, more sophisticated. Through the period from 1830 to the early 1840s the Island newspapers are sprinkled with reports of arrivals of parties of emigrants, not only from Devon and Cornwall but in large numbers from Scotland, Norfolk and Suffolk and Ireland, and a few from the Devizes area of Wiltshire. At a meeting of the Agricultural Society in January 1842 it was announced that 2,000 emigrants had arrived at Charlottetown alone in the navigation season of 1841. John Hill, then settled in Exmouth, advertised in 1830 in the hope of recruiting labour for his Cascumpec lumber business. An announcement in the *Western Luminary* in June of that year read :

Emigration to British America—Industrious husbandmen have now an opportunity of Providing for themselves and families, and, by Perseverance, acquiring in a short time Independence, by Cultivating Fertile Lands on the Island of Prince Edward.

The Advertiser is possessor of 80,000 acres and Proposes to Let or Sell a proportion, in parcels of 100 acres or less. . . . The lands are situated in the above mentioned British Colony, where English Laws and English Custom prevail, only one Month's sail from England, and a Vessel will be provided for those who wish to engage, at a moderate rate for the passage.

In this most healthy and delightful Island, where there are NO TAXES or GAME LAWS, except a Quit—Rent of 2-3/ for 100 Acres, the Proprietor's lands are situated on the Banks of a Navigable River, abounding with Fish, not four Miles from the Sea, and will be warranted fit for all purposes of Agriculture, and to produce every article that is raised in this Country, to the greatest Perfection; consequently those who are industrious cannot fail of doing well. And, in order to encourage some of those who have not the means of supporting themselves while their Crops are getting forward, will find occasional Employment amongst such as are already settled, till their own Farms are Productive, and during the winter by cutting Timber. . . .

Between 1827 and 1833 the population of the Island increased by nearly a half, from 23,000 to 32,000. In the latter year there were 275 people on Lot 13, and Yeo was supplying store goods not only to them and to the 127 people on Lot 12 but to people all over Prince County. His marketing area was the whole of the Island north and west of the narrow neck between Richmond Bay and the Northumberland Strait—more than a fifth of the whole colony—and he shared it at first only with John Hill and then in the mid-1830s with Thomas Chanter at Cascumpec. It was still, and remained for some time, one of the more sparsely populated parts of the Island, but in 1833 it contained about 4,000 people. The goods they bought are indicative of the social and economic state of Prince County and of Lot 13 in particular. A great many of the transactions are still summed up in the accounts by the single word 'rum'. But the settlers also purchased tobacco, salt, tea, nails, shoes, barrels of herrings, potatoes, molasses, meat, salt cod, seed of various kinds, the services of the

English bull, cloth, thread, charcoal, shovels, sail-making twine, pitch, varnish, earthenware, peas, rope, south-westers, rope matting, pit saws, handsaws, cross-cut saws, augers of various sizes, indigo and coals. Besides these material purchases all the surviving accounts show many banking transactions. Goods and services were paid for in various ways. Joseph Higgins paid his accounts with Yeo in 1833 and 1834 in small quantities of cash, in provisions provided for Yeo's men, in herrings, in '2 Horse Shoes to William Yeo', 'Collecting Lumber—£5', and in work at rafting lumber. James Gillis of Lot 16 paid off a bill of £24 by such varied means as hauling timber at Egmont Bay (which was a long way from his home), 'rafting part of a night—3s 6d', '6 days work on board *Despatch* at 5s—£1 10s', '4 Trees of Poor Timber at 8s'.

Tastes in the Island capital became more sophisticated during the 1830s. By the end of the decade there were several shops advertising luxury goods. In 1841 J. M. Tucker opened shop with a big consignment imported in Thomas Chanter's current *Isabella*. This included 'Ladies' dresses of the latest fashion', prints, shawls, ribbons, bonnets, parasols, saddles, 'a set of very good covered furniture'. Chanter's bark *Glenburnie* in the same month brought to George Hooper of Bideford, who had also opened a shop in Charlottetown, ready-made winter clothing, muslins, gauze handkerchiefs, veils, table linen, rosewood workboxes, tea caddys, writing desks and toys.

Such goods were bought by a small, relatively wealthy group of land agents, merchants, shipbuilders and professional people which was growing up in the capital. There are many other signs that a moderate prosperity was developing generally in the Island. People could afford to build brick chimneys for their wooden houses and in 1835 the *Mary Jane* brought 50,000 bricks from Bridgwater. Finished furniture was imported as early as 1832. In the same year the first pleasure boat was built. In 1835 Mr Dixon found it worth his while to advertise classes in English grammar at £1 6s for a month's course and Mr and Mrs Beer set up a boarding school for boys and girls in Sydney Street. The Misses Beer and Miss Mitchell advertised bonnet and dressmaking to order, and a daguerreotype photographer started business in competition with the first professional portrait painter. In 1842 the *Royal Gazette*, which since it was founded in 1823 had been the Island's only real newspaper, found it had serious competition from *The Islander*, established by John Ings, the lively and extremely able son of a British Naval Dockyard draughtsman who had emigrated to the Island ten years before and settled on Lot 49, advertising lessons in naval architecture for the Island's shipbuilders.

In Charlottetown in the 1830s the empty lots were filling in. Some of the best buildings of the modern town were constructed. The pleasant white-painted wooden house of the successive Lieutenant Governors with its pillared front overlooking the harbour was built (not quite in the form it is in today) in 1835. An authoritative British magazine has recently put it on record that students of the Georgian style consider the house among the finest examples of its type in North America. In 1843 a new building for the Colonial Assembly was begun. Of grey stone brought across the Strait from Nova Scotia, it is still one of the most conspicuous features of the town.

Although most people still lived near the coast or on the bank of a creek, pockets of inland settlement were growing up, like New Wiltshire, almost in the geographical centre of the Island. The growing population and the push inland meant more roads. Princetown, New London and Rustico on the north coast were linked. On the coasts a long and very detailed survey had begun; it remains the basis from which some modern charts are still ultimately derived.

There were developments at Port Hill as well. In January 1831 the Society for the Propagation of the Gospel missionary at St Eleanors, near Bedeque, reported to the Society that he was now holding a monthly service at Port Hill. A small church was built there ten years later and consecrated in 1843. On that occasion the Bishop spent the night at Lemuel Cambridge's on Grand River and next day :

> Friday, June 23. Mr and Mrs Cambridge joined us, and
> we were rowed in a little boat to the ferry-house on Port Hill

side of the river (two miles). From thence we drove to Mr
Yeo's a settler from Cornwall, and much respected (four miles).
Having an hour to spare, I occupied it in walking over a glebe
which had been given by Sir George Seymour, a principal
proprietor in this parish, who takes a lively interest in its
welfare, and feels that this welfare will be best promoted by
aiding the influence and promoting the prosperity of the
Church. A part of the Glebe has been cleared, and will have
an increased value. We next proceeded to the Church at Port
Hill, which, though small, is compact, and suitable to the place,
to which it is very creditable. Mr Yeo's subscription to the
building was £50.[6]

It was 1845 before the little church had a resident priest. It
was, and still is (for apart from the spire, which was taken down
in 1890, it stands unchanged today), a charming little shingle
building with wide corner boards, in its style very similar to the
house Thomas Chanter had built on Port Hill farm. Part of
James Yeo's fifty-pound donation was probably in labour and
timber, and it was in no way surprising that the little church
should have been dedicated to St James. He had been christened
in St James' Church at Kilkhamton fifty-four years before.

The successful and popular John Ready left the Island in 1831
and he was succeeded by Sir Aretas Young. During the troubled
reigns of the two Lieutenant Governors who had preceded Ready
the Legislative Assembly had established its right of discussion and
criticism. Under Ready it was summoned regularly, but the
situation was still very different from that in Britain, where the
Throne was advised by men who held seats in Parliament, many
of them accountable for their actions to the House of Commons.
In the Island the Lieutenant Governor was advised by appointed
Councillors who were not members of the Assembly or accountable
to it and whose policies were often contrary to those of the elected
body. To make matters worse, many of them were paid officials
of the Colonial Administration and the 'family compact' of
interrelationships between them was self-perpetuating. As late as
1841, when a Committee of the Assembly investigated the family
connections of members of the Executive Council, it was found
that all nine of them had blood relationship or marriage

connections with at least one other member and most with several members. T. H. Haviland was connected in one way or another with almost all. The Assembly resolved :

> That conviction is forced upon the mind that a family compact of such magnitude, however well disposed in advising the Executive, will take care of themselves and their friends in the first place, and the interests of the Colony only as a secondary consideration.[7]

Young's successor, Sir John Harvey, described the functioning of his Council in revealing terms in a despatch to the Colonial Office in 1837. First the Council met as a law-making body with the Chief Justice in the chair. Then the Governor took the chair and gave his agreement to the bills which had just been passed. The Council adjourned for a few minutes and reassembled as the Lieutenant Governor's Executive Council to discuss the day-to-day running of the Colony. Eight people only were involved in this charade, seven of them paid officials, all living in Charlottetown, and several of them proprietor's agents and therefore almost by definition unacceptable to most of the settlers.

The elected Legislative Assembly tried to break this system by stages, and in the long run succeeded. The members' first object was to weaken the Council by splitting it into separate Legislative and Executive bodies and to get some members of the elected Assembly on to the Executive Council, and they wanted a Legislative Council which had no paid officials on it. The Assembly petitioned the King for these arrangements in 1834, but it was not until 1839, when Harvey had been succeeded by Sir Charles Fitzroy, that the British Government agreed to separate Councils. Even then their members were still appointed by the Governor (though he was told to select from all parts of the Island men who held public confidence) and they could and did still hold 'offices of emolument under the Crown'. Many of the old Council members still continued to serve and some of them were members of both the new Councils. Though Fitzroy appointed some Council members from the elected house, they were not necessarily the people that the lower house would have voted for.

The Assembly could lay down the terms of its own membership. It passed a Bill in 1835 which provided that none of its members could accept an 'office of emolument under the Crown' without resigning his seat and being re-elected. In the end this device got around the difficulty referred to in the last sentence of the previous paragraph in a devious way, for appointment to a seat on the Executive Council was interpreted by the Assembly as accepting an office of emolument and therefore as necessitating resignation and re-election by an electorate aware that it was in effect endorsing or otherwise the Lieutenant Governor's appointment. Slowly the Island was moving towards responsible government.

Political battles similar to these were being fought out, or had already been fought out, in the other North American Colonies, but they were given special significance in the Island by the ever present land question. In 1837 William Cooper, then the leader of the 'liberals', the party for reform and the abolition of the proprietary system, expounded the philosophy (on which he was already acting) that 'it requires a degree of public excitement' to bring home to the British Government the importance of the land question. He organised protest meetings and encouraged active opposition by the settlers, including the withholding of rent when it was demanded. He set the tone of high political and journalistic excitement and bitter mutual abuse in which the land question was fought out for more than thirty years.

The Assembly in the 1830s comprised eighteen members, as it had since it was formed sixty years before. An Act of 1838 increased the membership to twenty-four, a natural increase in view of the growth of the population and the improvement, slight as it was, in communications. Henceforth the first electoral district of Prince County, that is Lots 1 to 14 inclusive, all the Island from its northernmost tip to the north shore of the Grand River, one-fifth of its total area, was to send two members to Charlottetown. An election for the new Assembly to begin its four years of life in January 1839 was held in November 1838. James Yeo and Thomas Gorman polled a hundred and twenty votes each, as candidates for the first electoral district of Prince

Vernon River Valley near where the bark Civility *was built for William Heard. When this photograph was taken at the end of the nineteenth century the cultivated area in the Island was at its largest. Today the spruce has crept back a little and many of the roads are paved. Otherwise the typical Island countryside has changed little, even horse-drawn vehicles are still occasionally seen*

A typical nineteenth century North American country store. The stores at Port Hill and New Bideford were probably simpler

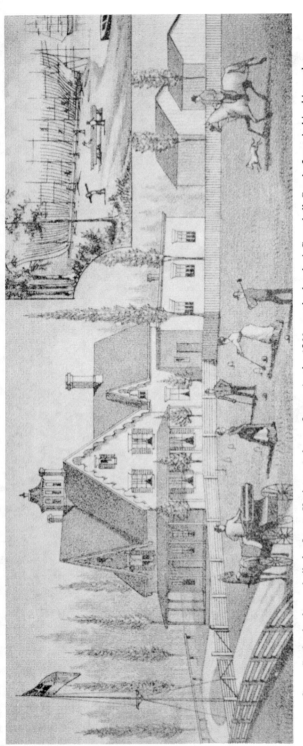

Green Park, the house built by James Yeo's second son, James, in the 1860s at the head of Campbell Creek. Inset is his shipyard on the shores of Campbell Creek. The ship in frame is the bark Ponemah, owned by John Yeo and Thomas Adams

County. Hugh Carr polled seventy-four and James Warburton sixty-four. Yeo and Gorman were duly declared elected.

Carr was a member of an old Island seafaring and farming family. Gorman was an Irish Catholic from County Kilkenny who, after working in the New Bideford shipyard, had settled on Lot 13 on the north bank of the Trout River. He ran a small store, farmed and taught in school. He was probably at this time a creature of Yeo's. He was to become the father of Larry Gorman, one of the great nineteenth-century composers of North American folksongs.

The traditions and family papers of some of James Warburton's descendants indicate that he came of an Anglo-Irish family which had acquired the estate of Garryhinch in Kings County, Ireland, soon after the Civil War in Britain. He was a younger son. In 1834, still a very young man, he came to the Island to become temporary agent for the proprietor of Lot 11, where he made his permanent home. At first working closely with Yeo, Warburton was to become his most outspoken critic. The bitter, noisy and abusive conflict between these two sharply-contrasted men, the impoverished younger son of Irish gentry and the Cornish carter in the process of building up a million-dollar international business, was to be heard as a constant undertone to the Island's politics for the first fifteen years of the second half of the century.

When the Assembly of 1839 met they were a motley crew. Lieutenant Governor Fitzroy reported on them:

... the qualification of a Member of the House of Assembly is the possession of either freehold or leasehold property to the amount of only fifty pounds currency—not more than thirty-five pounds sterling. ... The low qualification, while it enables Men of inferior station to offer themselves as candidates at the Elections, prevents persons of property of higher attainments and respectability—of whom there are sufficient in the several counties—to form a very intelligent House of Assembly—from coming forward; not only from a feeling of reluctance to enter into competition on the hustings, or sit in the Assembly with men of low character and gross ignorance, but also from a conviction, founded on experience, that in nine cases out of ten the ignorant settler will think that his own peculiar interests, ... will best be represented by one of his own chaps,

E

and occupying the same position in Society as himself; the general good of the Colony, and the encouragement or development of its resources being entirely lost sight of, or rather not being thought of.[8]

Of James Yeo he said that, while his principles were correct and honest and he had by his industry acquired a considerable property in the Island, he was not in his proper sphere in the Assembly. Be that as it may, his membership of the Island parliament continued with only one break until his death twenty-nine years later, and in the later part of this period he was to dominate the Colonial Government. It was natural that middle-range career public servants, whose connections were just good enough to secure them a Colonial governorship, should react strongly to Yeo, whose growing power and wealth represented the embodiment of a challenge. He was probably already richer than the successive Lieutenant Governors. His pragmatism took little account, when doing business, of traditional complexes of obligation and status unless they could be used to his advantage.

His interventions in his first four years in the Assembly were confined at first to the practical issues of road-making, the system of issue of Treasury Warrants, the improvement of the Grand River ferry, the provision of a Custom House at Cascumpec to allow vessels to enter and clear there. He was noted by the Lieutenant Governor as tending to follow the lead of his fellow West of England man, Joseph Pope. But a consistent political philosophy soon began to show itself. It was one of extreme conservatism. Yeo was with the proprietors and not with the tenants. The proprietorial system provided the environment in which he could work and he resisted every movement for change.

His views were first clearly expressed in a speech in a debate on the State of the Colony in the Session of 1841, when he told the Assembly that the prosperity of the settlers of Prince County varied exactly as the rigour with which rent was demanded of them by the agents. If they had to pay rents they worked hard and prospered. If they did not they drifted into a state 'worse than Indians'. But in this first session he had little to say on general issues. He was one of a minority, for the liberals who favoured the abolition of the proprietory system comprised the majority among the members. In the next election in the summer of 1842 a predominantly conservative Assembly was returned. Warburton did not stand. Yeo and Lemuel Cambridge represented the First District of Prince County for the next four years. Cambridge was an educated man, a Quaker of the Island's first great family, and he and Yeo must have made an odd pair.

Yeo now had the beginnings of everything he needed to become a man of great fortune. To all intents and purposes he was the agent of Lot 13. Through his store ledgers he had effective control of a significant fraction of the population of the Island. Many people did what he wanted. They had no choice. He was already a landowner and his timber-robbing went unchecked. Thus he had at his disposal a source of raw material. His growing fleet and the ships built for immediate sale were the means of transport. In William Yeo he had an energetic, competent and completely loyal agent in Britain. Thus he controlled the means of marketing the product. With the coming of the conservative majority in 1842 he began to acquire political power.

CHAPTER EIGHT

THE LEDGER GIANT
OF PORT HILL

IT was John Ings' newspaper which gave James Yeo this title, though it probably only put on record what was already current in everyday gossip. Ings was an able young man who in due course employed a formidable leader-writer, Duncan Mclean. Though *The Islander*'s heading bore the inscription 'OPEN TO ALL PARTIES : INFLUENCED BY NONE', and though it always maintained a degree of editorial freedom, it soon became the mouthpiece of the conservative elements in Island politics. Its position in this role was reinforced when in 1855 Ings married Mary Jane, the third of Yeo's five daughters, she who had kept the sentimental day book. Mclean's caustic and frequently abusive pen, uninhibited by any tradition of restraint in the Colony's political journalism or by an effective libel law, defined the position of the proprietors, the agents and the merchants, in both positive and negative terms. *The Islander* said what their official and public policy was and sometimes made the policy in the process. More frequently it attacked the liberal elements who sought land reform and a measure of self-government. Even now, when the issues over which these gales blew so strongly in the teacup of the Island's political life have been dead, like the participants in the squabbles, for nearly a century, *The Islander* can still make zestful reading.

Yeo's numerous interventions in the debates of the Parliament which began in 1843, as recorded in *The Islander* and the *Royal Gazette*, reveal much of his personality. There is about these early speeches something which suggests wonder at his own achievement. This product of the education provided by a literate father in a cottage in eighteenth-century Cornwall, this graduate of the

school of hopeless poverty in a highly stratified society, was
constantly probing to find what could be made of his new
environment. The main influence in his formal education is
revealed clearly in these early interventions. They are the speeches
of a man steeped in the Authorised Version of the Bible. He
expressed his thoughts in the periods of James I and illustrated
them with parables and tags of his own making. Speaking in a
debate of 1843 on the State of the Colony he is reported to have :

> 'remembered that a petition was once got up in his part of
> the country to beg some favour from the proprietor; but from
> some cause it was not sent to him. When he came round, about
> two years afterwards, the petition was shewn him, and all who
> had signed he relieved, and even some of those who had paid
> him he reimbursed; he even went round and gave money to
> those in distress. He forgave arrears of rent, he also took back
> such bad land as was unfit for cultivation. But those who had
> not signed, and were opposed to him, he knew them not.'[1]

Next year he said of one of his colleagues :

> this trick of the Hon. Member reminded him of a rogue and
> a vagabond, who by changing his dress, obtained alms at the
> house there several times in one day. Some cunning was therein
> displayed it must be admitted, yet it was seen through, ...[2]

In the same year a good-humoured exchange with Duncan
Mclean (at that time a Member of the House and inclined to
liberal views) he :

> compared Mr D. McLean's association with *'the Cooperites'*,
> or *'Malignants'* to that of a sailor, who, having carelessly
> entered himself on board a *strange* ship, is horror-stricken to
> discover, when too late for retreat:—When she is many a league
> at sea—that her true character is piratical, and her captain
> and crew nothing but a lawless band of desperate *pickeroons*:
> in such a *'fix'* the *hones*t fellow can only secretly determine
> within himself to desert the ship the very first favourable
> opportunity.[3]

His tags became part of the currency of the House. He would
blame views put forward for the opposition on a single one of
their members, saying 'one scabby sheep infects the whole flock'.
The attitude of the House to the proprietors was generally wrong,
he maintained; the proprietors were criticised too much; 'we

cannot expect figs to be produced from planting thorns'. He believed in people and cases being taken on their own merits; 'let every tub stand on its own bottom'. All this was uttered softly in the dialect of the country between the Torridge and the sea (for instance *pickeroon* was a Clovelly term for a pirate), so softly that sometimes the reporter of the House had difficulty in hearing him. He often had the House convulsed with laughter into which in later years, as he became more powerful and at the same time more sardonic, there sometimes crept a nervous note. Certain of his tricks of speech passed into the usage not only of the Assembly but of the Island generally. He had a habit of saying he was ready to do something for a con-si-der-a-tion, spoken with deliberation as a word which was not part of his youth. He frequently used the word 'whatever' for emphasis.

Though he was tolerant in religious matters, his social attitude was patriarchal. He saw himself as the 'active man' of his principality. To him this position involved great responsibility, but it also conferred absolute authority. He would do a great deal for the people and for the Island, but he would do it in his own way and with his own long-term interests in mind. He assured the House again and again of a truth that was obvious to them all : 'I do not like working for nothing'. He was ready to make big financial sacrifices when he saw it to be in the interests of the economy to do so, since he could not increase his fortune and influence in an impoverished society. In the hard years of the late 'forties, when the crops failed generally in the western districts and the Irish potato blight came to the Island, he argued strongly for a prolonged embargo on the export of grain to reduce its price and keep food in the Colony, even though this would mean that he had to stop his profitable large-scale shipments of barley and oats to Britain and the neighbouring colonies. Consistently, he consoled himself in the year that an embargo was enforced by buying up grain and subsequently disposing of it to the settlers as seed at the highest price they could reasonably afford—which meant that more people passed into his debt and his influence was further extended.

The records of the land office in Charlottetown show that by the mid-1840s his dealings in real estate were extensive. He referred to this in 1844 in a speech in a debate on the land question :

> I am . . . now designated as a Proprietor, such I admit sometimes is true enough; I buy to sell again, but I will not do it for nothing!!! The 1,800 acres I bought last year soon passed into other hands, and whether I am a proprietor or whether I am not, my interest for the prosperity of the colony is not abated, any one that applies to me for employment meets with it, at the present time I have not less than three hundred men in my employ in various improvements, &c; and so far as to the payment of rent, any thing they bring I take of them, and frequently give them cash for produce.[4]

He expressed his beliefs again in round terms in a speech at his nomination for the election of 1846 :

> Gentlemen, this is the third time I have presented myself for your suffrages: twice I have been returned to represent your interests in the House of Assembly. The most popular question at these times was that of Escheat [the proposal that the land should be taken from the proprietors]. Gentlemen, I need not tell you that that question is now worn out; it appeared to me to be unjust, and consequently I opposed it. I can assure you, gentlemen, in this, as in every other public question, my conduct for the last eight years has not been regulated by any selfish or unworthy motive, but entirely approved of by my own conscience, well knowing that while I was furthering your interests, I was promoting my own; and how, I would ask, gentlemen, can it be otherwise? when you consider what I have at stake from one end of the district to the other, what other conclusion can you come to than that your interests and mine are one?[5]

In all questions in which the interests of the proprietors, the merchants and the agents were involved, he took his stand to the right of the right in the political spectrum of the Colony. Over the great question of responsible government, the battle won in 1851 for a greater degree of self-government for the Island, and in the subsequent political disputes of the 1850s, he took up a position less compromising even than that of the absentee proprietors themselves.

*   *   *

British North America was still a vast emptiness. Though in the 1850s the railway was extended from Rivière de Loup on the south shore of the St Lawrence estuary to Windsor in the extreme south of Ontario and linked with the American lines down to Portland, Maine, and in Northern New York State, real settlement was still a very thin line along the St Lawrence, the Ottawa and the north shores of the two most easterly Lakes. There was nothing west of Sault Ste Marie, except a few scattered trading forts.

But settlement in the United States was advancing westwards like an irresistible tide. By 1850 the Oregon Treaty, the annexation of Texas and the Mexican Cession had consolidated the nation from coast to coast. By 1859 the whole of the area of the present contiguous States was broken into established political divisions of one kind or another. These were the years of 'manifest destiny', which, as one of the greatest of the historians of the United States put it, 'laid a golden egg' in that the Great Plains, at first thought of as the American desert, in fact proved the key to the nation's further phenomenal expansion. In the 1850s regular coast-to-coast communication was established by stage coach and pony express. By 1860 there were 6,000 freight wagons on the overland trails and a year later the continent was to be crossed by electric telegraph. The network of railroads in the east and mid-west was growing like a spider's web. But behind it all there were growing undertones of strain.

The population of Prince Edward Island was rising steadily and by 1855 it had reached 71,000. Charlottetown was the home of over 6,000, but at last a second big settlement was rapidly growing up. Green's Shore, the land on the south side of the narrow neck between Richmond Bay and the Northumberland Strait, was being turned by the growth of shipbuilding and the building of the New Brunswick railway from St John to Shediac (for which Green's Shore was very favourably placed as a potential trading point) into a town in its own right, and soon custom gave it the name of Summerside.

Though the Island escaped the worst of the complex effects of the potato blight in Ireland, in the years after 1844 more than one 'shipload of Irish paupers' arrived and coincidentally in

Prince County there were failures of several crops for several years in succession. The consequent distress horrified the Rev W. H. Cooper, a newly-ordained missionary who in 1846 became Port Hill's first clergyman.

The Island was less cut off than it had ever been before. The Atlantic Steam Packet Service meant quick regular communications with Europe. On 21 July 1853 the first telegram was received in Charlottetown and the winter isolation was ended. The first steps were taken towards lighting Charlottetown by gas, William Heard of Bideford imported an ever-increasing range of fancy goods for sale in his Charlottetown shop and his wife set herself up as a purveyor of women's hats. He launched the first steamer to be built in the Island, the *Rosebud*, and although she was too weakly powered to be successful commercially, she laid a cable across the Northumberland Strait, carried parties of townsfolk on picnic pleasure trips up the river from Charlottetown, and acted as the Island's first regular steam-tug. In December 1856 she went round the coast to Richmond Bay and towed the *James Yeo* out from Port Hill before the ice closed around her.

But despite these developments, travel to the mainland in winter was still an ordeal. None of the steamers so far employed had nearly enough power to break through the packed ice in the Northumberland Strait. The journey was made in 'ice boats', sixteen or eighteen feet long, and all the passengers were required to join in the arduous process of getting them from shore to shore. Where there was open water they were rowed or sailed under great dipping lugsails. But at each extensive mass of ice they had to be hauled out and dragged across the floe, the passengers donning harness and pulling for all they were worth as they stumbled and slipped over the uneven surface. It was a hazardous business, and however careful the ice boatmen were there was often great hardship and sometimes even disaster. For days on end it was not possible to leave the Island.

*   *   *

For a time after the middle of the 1840s the land question gave pride of place in the debates in the Island Parliament to the issue of responsible government. The reformers demanded that 'the advisors of the Representative of the Sovereign, constituting a Provincial Administration under him, ought to be men possessed of the confidence of the representatives of the people'.[6] In other words they wanted to go several stages beyond what had been achieved with the separation of the Councils in 1839. They wanted a system in which the Executive :

> would be chosen so as to conform with the party pattern of the popularly elected house and which would change with the rise and fall of party fortunes. It required a number of available and suitable Executive Councillors, not a scarce supply of paid officials sent out from England, and the presence of alert and effective political parties, not a number of mere factions based on personal and group rivalries. It assumed also an interested public opinion and a degree of independence from the Colonial Office.[7]

The Lieutenant Governor of the first half of the '40s, Sir Henry Huntley, was of the view that these conditions were not met in the Island. The Colonial Secretary in London, William Ewart Gladstone, agreed with him, but criticised the intemperateness of his reporting of the successive crises in the Colony's affairs. Gladstone's successor, Earl Grey, had to deal with a predominantly liberal Assembly returned in the general election in the Island in 1846.

Huntley's successor, Sir Donald Campbell, found conservatives and liberals equally set on obtaining a greater measure of independence for the Colony, but greatly differing as to exactly what it should be. The conservatives saw responsible government as a system under which a minority of the seats in the Executive Council would go to members of the elected Assembly regardless of party. This they saw as a compromise which might buy off the liberals but leave the conservatives with the effective control of the Council which they already had. The liberals were seeking a system under which the Executive Council would be under the control of the majority party in the Assembly and thus the family compact would be broken for ever. Campbell was a proprietor's man and he advised London against responsible government on the ground that the population comprised largely ignorant tenantry from whom a party had been formed by men who were intent, at first, on obtaining the forfeit of the proprietor's lands, and then, when this had failed, sought to obtain responsible government and use it to confiscate the land. Earl Grey accepted his advice.

But to do so was inconsistent with the general policies of the British Government of which Grey was a member. From one cause or another that government decided to withhold the sum of £3,000 which had been voted annually by Parliament since 1776 to meet the costs of the government of Prince Edward Island. At the same time as he announced that the Colonial Office had refused to grant a greater measure of independence, Campbell had to tell the Assembly that the power of the purse had been given into their hands. Immediately the majority party introduced a resolution 'that the question of paying the Civil List be postponed until the system of Responsible Government is introduced into this Island'.[8] The conservatives recognised that for the time being their best hope lay in compromise, but they were not successful. An election held in February 1850, when the snow was at its deepest, resulted in a sweeping victory for the liberals. George Coles, their leader, was resolute, and one of the stormiest sessions in the history of an Assembly which for years had never been peaceful came to an end with a petition to the British Parliament. The representatives in the Assembly of the tenants and of the proprietors came into headlong conflict for twenty dramatic days.

In the fall Sir Donald Campbell died in Charlottetown. His successor, Sir Alexander Bannerman, left London with clear instructions that responsible government as the majority in the Assembly saw it was to be introduced. It took a winter of argument to come to a settlement, and at the end of April 1851 Bannerman summoned Coles and requested him to form an Executive Council possessing the confidence of the House. After over eighty years the settling of the land question was coming into sight. But the conservatives, the agents and merchants, did not after all find that their position was put in jeopardy by temporary loss of control of the government. The power they had among the tenants by virtue of the ledger and their control of available capital made it possible for them fully to exploit the great trading opportunities which were now opening up with the industrial development of Britain and the United States. Apart from the short period of Coles's first Government, which lasted from 1854 to 1858, the conservatives did not lose even the façade of power until it was eroded in the late 'sixties and early 'seventies.

Coles's four years of government were marked by a vigorously-executed programme of reform. He sought to improve education in the Colony, to diversify its industry and by purchases to increase the area of the Island which belonged to its own people. He was up against a vigorous and able group of conservatives who, when the Assembly came to its natural end in 1858, had succeeded in stirring up confusing issues, especially the question of whether the Bible should be compulsorily taught in schools, to such an extent that they were returned, at first with a majority of one and then on a second election with a working majority. They used their recovered power, among other things, to do what they could to reinstate the system of family compact. In this James Yeo took a leading and very practical part.

*   *   *

His rôle in these stirring events was consistent. In the Assembly the conservatives sought, by long-drawn delaying action, to win a decade or two more of power. Yeo was more concerned with exercising power than debating it. As he never tired of writing and saying, 'I am not short of employment, I have a deal of business to do'. His part in Island politics became apparent when it was dramatised by the spectacular conflict with James Warburton. Warburton had come to the Island as an agent and he had stood for election and failed in 1838. In 1846 he stood again, running in double harness with Yeo for the First District of Prince County. Ten minutes before the close of the poll, when he had 336 votes in his favour and Warburton only 207, Yeo resigned in favour of Warburton, who sat in the House as what *The Islander* described years later as a 'political bantling' of Yeo. But this happy arrangement did not last for long. Perhaps the characters and backgrounds of the two were too much contrasted. Warburton, 'a gentleman by birth and education' as Sir Henry Huntley described him, soon began to show liberal tendencies. He used his good connections, and in 1847, at Lord Stanley's suggestion, he was made a member of the Executive Council. Governor Campbell found him too much a liberal and tried to prevent the confirmation of his appointment, but with much reluctance, for he wrote : 'As for my intercourse with Mr Warburton, I have formed a high opinion of his character, attainments and private worth'.[9] He was confirmed in his position, but because he had taken an office of profit under the Crown the Assembly duly declared his seat vacant and a by-election was held in the summer of 1848 at which Yeo, standing against him, was successful.

Yeo came back into the House in time to join in the debate which followed Campbell's arrival in the Island. He early made his views on the subject of responsible government perfectly clear :

> For his part, he had never sought for any office. He could always find plenty of employment elsewhere. In his opinion, what was called Responsible Government was a mere fallacy. Honorable members, whose minds are now so much bent upon this subject, are just expecting to step into the shoes of the gentlemen who now fill the public offices of the Colony. . . .[10]

When Campbell held the snap election of February 1850, both Yeo and Warburton were elected. Such was the power of Yeo's ledger that, although he was on a visit to Britain when the Assembly was dissolved, he was nominated and re-elected without even the formality of his presence in North America.

It was at this period that *The Islander* developed its style of uninhibited attack on political opponents. The great struggle for the Island's future was fought out in the press in petty charge and countercharge against prominent individuals of either side, made and denied in extreme and abusive terms. George Coles, a Westcountryman from Somerset, was invariably Jarge Coals, out of respect for his dialect, unless he was the 'whiskey dragon' (he was a brewer by occupation). Those who would see the land taken from the proprietors were always the 'snatchers'. Edward

Whelan, a major liberal figure who was later to play a prominent part in the making of the Canadian Confederation, was 'the dirty faced urchin'. Warburton was lucky to escape with Wearbutton or Waterproof; it was more likely to be Warebottom. When the first responsible government was formed in 1851, the attack in the press was made on two principal fronts. The liberals were accused of promising that responsible government would bring free land in its train, and, more specifically, Warburton, now Colonial Secretary, was accused of promising his constituents that the introduction of responsible government would mean that the 'Queen's Assent to any and every Bill would not be prerequisite'. In other words, it was said that he had offered complete independence in which laws could be passed to free the tenants of the obligation to pay rent without compensation to the proprietors, and, more especially, Yeo could be deprived of the power of his ledger. This accusation led to an almighty slanging match in the newspapers. Correspondents swore they had heard Warburton say in a public meeting at Grand River on Lot 14 that responsible government meant the elimination of the Crown from the constitution. The liberal *Examiner* gave as good as it got from *The Islander*, weighing into James Yeo as 'Jemmy Twitcher' or the 'Great Potentate of Port Hill' and asserting that the correspondents were in his pay and 'would endorse any statement he might choose to make, and swear, to boot, through a three-inch plank, for a con-sid-er-a-tion'. They accused Yeo of opening the mail at Port Hill post office and of overcharging rent. John Ings himself received a fair sample of the local invective when the *Examiner* described him as a 'disgraceful, slandering, self-convicted liar'.

The election of 1853 again brought Yeo and Warburton back into the House, but before it there was a vigorous and prolonged exchange in the Press in which Yeo accused Warburton of attacks on the Catholic settlers. In 1854 and again in 1858 both were returned, and in the latter election Yeo's youngest son John and a close collaborator, David Ramsay of Port Hill, were returned to the Assembly as well.

*   *   *

By the mid-1840s Yeo was the biggest business man in the Colony. In November 1844 five large ships sailed from Port Hill in one week, laden with timber, oats and dried and salted codfish; all of them, and their cargoes, his entire property. His shipments of grain now became an important part of the economy of the western part of the Island. It was not surprising that when the inefficiency of the unfortunate Sidney Dealey, Sir George Seymour's agent on Lot 13, became intolerable, T. H. Haviland should recommend Yeo as the obvious successor. He did so in frank terms in a letter of March 1846 :

> I do not think we can do better than adopt your suggestion by giving the requisite authority to Mr Yeo; as he has already pretty well stripped the Lot of what little timber it possessed, as was evident upon your visiting it is scarcely susceptible of further damage and there is no person better calculated to convert the rents into a remittance than Yeo, or by his Great knowledge and the opportunity afforded him by the arrival of emigrants in his ships of which he owns several to advance the settlement of the Lot.[11]

Yeo accepted, with delight, in a letter from Charlottetown which showed that he had not failed to bring Sidney Dealey's shortcomings to the attention of the Seymours. It ended characteristically :

> I am going to leave town this morning early I am at a loss to find some ink or paper for to write on as the people are not out [of bed] you will have to excuse it I am myself ashamed for it but I am anxious to be gone as I expect a vessel to be arrived from Bristol—[12]

Bristol was now one of his principal trading points. His agent there worked in close association with William Yeo in Appledore. A few months later James Yeo wrote in a revealing letter :

> I have received a letter from you dated in Jan I am sorry I did not answer you before this but I have so much to do this Summer that I can scarcely find time to write I never had so much business at one time as I have had this season I hope if all is well to get clear of the greater part of it in the course of another month or two but all the vessels will be gone then I shall have time to look about all I can state to you respecting

of Lot 13 the people are all in good health and I hope in a pretty state of doing well the crops this season are pretty fair the potatoe crop not over good but the wheat was a good crop and the oats not bad—I hope I shall get most of the Tenants to pay their rent as I will take produce from them I was sorry to think you should have any mistrust of my having to much power over the Tenants on the Lot to be hard on them in any way I am happy to say the Tenants on the Lot was glad to hear I was appointed the agent as I mentioned to you before I have for many years past paid the greatest part of the rent for the Tenants and taken produce from them in no other part of the Island have they same privilege as they have in this place—as it is my wish to do everything lies in my power to do the people good.[13]

The last rent-roll sent by Sidney Dealey to Seymour in May 1846 shows William Ellis as the tenant of Port Hill Farm. The first return by Yeo a few months later shows the property in his occupation. Only a year before Ellis had given up the lease of the New Bideford shipyard site. For the rest of his life he occupied fifty acres of Port Hill Farm as a sub-tenant of Yeo, and from the records of ship registration it would appear that he continued to supervise the building of ships. The old master craftsman lived on in this semi-retirement until his death on Christmas Day 1855, 'an old and respected inhabitant of that place, aged about 80 years', as *The Islander* put it. He was in fact eighty-two and he left behind numerous grandchildren, some of whose descendants live in the area today. The shipbuilding traditions he established and the skills he taught were his memorial; these and the small tragedy of the loss of his inheritance to the greater dynamic and smaller scruples of James Yeo. The story of the slow reversal in fortune of these two contrasted men and Yeo's rise has already in the late twentieth century become a myth in the Island.

So the small robber baron at last acquired the best site on Lot 13 as his own and, together with two hundred acres around his house, it formed the 'home farm' of his growing principality. From the low cliffs at the foot of the peninsula of Penman's Point out into the sound between Lot 13 and Lennox Island he built a new wharf. As he wrote to Francis Seymour:

The New Bideford shipyard at the peak of its prosperity in the 1870s, when it was owned by William Richards. A vessel is being built above the pool where the Peter & Sarah anchored. Another is being loaded with grain for export at New Bideford wharf. The bagged grain is coming down in carts

A shipyard near Murray Harbour in the shipbuilding boom of the 1870s. This was the area in which John Cambridge and his sons first established large scale shipbuilding and lumbering during the Napoleonic Wars

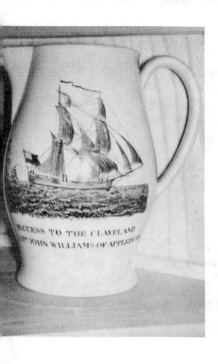

1778. *Clevland of Barnstaple, 69 tons, a brig built at Appledore, owned and sailed by John Williams and later by his son Joshua Williams. The spelling of her name on this commemorative jug is phonetic*

1809. Peter & Sarah, *of Bideford, 59 tons, a polacca brigantine built by Richard Chapman at Cleave Houses. Before her pioneering expedition to Prince Edward Island she made several voyages to Southern Europe but after it she was employed for 41 years in the coasting trade. This very early photograph, taken at Padstow where she was registered for the last six years of her life, shows a vessel in all respects identical to the description of the* Peter & Sarah, *and almost certainly her*

1827, Jessie of Bideford, 136 tons, a brig built at New Bideford by William Ellis and owned at different times by Joshua Williams, William Henry English Burnard and Thomas Chanter

1845. This Bideford harvest jug commemorates the full-rigged ship Ocean Queen, 630 tons, built at New Bideford in 1845 for James Yeo and owned by him and William Yeo until her loss in 1865

... there is considerable improvements can be made on the Lot as soon as I get clear of the Vessels I have on hand I will attend to it if all is well I am in hopes to get many more settlers on the Lot next year—I am shipping of oats and some potatoes for Britain from here I have a wharf built on my shore three hundred and twenty-seven feet long at my own expense a vessel of three hundred tons can come alonside it a great comodation to the people to ship of their produce—[14]

This wharf, which was in a very exposed position and was damaged several times over the years and eventually washed away, did much for the prosperity of Port Hill. In the year it was built ten ships loaded at Port Hill for Britain, forty small schooners for New Brunswick and Nova Scotia, all on Yeo's account, £6,700 worth of goods came in, £8,300 worth (excluding the new ships themselves, which were worth at least another £7,500) went out.

For the next year or two the community around Port Hill needed all the fat it had built up to survive at all. These were the lean years of the late 'forties when, as Yeo reported to his employers:

The times in the Island are most awful the Crops Entirely failed the last year times have been very bad the Two years past but they are this year (1848) tenfold worse the potatoe crops failed and the wheat also failed what the end will be I am not aware. . . . I'll advise you I have to feed now weekly of the Tennants of the Lot as many as Ten Familys that are entirely destitute for want of provisions I keep the poor creatures to work at something or other to help pay for it. . . .[15]

Despite the general depression, Lieutenant Governor Huntley was properly entertained when he paid a formal visit in the same year. A piper was in attendance on the north side of the Grand River ferry when his Excellency crossed over. Carriages were waiting for him and he was driven by Yeo (who was, after all, a professional driver) to his house at Port Hill where an address of congratulation was presented.

Three years later, when conservative fortunes were in eclipse, and Lieutenant Governor Bannerman was on the verge of calling upon George Coles to establish the first responsible government,

Yeo judged it politic to appoint his close associate David Ramsay to be the Lieutenant Governor's host. But he could not resist one gesture, and as the Governor's carriage passed Port Hill house at the head of a procession of fifty vehicles it received a salute from a twelve-pounder gun. The procession was watched by a very new settler. Thomas Adams, a sixteen-year-old nephew of James Yeo from Kilkhampton, had arrived at Port Hill wharf with his parents and spent the first night of his life in the New World (which was Hallow'een) in the old Port Hill house that Thomas Chanter had built. Soon he moved into the new house and there for twenty years he shared a small room with John Yeo, who was one year older. He was employed as accountant and in due course as general manager of James Yeo's interests, and he dabbled in shipbuilding and timber cargoes himself. He played no small part in the establishment of Yeo as the Colony's richest and most powerful man.

Soon Yeo was a Justice of the Peace, but his duties were liable to take second place to business, as a couple whom he was to marry discovered. Arriving at the appointed time they found his gig at the door. He was sitting in it and he was anxious to be off to see about a cargo. 'So ye wish to be married,' he said, 'are ye both agreed?'—'Aye'—'Well, in God's name I pronounce you man and wife. Gee up!' Their children were regarded as legitimate.

At this period there occurred the incident of the Frenchman's horse. The story of this exploit has survived in the traditions of the Island in several versions. It seems a vessel was in trouble off the northern shore and Yeo was not satisfied with the way the situation was being handled. Arriving on the shore with an exhausted horse, he commandeered a grey belonging to a French-speaking Islander. He swam this horse out to the ship, released it to find its own way ashore, successfully took charge of the situation on board and saved the vessel. Later he sought out the horse and bought it for his personal use.

He was used to swimming horses. When the Grand River ferry was not working, which was often, he would swim his horse across the mile-wide river, resting on an oyster bed half way over. There are many legends of him in those years, of his suddenly arriving among startled gangs of idling men who thought him fifty miles away, taking charge of situations which defeated technical experts, of fights, of sudden acts of generosity, of drinking bouts during which foolish people would seek to persuade him to sign his name on a blank sheet of paper; they were never successful and were made to regret it afterwards. He was quite uninhibited about his drinking habits, telling the Assembly more than once that he liked his glass, but could take it or leave it alone and usually felt much better when he did the latter.

Out in the Gulf every day in late summer and fall the white sails of the hovering fleet of American mackerel schooners could be seen glinting on the sparkling sea. In September 1851 250 schooners came into Richmond Bay together; in that year New England had 1,000 vessels in the fishery and Lunenburg, Nova Scotia, perhaps another 100. The Lieutenant Governor described them as beautifully-equipped vessels of from sixty to a hundred tons with from ten to twelve men each. One afternoon about 1,300 American seamen descended together on the Agricultural Show in Princetown and, 'behaved as well and peacefully as so many sailors congregated together could be expected to do'.[16] For what other business these schooners put men ashore besides agricultural shows was nobody's concern. Except in periods of reciprocity in free trade with the USA they were notorious throughout British North America for their smuggling activities. Port Hill was a remote place and Yeo's word was law, questioned by few. One man who questioned it to the extent of attempting a murderous assault on him was lucky to escape with six months in gaol.

To try to enforce some control over this great fleet from New England a small British naval force was sent to the North American Colonies under the command of Vice-Admiral Sir George Seymour. This tour of duty brought the Admiral once more into close touch with his property on Lot 13. He had been receiving small sums by way of rent in the form of bills to be drawn on William Yeo, but they did not amount to a great deal and, as Sir George was an able and conscientious man who took a great deal of interest in what he was called upon to do, the Lot took up more of his time than it was worth. For the second time it became apparent that the enterprise, now so enormously grown, which had begun with the visit of the *Peter & Sarah* to the deep pool above the spit of red sand off New Bideford was exploitable to its full potential only by the man on the spot. Twenty-five years before, 630 acres of forest with a few small clearings had passed from Martha Burnard through Thomas Chanter into the uncertain hands of William Ellis. Now in 1857 16,000 acres were conveyed from Sir George Seymour to James Yeo Esq., who in the years immediately before had acquired also parts of Lots 7, 19 and others, half of Lot 3 and most of Lot 8, and the agencies of Lots 9 and 61, and thus was already a large proprietor. In the same year the Ledger Giant's seaborne ventures achieved a new high. Eleven of his ships, laden with his own cargoes, arrived in British ports within one month.

Once William Yeo was established in Devon his father began to make regular visits to Britain. James Yeo was always pleased to meet and talk with the Seymours, but he who was so much the master of his own environment was lost in a more sophisticated community. George Henry Seymour, who had crossed the Island with him in 1840, wrote to Sir George that Yeo was 'all adrift' in London. Each of these visits was followed by a development in Appledore. In 1845 William and Elizabeth Yeo moved from the rented house in Market Street to one purchased in Bude Street, among prosperous shipmasters and the smaller shipowners and merchants. During a visit in 1849-50 a momentous and imaginative decision was taken which was greatly to affect the history of the Torridge estuary. This was no less than to turn the shallow triangular bay around which Appledore was built into the European headquarters of James Yeo's growing commercial principality.

The ships built in the Island were not finished there. On arrival in Britain they were re-caulked, given deck houses fastened with galvanised iron or copper bolts in addition to the wooden treenails with which they were pinned together in the Island.

Sometimes they had strengthening members built into the hull, sometimes there was extensive rigging work to be done on them. Appledore was already established as one of the cheapest and best repair ports in Britain, but the ships being finished had to lie on the sands among the mooring posts or alongside the new quay which had been opened in 1845 after the householders in Market Street, encouraged by Thomas Chanter, had joined up a series of private wharves which had gradually been built behind the houses, to make a long narrow quay faced with rough stone and paved with gravel. There was much controversy in the local press as to how safe the moorings at Appledore really were, but, however sheltered they were and however hard the ground, ships could only be worked on at low tide, and this was not economical with the scale of the Yeo enterprise growing so that fifty-five ships from the Island came to be finished in Appledore between 1843 and 1853. A dry dock was wanted, with proper industrial installations, a foundry, a smithy, a sail loft, block-making shops, a mast house around it where the ships could lie in complete safety with men working on them all day and all night if necessary. More and more ships could be poured through such an industrial complex in a continuous stream. There was some difficulty because the land and buildings belonged to several different people and the foreshore rights belonged to the public. It took six years and another visit from James Yeo in the summer of 1855 before the land was bought and filched, some buildings torn down, including the almshouses which had been given to the poor of the parish more than a century and a half before. But it was done, and the great dry dock, 330 feet long, big enough to take four of Yeo's smaller ships together, was cut into the bay with its head in the shallow valley which ran down to Benson's New Quay. To make the south wall a great enclosure was made of the foreshore. On the other side the strand was built up and a new road was made down to the sands. To provide the stone for the dock a tramway was run under the low cliffs along the edge of the Torridge to a quarry which the Reverend Jerome Clapp, pastor of the local Congregational Chapel (whose son Jerome was one day to write the Victorian comic best-sellers

Three Men in a Boat and *Three Men on the Bummel*), had developed on his property at Bidna on the hillside below Thomas Chanter's signal tower.

But not only the dry dock and the foundry, a forge, wharves, sail lofts and stores were built. High up on the hillside above the dock a great new house took shape, a house with terraced gardens, lodges, coach houses and paved stable yard, surrounded by extensive grounds, the whole encompassed with a high stone wall. It was a house whose great reception rooms had corniced ceilings twenty feet high, with a warren of bedrooms, attics, servants' quarters, kitchens, wash-houses, cellars and store-places. The tall windows of the great drawing-room looked insolently across the Torridge over the roofs of Appledore straight at the grey shape of old Tapeleigh, for so long the home of squires. There was something symbolic in that it looked also on to a tall obelisk, a memorial to Augustus Saltren Willett's only son, killed in the Crimea two years before. The Clevlands had at last come to the end which Augustus's inheritance and change of name had only postponed.

The great house of the Yeos established James Yeo's son and agent for all to see as among the richer men in Devon. The house, so much bigger and finer than any other building in Appledore, was designed to show all opposition to be absurd, to symbolise the turning of Appledore into a transatlantic fief of James Yeo's Island principality. Henceforth Appledore, like Port Hill, much of Prince County and soon to an increasing extent the government of Prince Edward Island, was going to be run in the interests of Yeo. The power of the ledger, giving employment or denying it in any form, had reached across the Atlantic. Thirty-three years after Thomas Burnard's death his heir had come home to claim his heritage. To mark the fact the dry dock, the house and the road between the two were each named Richmond, after the great bay which fronted Port Hill, and Richmond Road was lined with saplings from the Island.

On 17 July 1856 the bark *Elizabeth Yeo* entered the dry dock to be completed to the accompaniment of firing guns, waving flags and cheering crowds. A few months later, in the record time of two weeks, the *Susannah* was repaired and completely sheathed in metal against the marine worms which attack wooden ships. On the beach, where she would have had to go a year earlier, the same work would have taken two months of the ship's earning time. The local correspondents of the press broke into superlatives in their enthusiasm for the economic benefits the dockyard would bring to Appledore and the whole Northam Peninsula, and they awarded the unanimous thanks of the community to 'the gentleman whose public spirit has supplied so great a desideratum, and who is ever foremost in any movement towards the improvement of the town'.[17] They meant William, who was there to receive the plaudits, his father being busy on the other side of the Atlantic, where he 'did not lack employment'.

CHAPTER NINE

HOW THE CAPTAINS
GOT THEIR BREAD

'I DO not wish to own more than one or two vessels at a time for the Captains get their bread when the owners are going to ruin,' wrote Thomas Chanter to William Ellis in the early spring of 1835. He followed his own advice, and henceforth never owned more than a few ships at a time. He built up his fortune from timber bought in North America and sold profitably in Britain, from consumer goods bought cheap in Britain and sold dear in the Island, from ships built at low cost, used to carry his own cargoes, and then sold at a profit when the market for tonnage was good. Neither he nor any other of the Devon Islanders made much money as ship owners in the modern sense, that is as owners of vessels with cargo space to be hired out to carry goods in which the shipowner had no interest.

Thomas Burnard's venture with the *Peter & Sarah* led directly to between 1,500 and 2,000 crossings of the North Atlantic by sailing ships of various kinds and greatly differing sizes during the next seventy-five years. Three generations of men were employed in this little world of Atlantic seafaring, two generations inherited it as their way of life.

As sailing ships recede into the past they have been glamorised, and the sordid discomforts and hardships involved in their use have been written of as if they had special virtue, rather than being the incidental products of circumstances in a society relatively still poor and technically primitive. It is true that many sailing ships, both square rigged ships and schooners, were beautiful in the shapes of their hulls and the combinations of hulls, masts and rigging and sails, brown, white and grey, wind-distended or hanging slack in a calm. Both as objects of interest for their own sake and for the very important part they played in the development of what was to become Canada, these Island ships and the human life and economy which went with them deserve far more study than they have yet received. Canada should be proud of them, as of the ships of Nova Scotia and New Brunswick, and the masters who drove them. They were far-travelling emissaries of a new world opening up north of the United States' frontier. They carried the ethos of this new North Atlantic society in its early formative years to the narrow seas of Northern Europe, to the Mediterranean, to India and the islands of the East, around Cape Horn and across the Pacific to Japan. For a few brief years they were at the heart of a great burst of enterprise and outward-looking activity. Then they vanished, like monuments made from snow, leaving behind no frontier myth and, until now, no history.

Symbols of a great era of human activity they may have been, but in all the long record of seafaring enterprise which is the constant background to this story there is no contemporary mention of romance, or of the virtues of misery, poverty and primitiveness for their own sakes. These ideas are products of a later era of technical and social change. The men who sailed these ships, though physically small, undernourished and very prone to certain diseases, tended to be strong and able to endure acute discomfort. This was a result of natural selection. In an age when the expectation of life was still very low, only those who were most resistant survived as labourers on sea or land. Success was measured by the number of years before enough money had been made to live ashore. As a general rule only the masters could hope for this kind of prosperity. Some of them got bread enough and to spare.

Though few except masters could hope to retire, both they and the crews who served them had markedly more opportunity for bettering their position than had their equivalents ashore. Lewis Grossard, James Lowther, Joshua Williams, William Marshall and William Chappel all became ship owners themselves. It was a measure of the position and importance of the masters to their ships' reputations and success that in reports of shipping affairs in the press their names were always given whenever their ships were mentioned. But their occupation was a dangerous one. Of British merchant shipmasters generally during the years 1835-48, less than two-thirds died natural deaths and nearly a quarter lost their lives with their ships. And by the time they became masters these men were already the survivors of lower ratings where the casualty figures were even higher.

Most of the events in this story happened before communication by transatlantic telegraph became part of the regular pattern of business. In the earlier period a ship's arrival back in Britain often brought the first news of her outward voyage. The master's responsibilities and opportunities were considerable. He was both the bearer and interpreter of his instructions, which were frequently in very general terms. The owner merchant was in his shipmaster's hands and this was the situation which led Thomas Chanter to write the words which open this chapter. The position has been admirably summed up by Ralph Davis :

> . . . The greatest problem of management, indeed, can be put in a nutshell; to find a paragon to be master, and then devise means to assist him if he really were perfect, rescue him if he turned out a fool, and then restrain him if he turned out a scoundrel. . . . This is one reason why owners so often sought to appoint masters who would be bound by more than mere financial ties; a reason for the frequent employment of sons, brothers, nephews or cousins of the owners or their business associates; for the difficulty which seamen who had nothing to offer but a record of competence and reliability faced when attempting to become masters, unless they could find the money to become major partowners.[1]

In the Northam peninsula the position was a little different. Here forces in a tightly organised local society tended to keep the master under the merchant's thumb. Even Lewis Grossard, who must have been a master of quite remarkable experience and a very valuable man, could not afford to risk Thomas Chanter's chances of a second voyage for the *Calypso* in the summer of 1832, for in the course of the dispute over the landing of the immigrants on the shores of Richmond Bay *(Chapter 6)* he said 'my orders are to land you at Princetown, and it would be at my peril to take the vessel to any other Port; if I did so, I could never show my face in Bideford again'.[2]

The early Atlantic masters were recruited from among the successful home trade captains of Bideford and from local men who had been employed in the ships of other ports. Some of them were the sons of shipowners who held shares in vessels with Thomas Burnard, who was therefore ideally placed to assess their likely performance as his agents and managers and to make sure they served his interests to the best of their ability. Sometimes the man who was entered as the master when the vessel cleared was the manager rather than the man who sailed the ship.

Among these early masters were men who acquired great experience. When Joshua Williams gave evidence before a Royal Commission on Harbours of Refuge in 1858 he was able to say that he had been forty years in command in the American trade. He must have made at least 150 crossings of the North Atlantic. Richard England of the *Lord Ramsay* spent at least the twenty-one summers from 1820 to 1840 in command going backwards and forwards across the Western Ocean. But experience was bought at a price. All these men except Joshua Williams lost ships. James Lowther lost four or five in his long sea-going career.

They were men without paper qualifications. Not until the middle of the century was a system of compulsory examinations for masters and mates introduced in the British Mercantile Marine Act of 1850. There was nothing scientific about their navigation, which, from contemporary reports, appears to have represented no more than attempts to travel in a straight line across the chart. Where more detailed information is available it shows the complex uncertainties of a sailing vessel's course, the scores of wasted miles sailed, particularly in a westerly direction.

As the years passed and the Atlantic trade grew, a second and then a third generation of masters formed an élite corps serving the growing commercial empire of James Yeo. These men could handle any sort of sailing ship of their period in any conditions. Some of them became masters of clipper ships in the China trade, one became master of the *Great Eastern*.

Though over the years the safety record of the Devon Island

ships was good, by the standards of the time, they had their adventures. Ships were trapped in the ice for the winter as the second *Bacchus* and the *Margaret* were at Quebec in 1853. They were wrecked on the British coast at the end of their easterly voyages, Thomas Chanter's last *Collina* being lost by breaking her back on a rock at Crosspark in the Torridge opposite Bideford Quay. They were abandoned at sea, as the aged *Bellona* eventually had to be in 1844, or lost on the shores of Prince Edward Island like one of the five *British Ladies* in 1848. Thomas Chanter's *Glenburnie* sank after a collision in the Gulf of St Lawrence, the *Telegraph* was captured by pirates off the East coast of Africa and the crew set adrift in a boat. In 1865 the *Juniper,* which had been caught in the ice and frozen in for the winter at West Cape in the Island, was blown with her surrounding ice away from the shore, her crew of six still on board. They had provisions, wood and water to last four months. They spent three months drifting around the Gulf and did not break loose from the ice until early April when off Newfoundland. Next year the *Isabella Saunders,* when she was fourteen days out from Quebec bound towards Sharpness, was pooped by a great wave which smashed her after-cabin, washed out the stores and carried away the deck cargo, the master and three of the crew. The three-masted schooners *Bride* and *Bridegroom* were both abandoned near Cape Horn and the barkentine *Clansman* went missing in the same area. The *Alma* was lost in the ice of the St Lawrence, the *Transit* was wrecked on St Pierre at the beginning of her delivery passage and her name boards, cut out but never fitted to her, are still in a house at New Bideford. The *Esperance* was lost on the coast of Lapland and the *Minna* off the coast of Brazil.

Accidents happened to small ships in the Bristol Channel as well. In a savage gale in October 1859, after fifty years of sailing, the *Peter & Sarah* was smashed to pieces on the rocks outside the harbour at Ilfracombe. Her master, who could have been taken off, was lost because he returned to the cabin to try to save twelve sovereigns he had on board.

But not all adventures were disastrous. James Yeo's bark *Malakoff* assisted four ships in the course of one stormy Atlantic crossing in the fall of 1858 and rescued the entire crews of two of them. In 1844 his schooner *Isabella* came across the *Pandora* of Waterford, St John for Bristol, waterlogged and on her beam ends. The *Isabella* had no boat adequate for rescuing people in the conditions prevailing, so the master hazarded his ship alongside the *Pandora* and rescued her entire crew. In 1830 the *Bellona* rescued part of the crews of a bark and a brig in the course of her first voyage of the year to the westward. For twenty-nine years the *Bellona* crossed the North Atlantic sometimes twice, usually four times, and occasionally six times each year. Under Joshua Williams she established a record few ships can have equalled in all history.

A crossing from west to east was sometimes all too easy and the century is littered with records of schooners setting out to go from one small North American port to another and ending up in European waters, blown out from the land and across the whole North Atlantic. In 1854, James Yeo's brigantine *Margaret*, having fought her way to within 100 miles of Newfoundland, was driven all the way back to Appledore again. But these same relentless winds could sometimes be used to make outstanding passages. In 1833 Thomas Chanter's *Sappho*, under William Howes, sailed from Nova Scotia to Bideford in twelve days, one of the fastest Atlantic passages ever made under sail. In October 1857 the *Alma*, William Richards, made a passage from Port Hill to the Mumbles in the Bristol Channel in fourteen days from land to land. The regular sailing packets from Britain to New York, which were the liners of the middle nineteenth century, did not at their best make better passages than these. Yeo's bark *Florida* once spent only eleven weeks on the round voyage from Devon to North America and back. Passages to the westward were, of course, longer. Forty-two days was average, crossings of over seventy days were not uncommon. But the ships of the Devon Islanders made many quick passages to the westward. In 1827 the *Bolivar* sailed from Plymouth to Charlottetown in twenty days. In 1843 the *Lord Ramsay* crossed from Devon to Quebec City in only twenty-two days. William Heard's *Civility* once made the spring passage to Charlottetown in twenty-three days, and in 1852 his *Secret* bettered both these passages and made Quebec City in twenty-one.

*   *   *

The most successful of all the North Atlantic masters employed by the Yeo enterprise was neither an Islander nor a Devonian. His name was William Richards. He was born in Swansea in 1819, the son of a master mariner who had made a comfortable fortune. He may have had family connections both in Bideford and in the Island. He went to sea when he was eighteen and when he was twenty-five he was made master of the *John Hawkes*, a brig of 175 tons which had been built in the Island and was partly owned by Joshua Williams. Williams sold her to a Swansea firm, Beynon and Tucker, whose representative in the Island, J. M. Tucker, ran one of the stores in Charlottetown.

The first contact of the *John Hawkes* and her young master with James Yeo came in 1845 when she loaded lumber at Richmond Bay. Richards traded with the Island for the next four years, interspersing his voyages there with other ventures, such as passages to the Miramichi with Irish emigrants who were mis-informed by the Limerick agent that the Miramichi was somewhere near St Andrews, from whence New York could be reached any day.

In 1849 Richards married Yeo's second daughter Susannah, the first child of his second marriage, in the little church at Port Hill. As befitted the robber baron's daughter, Susannah began her married life at sea. The couple arrived at Limerick in the *John Hawkes* exactly a month after their wedding and they were back in Boston two months later.

Richards abandoned the *John Hawkes* on a voyage from the Island to Bristol in the summer of 1851. For the next few years he worked as a master for James Yeo. In 1853 his brother Thomas Picton Richards, also a prosperous master mariner whose wandering young manhood had included the Californian gold rush of 1849, visited Port Hill and bought a brigantine which he called the *Queen*. He may have had in mind Yeo's third daughter Mary Jane, but if he did nothing came of it and he had to be content with an invitation to write a poem in her commonplace book. He responded with a realism which contrasts with the more conventional verse of most of her friends :

The Apple

Lady; the apple you'v sent me; such I'll prize;
As your fairy form; which I Idolize;
Your beaming smile; your generous heart;
Within my memory; bears a part;
Tis but an apple; yet; the Gift is rare;
The same, which Adam took from Eve; when paradise was there
The same; perchance; analogies must suit;
Aspiring to your love; would be forbidden fruit;
Nay; do not frown; for I would fain;
Give place unto your favoured swain;
Some others smile perchance; will raise me from dispair;
And for the apple that you sent me; make a pair;[3]

In 1854 William Richards took charge of Yeo's new bark *Alma,* named after the Crimean battle which had just been fought. He bought her a year later and henceforth from the base at Port Hill he proceeded to make his fortune. He had eight ships built between 1858 and 1864, operating some of them in partnership with his father-in-law and sailing in some of them as master. But after 1859 Thomas Picton Richards started to build up a shipowning and broking business in Swansea and, thus provided with a reliable agency, in 1864 William Richards persuaded his father-in-law to allow him to settle down at New Bideford. He had a house built (part of which is still in use as a farmhouse) on the brow of the hill above the pool where the *Peter & Sarah* anchored. Around the house stores and sheds were built and soon the New Bideford shipyard was booming again as it had not since William Ellis' great days in the 1830s. Between 1866 and 1892, out of the ninety-four ships William Richards had built in the Island, about forty were built at New Bideford, many of the earlier ones by sons of William Ellis. Some of the later vessels showed great enterprise in developing and adapting wooden sailing ship design to the economic conditions and technical possibilities of the late nineteenth century.

*   *   *

Until the end of the sailing emigrant trade at the beginning of the 1860s the captain had as one of his chief responsibilities the survival of his passengers, scores of them packed in temporary berths built on temporary decks in the hold of a timber ship. In writing of emigration it has become customary to stress the hardships frequently undergone by the passengers. It is refreshing to examine the record of the North Devon Island ships and to find that by the standards of their time travel in them was no worse and often a great deal better than might be expected. Above all it was safe. Neither the Burnards nor Chanter nor Yeo ever lost a ship laden with emigrants, or even any substantial number of passengers through disease. Nor were many complaints made against them when in later years the passing of successive Passenger Acts made conditions sometimes better and complaint possible when they were not.

If the first exodus of roughly 2,250 people from North Devon ended with the waning of Chanter's interest in the emigrant business in the early 1840s, a second and greater exodus began with the emigration to Prince Edward Island of 100 people from the vicinity of Kilkhampton in James Yeo's *British Lady* in the spring of 1842. It is not possible to write of this second exodus in the fairly definite terms which can be used of the first. The records are much less complete, emigration was now commonplace and, although they continued to record the arrivals and departures of the timber ships, the newspapers on both sides of the Atlantic no longer gave as a matter of course the approximate number of passengers they carried. The incompleteness of the British official records of emigration is well known. Moreover, after the late 1840s, improved transport inside Britain meant that emigration ceased to be a local affair in local ships, and people travelled from Bideford or Kilkhampton to Plymouth, Bristol or Newport to sail to America. All possibility of forming reliable conclusions as to the extent of local emigration from shipping records therefore ceases. In 1849 Richard Heard advertised the *Civility* and the *Secret* as sailing from Bideford for Prince Edward Island and Nova Scotia and for Montreal

1852, Nugget, *of Bideford, 80 tons, the polacca brigantine built by William Heard at Charlottetown which took the entire horses from Bideford to Prince Edward Island in 1853. This photograph shows her in her old age rigged as a ketch*

1854, Alma, *of Charlottetown, 356 tons, the bark built by George Ellis of New Bideford for James Yeo which William Richards bought and owned for fifteen years. This painting shows her off Naples*

Loading small timber through hold ports from a sailing scow at Quebec. Tackles have been rigged on the forecastle head for lifting the timber to the hold ports and swinging it into the hold. The jibboom and martingale have been rigged in so that the ship will take up less space at the wharves. She is the Parramatta, a full-rigged ship built in 1853 in New Brunswick. She is smaller than the largest ships built for the Yeo's at New Bideford and Port Hill and Quebec respectively, and the bark *Devonia* as sailing from Bristol to New York:

> This splendid Ship is quite new, only having made one voyage. She has been fitted up under the immediate super-intendence and inspection of the Government Emigration Com-missioners, with every possible convenience for the comfort and accommodation of Passengers; has very roomy 'twixt Decks, being seven feet in height; and as this Ship will sail in ballast trim, and at such a favourable season of the year for making a speedy voyage, it affords such an opportunity to passengers about to emigrate to New York as rarely occurs.
> The Master, being the Owner's Son, will afford every assist-ance and comfort to the Passengers in his power. . . .
> Passengers forwarded from Bideford to Bristol free, by the 'Water Witch' Steamer, or Sailing Vessels, which sail regularly three times every week.[4]

After Chanter's enthusiastic promotion had brought the 'Bideford Extension Railway' to East-the-Water in 1855 many emigrants left by train, bound for the big ports, and the whole nature of the trade changed. The *North Devon Journal* reported in 1857:

> It is said, that within the last week little short of 200 persons have passed up the North Devon Railway *en route* for the emigration ports—those for the North American Colonies proceeding chiefly to Plymouth. . . .[5]

When the Plymouth bark *John* was lost in scandalous circum-stances with nearly all her 263 passengers a few hours out from Plymouth in 1855, it was reported that most of them came from North Devon—'the great source of American emigration in the west of England'.[6] Nevertheless, Yeo's ships carried emigrants from Bideford until at least 1859.

Reports of arrivals and departures indicate that during the fourteen years from 1842 until 1855 at least 3,000 emigrants sailed from Bideford for Prince Edward Island, Quebec and Montreal, New York, Boston, St Andrews and Halifax. There were certainly very many more whose departure was not recorded in any way and more still from the neighbourhood who sailed

F

from Plymouth or Bristol or the Port of Padstow, which had a thriving emigrant trade with regular sailings to the St Lawrence taking several hundred passengers each summer. Altogether over those fourteen years, probably about 7,000 people left the Torridge and Taw valleys and the hill villages and market towns for North America. In some areas the exodus had marked social effects. Why did they leave?

A tradition of movement was now well established. An Atlantic voyage was thought of as fairly commonplace. There were plenty of relatives in North America who wrote home encouraging letters and provided introductions and money and a feeling of not being alone on the other side. James Yeo was well known by repute in Devon and he was always ready to help a settler get a start (and a start in debt to him) in the Island. His many ships were familiar sights on the river and they provided a cheap passage from a port convenient for the whole of North Devon and North Cornwall. They had an excellent reputation for delivering their human cargoes intact and their masters were reputed to take an interest in the welfare of the passengers. But there was more to it than that.

North Devon was still backward socially and economically. There was truth in the allegation the *North Devon Journal* sought to refute when in 1854 it said :

> It has often been said in disparagement of the North of Devon that in all the arts of civilisation, the refinements of life, and the several factors of moral, intellectual and social improvement she is half a century behind some other parts of the Kingdom.[7]

Prospective settlers were influenced by such stories as the following, reproduced in the same paper in 1857, which gets near to the heart of the whole matter of emigration to North America :

> About seven years ago, a young farm servant from a neighbouring village went to America leaving his sweetheart behind in a state that added nothing to the good reputation of either. When he had been there about a year, he sent home for the latter; she went out to him, and they were married. He now writes home that he has maintained his increasing family during

that period, and has worked himself into a farm—not a hired one—but 50 acres of purchased land, to which 10 more are to be soon added. Besides the land, there is the stock enumerating 25 bullocks besides other animals with the rest of the et ceteras of a farm. A few miscellaneous particulars were added, such as that they had to be their own tailors, in the spring make their own candles and soap, &c. Suppose this couple had been married seven years ago in this country, where would they have been now with their half dozen children? Where would have been the acres, the bullocks, the sheep, the corn, the candles, and the soap? Not only would there have been no where for them, but instead there-of hopeless poverty, dirt, drudgery, the Union, and a pauper's grave.[8]

The 1840s were a period of depression and hardship for many people. In 1849 the *North Devon Journal* reported :

The extent of emigration from this town and neighbourhood will scarcely be credited. Upwards of 50 are on the point of leaving Bideford alone; and in almost every Parish of the Union able bodied men and women who have been compelled to apply for partial relief are 'picking up their alls' and preparing to begin life *de novo* in another clime.[9]

Four years later the effects of this migration began to show :

We understand that not less than 60 persons, mechanics and agricultural labourers, and their wives are about to emigrate to the US from Swimbridge and the neighbouring parishes. So large a drain from the labour market is producing its effect in the enhancement of wages of those who remain at home . . . in the parishes of Holsworthy, Buckland Brewer, Yarnscombe, and throughout all those districts where emigration has thinned the agricultural population labourers are not to be had for money. Everywhere in fact we hear of wages being advanced and the labour market never before looked up so well—a large number we hear are preparing to go from hence both to America and Australia.[10]

In some local areas there were special reasons for migration. Appledore suffered a loss of population between 1841 and 1851 which was certainly in part the effect of migration and was at the time attributed to the gradual decline of the limestone trade and the general lawlessness of the place which 'prevented many families of respectability from residing there'. Throughout the century the whole county suffered a slow rural depopulation as the effect of the movement of its industries to other parts of Britain, of its poor communications and small farms, became more felt in the face of rising prosperity elsewhere. Besides those who went overseas many more moved to the towns and to other parts of Britain.

The conditions which brought about migration in some individual cases are clearly brought out in a series of letters written to William Ellis in the Island by members of his family in Britain. His son Robert, who had been in the Island for a short time but returned to Britain, wrote in July 1844 :

> Dear father this coms with my love to you hoping it will find you and my Brothers and Sisters all in good helth as it leves me and my Wife and my three Children thank the all-mighty god for it i receved your kind and wolkim letter datled October 23 1843 and glad to your from you all Dear father be not a fended at me for not writing to you be for for i wos in Ilfracombe i was thear 9 wieks to work and by the time i came back all the vessels ware gon out since that i have bin to Barnstaple to work and now i am working at Mr Jonsen for 13 Shilings pear Wick i ham the onely jonnenen that is imploud in Bideford i have not work for Mr Brook not six months he is still oying me ten Poundes he as Pead 20 Pounds of him he as not Sold nether one of the 3 vessels Dear father thear is very fine crops of weat in the country by Brley is nothing great and pattates is very Bad for i planted 58 yards and not one out of fifty that grw and i planted them the Seken time and not the inseak is eating them of as fast as the come above the grond tis not my complent only but all Rond for mils Dear father it as binn the dryeas sumer that as binn for great many years if you have a bushel weat or Barley you cant gilil gon grond plest to give ouer loves to all Brothers and Sisters and to ther littel ones ant gurven desears to be remembered to you all unkel Robert and Unkel Gorge Ellis desears to be remembered to you all unkel Jams is dead he did about 8 munths agun mary ann and elizabeth & agnes gives thers loves to lille William and to all ther litle cusens so no more at present from your affectnet Son and doter.
>   ROBERT ELIZABETH ELLIS.[11]

Next year another member of the family wrote :

Dear Uncle, I have taken the opportunity of answering your kind an welcome letter hoping it find you still in good health as I am happy to say it leaves me at present thank the Lord for it Dear Uncle I received your kind letter of the 23 of July Dear Uncle I am thinking weither I could do you any service or no as you mentioned an your Letter that you had upwards of seventy Grand Children an could not get one of them to drive a Plough for you an as wages is so high an you have no one to trust to our term his out of the road next Summer an if we did not take it again I am thinking of trying America as there is nothing here to look to for a living for the inhabitants is so thick and Labour his so dead there is nothing going on an if ever I come to America I think it will be next Summer For I am thinking then to take a Wife an after people get settld it is a great Difficulty of removing again so I think if ever I come to America it will be next Summer the youg Woman that I entend to make my wife has got a Brother on the Island an he is Doing very well an he rather persuads one to come he lives 13 Miles from Charlotte Town Dear Uncle I should Be Glad to have a few Lines again from you Between this an Chrismas if I am not troubling you to much For I am always Glad to hear from you an to hear about America as I am very often thinking about it Dear Uncle I have remembered you to Uncle George and to the greater part of My Cousans an the all gives their kind Love to you in regard to the times here in England it just to one stay there his but very little doing.

Carn his selling prety well at preasent wheat his from 7s to 8s per Busel Barly 4s 6d Oats from 2s to 3s per Bushel Meat has been very Dear all this Sumer on account of the scarcity of house meat Last Winter Beef his 6d per lb Mutton 6d per lb Pork 4d per lb it his coming back a Little now what it hath been their his fine likes of cr of every kind this year corn an potatoes an turnips harvest his just beginning But it hath been very ruff whether for a long time the corn that his cut is growing very much and somewhere it stands But I be in hopes it will char up now So Dear Uncle If I do come if I can do you any Service I shall be most happy to do so But if we never See each other more in this world I hope we shall meet in Heaven where we shall part no more for ever Pleast to give my kind love to James Ellis that was here and to the rest of my cousans so not more at Preasant from your

Affectionate Nephew, JAMES ELLIS.

> If you send by post do not pay anything with the letter for
> I will pay for it.[12]

The migrants included many small farmers and labourers.
When Thomas Chanter's bark *Falcon* arrived at Quebec from
Bideford in June 1842 with 78 men, women and children, they
were reported as farm servants, mechanics and labourers and their
families, able to pay their way on to their destinations which were
Kingston, Bytown (Ottawa), Toronto and Hamilton. Next year
the London-owned *St Ann's*, built by Richard Chapman in 1812,
brought 309 people to Quebec from Bideford; they were described
in the emigration reports as including 'some respectable farmers
and farm labourers who, with the exception of four families,
were able to pay their way; they are going to the Huron and
Newcastle districts to friends. A few go to Ohio and Illinois'.[13]
In September 1846 How's *Arab* brought out some farmers with
considerable capital; some of whom went to Upper Canada and
two or three families to New York State. Two years later James
Yeo's *Ocean Queen* brought in more 'respectable settlers of good
means' and the same year the *Civility* brought a cargo of farmers,
all of whom went up country. The reports from Quebec of the
general acceptability of the emigrants from North Devon go on
into the 'fifties.

What sort of conditions did these respectable people meet with
on the passage? They embarked often in considerable excitement :

> On Saturday evening the *Electric* was taken in tow by the
> *Princess Royal* Stmr. and moved to the Pool. For some days
> previous much excitement had prevailed in the vicinity of
> her berth. The constant arrival of wagons laden with luggage,
> crowned with real Devonian roses blooming in beautiful fresh-
> ness. The peculiar expression depicted on their contenances
> as they realised the novelty of their situation—the hope that
> beamed forth from happy faces—the joy that lighted up the
> eyes of some—the thoughtful and pensive countenances of
> others—Many spoke of the attention and kindness of the Capt.
> and owners and were in good spirits.[14]

This was a highly competitive business. In 1843, for example,
John How had two timber ships seeking emigrants from North

Devon, Thomas Chanter one, Richard Buse one, William Heard one, James Yeo two and the London-owned *St Ann's* was competing as well. Passengers represented pure gain over what would have been westerly passages with empty holds. Ships with good reputations, and this depended chiefly on the master, got the passengers and made the money. The owners themselves were equally anxious to develop an image of benign paternal preoccupation with the welfare of human cargo. William Yeo, not a man to bother himself over much with other people's troubles, took particular pains to present himself as a humane and careful shipowner, accompanying his ships out over the bar at the start of their passages and achieving satisfactory publicity for such gestures as the returning to land of visitors who inadvertently prolonged their farewells and found themselves unexpectedly bound for America.

The masters, local men, depended for their employment and their standing in the community on the commercial success of their voyages. All these factors were working to ensure that emigrants who sailed out over Bideford bar arrived safely after a passage no more unpleasant than was inevitable, though travelling in an emigrant ship was not a way to get fat. In 1851 Richard Heard advertised,

> Provisions supplied weekly to each passenger—$2\frac{1}{2}$ lbs of bread or biscuit, 1 lb wheaten flour, 5 lbs oatmeal, 2 lbs rice, $\frac{1}{2}$ lb sugar, $\frac{1}{2}$ lb treacle or molasses, 2 oz Tea, 21 quarts of good water.
>
> For terms of passage, which will be Much Lower than is charged by any other vessel including similar comforts and provisions apply to the owner.[15]

Only John How's ships were occasionally criticised for poverty of food and hardships incurred by the passengers.

Many years ago one of the authors of this book made a passage out of the Bristol Channel in a square-rigged ship without an engine. This was in the teeth of a moderate gale from the southwest which made it necessary to beat backwards and forwards between Bideford Bay and the Welsh coast to weather Lundy. The very strangeness of the environment of a sailing ship must have been frightening to the labourer or craftsman and his family making their first acquaintance with the sea, even though they were bred to hard lying, wet, cold, overcrowded quarters and poor food. Thirty years later strong impressions of this passage still remain; the roar of the wind in the complex web of the inefficient rigging, the squeal of the blocks and the beating of the feet of the hurrying crew on deck as the ship was put about, the strange smells, the mist and driving spray, the wash of the looming dark seas, the scent of the bracken coming down off the land, which must have been deeply nostalgic for the countryman, and the violent three-dimensional mobility of the world.

There survive at least two first-hand accounts of emigrant passages from Bideford to North America. These are William Fulford's (Uncle Billie's) *Journal*, kept aboard Richard Heard's *Civility* on a passage from Bideford towards Quebec in 1848, and a journal kept by W. Gliddon of Barnstaple on a passage from Appledore towards Quebec in James Yeo's *Ocean Queen* in 1855. This particular passage was notable because the emigrants were 'a number of young persons from this town and neighbourhood'. These accounts convey in their different ways full impressions of what these passages meant to the most articulate of the people who made them.

The impression is of something of a communal venture, with passengers playing an active part in the sailing of the vessel, the craftsmen among them joining in her maintenance. Squalid as the conditions were, they were evidently no worse than was expected and accepted. The shared berths in the whitewashed hold entered by ladders through the cargo hatches are not thought subject for comment. There are no complaints, though the water in the *Civility* stank and had to be boiled and flavoured with peppermint. They had their adventures with bad weather, accompanied by the apparently inevitable 'females shrieking'! The gale experienced by the *Ocean Queen* on 12 April 1855 is graphically described.

Thursday, 12th. Weather dirty—about 4 p.m. orders were given to close-reef all sails as a storm was expected in half an hour every sail was furled and the ship pumped out, ready for the worst. By this time the rain had begun to fall and the wind to rattle through the ropes like thunder. This lasted but a few minutes, and we were all in hopes it was past over easily, but as it got dark the rain again began to fall, the wind to whistle and the sea to rise. By ten o'clock the storm was getting hot. Thunder is no more than a dog's bark compared with the tremendous roar of the wind and sea. Ten o'clock all but three passengers went below, to turn in and try to sleep, and I being the hindmost left the scuttle open, thinking the other three would follow. We had scarcely turned in when a sea struck her, making her reel most awfully. It came down the scuttle like a mill-stream, washing some of us nearly out of our beds. Two of our boxes broke from their lashings and rolled about from side to side, strewing their contents as they went.

It was an anxious time; females shrieking, the water almost floating our things and the pails, cans, etc., knocking about. It is impossible to convey an idea of such an awful sight. We had very little sleep this night.

About 4 o'clock a.m. Friday there was a dead calm which lasted until about 7 a.m., when the storm recommenced with all its fury. The sailors on deck were obliged to be lashed as they could not stand. We could cook nothing today, but the steward brought us some coffee, etc., and the Capt. comes down now and then to see us.

I went to the top of the steps this morning, just to see the sea. I never witnessed such a sight before; it was one mass of foam, and rolling as high as our topmast, threatening every moment to swallow us up. About 2 p.m. another sea struck the ship, smashing in the cabin skylight and some of the bulwarks. This completed the disaster of last night. We were now fairly washed clean out. This appeared to be the height of the storm, for it began to abate, and, thank God, by his aid we were carried safely through it.

But there were many compensations. The master of the *Civility* is friendly and relaxed with his charges and more tolerant of Uncle Billie's preaching and tract-giving than are some of the other passengers. The seamen raid a French fishing bark's long-lines for cod. There are crossing the Banks ceremonies. Discipline and crew conditions in the *Ocean Queen* were particularly happy and the relations between the master, Richard Dart, passengers and crew were excellent.

. . . We have plenty of amusement on deck today in the shape of chess etc., and plenty of singing every day from the sailors; they sing every two hours, when they pump the ship out. It makes one laugh to hear some of their songs:

'And now my boys we're outward bound,
    Young girls go a-weeping;
We're outward bound to Quebec Town
    Across the Western Ocean.'

We have had a complete merrymaking below tonight, a sort of return of our first night's spree.

Monday 16th—Weather still lovely.

'Away, haul away, haul away, my dandies,
Away, haul away, haul away Joe.'

When you come to 'Joe' you must pull. The crew leave work at 6 p.m., after which they amuse themselves and us, as they please. This evening they made their appearance on deck equipped as soldiers: they were capitally made-up: instead of a drum they had a tin box, and this greatly aided the burlesque. They marched aft to the cabin and one of the 'ossifers' handed the Captain a letter, the purport was that there was reason to suspect that one of their recruits was on board and that if he detained him any longer, he would have to take the consequences. The Captain gave them liberty to search the ship, and take him if they found him, which of course they very soon did; by this time two others of the crew had made their appearance equipped as countrymen. After some parleying of course they were enlisted and marched off to learn their exercise; not liking drill very well they ran away, and one was concealed in the long-boat, and when questioned as to the cause of his running off he answered that he 'ware towld to vall back, and valled into the boat'. The other's excuse was that he 'went to see the maester he was gwine to live wi', when they 'listed en, but when he got the gate, he seed his *apprehension*, and he wur frightened'. This is only a specimen of the wit and humour displayed by the crew and I do not think any ship possesses a better crew.

It was all very much a bucolic North Devon family affair in which the different dialect of a little group from Wiltshire is subject for amused comment.

*   *   *

Masters of Island ships in the North Atlantic trade sometimes had passengers of another kind to cope with. The bark *Prioress,* shared in ownership by the Yeos and the Popes, arrived at Charlottetown in September 1865 with five cabin passengers, five in the hold, and four horses, eight heifers, one bull, twenty ewes and three pigs imported for a newly established Colonial Government stock farm. With so few human passengers the *Prioress* was not subject to the restrictions on carrying livestock which controlled ships under the Passenger Acts. This was not the first time animals had been imported to improve the Island breeds. In 1852 the Colonial Government granted £1,000 to the Island's Royal Agricultural Society for the purchase in Britain and shipment of heavy working horses for use at stud. T. H. Haviland, who had recently retired from the presidency of the Governor's Executive Council and was then on what proved to be a temporary visit to Britain before he finally settled down in Charlottetown, was asked to purchase and ship them. He bought suitable horses, but there were long negotiations before they were shipped in two vessels, the *Attwood,* which sailed from London and Richard Heard's little Island built polacca brigantine *Nugget.* The *Bideford Journal* described the scene when the horses were loaded at Bideford Quay :

> *Exportation of entire horses.* On Saturday last some interest was excited in the vicinity of the quay, by the circumstance that Mr Thorne, of Prince Edward Island, was about to ship four beautiful entire horses on board the emigrant ship 'Nugget'. A large company assembled to witness the embarkation. The animals were hauled on board by means of slings. Some of them whilst slung aloft beat the air violently with their feet, causing all present to look on with bated breath. On the horses being lowered into their berths, a general rush was made on board the vessel, and not till the mate had dealt out a plentiful supply of water, which proved more potent than peace officers, could the crowd be dispersed. In the course of a couple of hours the animals were shipped safely without injury to horses or men. The beasts are considered perfect models for symmetery and power.[16]

The *Nugget* arrived at Charlottetown on 3 July 1853, forty-three days out from Bideford and the horses were all landed in good condition. Those on board the *Attwood* died of the effects of the prolonged violent motion of the ship during bad weather.

* * *

The lines of timber ships lying below Quebec City, loading squared timber from rafts through the hold ports, was one of the great sights of nineteenth-century British North America. The hold ports were square and were cut in the bows, and sometimes in the stern, to make the loading of the long timbers easier.

After the 1820s Thomas Chanter's and James Yeo's ships loaded from time to time at Quebec, but it was in the 'fifties and 'sixties, when the Island timber was showing signs of exhaustion and the great trade of the Miramichi was reduced, that the Island ships began to go to Quebec frequently. They loaded timber which had been cut in the winter up in the Ottawa, on the Lakes, and in northern New York State and Vermont. The great logs were hauled on sleds out of the woods relatively easily and floated down the rivers on the thaw, first as logs and squared timber, and then, as the rivers became wider lower down, they were made up into rafts, all to collect at Quebec with smaller timber brought by inland water transport. The timber ships came up the St Lawrence, sometimes among the ice floes, in the spring thaw in May, scores of them on a single tide, until as many as 500 have lain in the river below the lovely city. The rafts were brought up to the ships and the shore gangs broke them up and trod the logs and poled them into position. To sling the timbers in through the hold ports, gangs on deck with winches operated tackles rigged to derricks over the bows. As a historian of the trade, Frederick Wallace, has described it :

> But let us recall the brave days of sail, with the great timber rafts dropping down to the coves and the French-Canadian river-men singing *'en roulant ma boule'* or some such *chanson*: sun-bronzed, red-shirted men, with calks in the soles of their heavy boots, and surprisingly agile in leaping from log to log around the booms; hard, brawny fellows, who scanned the Irish timber-stowers for the sight of some opponent in past water-front *fracas* to seek or avoid. And the timber-stowers

with the brogue still strong, sweating and bawling lustily, 'Top up, starboard! Easy, port!' 'Hook on, Mike, an' heave in aisy as ye go!' or cursing in the dark holds, with the great slimy timbers charging at them, which must be grabbed on the move and swung into place.[17]

Timber cargoes presented many technical problems to masters and the legislation governing the timber trade has a history of its own. The contemporary work of reference on cargo problems, *Stevens on Stowage*, has twenty-six pages of advice and information for masters on the stowage of timber, much of it relevant to the American trade. There is advice on ballasting, very important when deck cargoes were carried, and on the distribution of cargo both in the length and breadth of the ship and in depth, so as to minimise the danger of damage through excessive weight bearing on the curved surfaces of the ceiling, as the inner lining of the ship was called. Wedging and securing against shifting of cargo was vital; each flat tier of cargo above the curved lower surfaces of the ship had to be separately wedged and care taken that the butts or joints of one layer did not fall directly over those of the tier below. The best and largest timber was selected for the upper layers in the lower hold and for the upper holds above the 'tween deck (where ships had 'tween decks) because the long runs and the space here made stowage more convenient and the big timber had to be moved about less. At Quebec, where red and yellow pine was shipped in great quantities, the heavy small red pine was placed below the larger, lighter yellow.

A master's horror in the timber trade was the deck cargo. The storing on deck of an additional quantity of timber could reduce a ship's safety margin dangerously, add greatly to the difficulty and hazard of working the vessel, and in winter involve a serious risk of ice forming on the cargo to a degree that made the vessel unstable. After 1840 it was illegal for British ships to carry deck cargoes in the North American trade between September and May. Various ways were devised to avoid the effects of this Act and in the 'fifties, when, after the Navigation Laws were repealed, foreign competition was felt in the trade, the deck cargo law was repealed too. In 1872 'timber ships from

Quebec and the Miramichi literally strewed their fabrics and cargo across the western ocean . . . during that year from May to December, the term of the St Lawrence season, fifty-seven vessels engaged in the timber trade were wrecked and abandoned'.[18] This débacle led eventually to the passing of a new Act of the British Parliament limiting deck cargoes in winter.

Prominent in the agitation for the passing of this Act, as he had been in the cleaning up of the Quebec waterfront, was an outstanding figure in the maritime history of Canada, Henry Fry. He was born in Bristol in 1826 and trained in the profession of ship broking by Mark Whitwell, James Yeo's Bristol agent. In 1849 he took half the shares with William Yeo in James Yeo's brigantine *Favourite*. Her first voyages were to Cuba with railway iron and back to London with mahogany and sugar, then 'from Shields to Venice with coals, thence with a cargo of wheat from the Adriatic to Donegal'.[19] Fry, now a partner in Mark Whitwell's firm, began to spend his summers about its business in Quebec and in due course settled there on his own account. He was the Yeos' Quebec agent.

*   *   *

Early in the twentieth century James Yeo's youngest son, Senator John Yeo, still owned several wooden sailing ships employed in general world trade. Two of them were the barkentines *Kathleen* and *Daisy*, named for the daughters of Thomas Adams, the manager and accountant from Kilkhampton, who played a large part in the fortunes of James Yeo. A British seaman turned journalist, F. C. Hendry, made a voyage from Swansea to Charlottetown via the Azores in the *Kathleen* and after he had turned to writing he used the theme at least twice, once in a short story and once in a semi-documentary account of the passage from Swansea to the Azores. From these accounts, fictitious though they both are in different degrees, there emerges the picture of a very happy ship, a slow but weatherly and seaworthy vessel. The food was excellent and the quarters adequate. Good relations between the master and crew were reflected in the general use of Christian names. All this was accompanied by a certain casualness in the way the barkentine went about the business of earning her living, but these were the last days and John Yeo had a sentimental streak. He wanted to keep representatives of the ships that had made his family's fortune for as long as he could.

CHAPTER TEN

TWO FIDDLES AND NO PLOW

SHIPS built in the Island, though they might be sold to British buyers after one or two transatlantic passages, did not appear in the statistics as exports. They could not, because the majority of them were registered at the Charlottetown Custom House as soon as they were completed and remained officially Island ships until, some time after their sale in Britain, their registers were transferred to their new home port on the European side of the Atlantic. No statistical record of these transfers was kept, though each represented an export from the Island of the largest kind. An examination of the Register Books, which are preserved in the Public Archives of Canada, strongly suggests that shipbuilding was very important indeed to the Colony's economy and that the picture of the Island commonly accepted, that, 'farming was its chief, almost its only industry and it lived by agricultural exports to the other provinces and to New England' is quite wrong. It is truer perhaps to say that for many decades the Colony lived by shipbuilding for markets in Britain and the other British colonies and by the earnings overseas of its own ships. In the great years of the 'sixties and early 'seventies a minor economic miracle took place and the Island became a considerable producer of ships for sale in the international market; in terms of numbers it probably contributed more ships to the merchant fleets of metropolitan Britain than any other place beyond Britain's shores.

Of the total of at least 350 ships built by, or for, financed by, or purchased immediately on completion by James Yeo, his sons and his son-in-law William Richards, between 1833 and 1893, at least 250 were transferred from Island registration to named British owners soon after their launch. Between 1842 and 1868, of the 40 or so ships built by, or for William Heard of

Charlottetown, three-quarters were sold through his father or brothers in Bideford.

Lieutenant Governor Donald Campbell, reporting the totals of exports and imports for 1848 to the Governor General in Quebec, came to the conclusion that the sale of ships to Britain had brought the Colony about £50,000. Without the exports of ships the Island had an adverse trade balance of about £37,000. In 1850 William Heard gave a lecture based on these figures to the Mechanics' Institute in Charlottetown. In commenting on this lecture *The Islander* came to the conclusion that the total value realised from shipping (presumably the value of vessels sold plus invisible earnings) in 1848 was about £58,000 and that shipping paid for more than half of all the Island's imports, while exported agricultural produce paid for less than one-twelfth of them.

In a debate in the Island Parliament in April 1849 on the levying of import duties on ship chandlery there was no dissension from the view that, though individuals might ruin themselves by speculative shipbuilding, the industry was, as Mr McLean put it, 'the principal and almost the only profitable industry the people of this Island can avail themselves of at present'. James Yeo said that it was 'well known that shipbuilding is, at present, the greatest support of the country', and the Solicitor General summed up, 'Our ships form the most valuable part of our exports, and it [the industry] gives employment to a large number of the inhabitants; and were it not for that species of trade we should scarcely be able to hold up our heads'.[1]

The numbers and total tonnage of ships built in the Island rise decade by decade after 1830 until the peak years of the 'sixties, when an average of ninety ships a year were launched. In the late 'fifties it became the custom to record on the register sheet of a new Island ship destined to be sold in Britain the name of the agent empowered to sell her and the minimum sum he was authorised to sell her for. Thus the register sheets of James Yeo's ships are embellished with notes to the effect that William Yeo of Appledore, Devon, in Great Britain, Merchant, had been empowered to sell the ship for a sum of not less than £X anywhere within twelve months, followed by entries of the name of the buyer, the date of sale (but not the final price) and of the return and cancellation of the Charlottetown Certificate of Registration. From the minimum prices recorded it is possible to form a general idea of the financial scale of the shipbuilding business of James Yeo and his family. Making certain allowances, and remembering that some ships were still sailed away from the Island unregistered on certificates of which apparently no record survives, a complete picture could be built up of the general significance of shipbuilding to the Island's economy. It is also possible to learn some interesting detailed facts about the business.

It was of great importance socially as well as economically. The felling, hauling and preparation of timber for building ninety ships a year and providing the cargoes of many of them, the cutting out and erection of the frames, the planking up, the multitude of small jobs around the building of a wooden ship, all done without the help of power of any kind except for a few water-driven sawmills, absorbed a great deal of the Colony's labour force. New families of settlers were brought out to do the skilled jobs. To Port Hill came the blacksmith Dennis and the sailmaker Strongman, whose descendants still farm there. As early as 1850 William Heard and *The Islander* questioned the effects of this concentration on one industry :

> . . . so long as farming is suffered to languish in its present degraded condition, vessels will continue to be a principal article of export—at least until the timber is consumed. But the abstract question, whether Shipbuilding enriches a young Colony, possessing a fertile soil, is an economical enquiry by no means so clear. Neither the ship timbers, nor the lumber forming her cargo, are of more value than the labour expended upon them; and it strikes us that a man nominally a farmer, but obtaining *liberal wages*—which ship-builders generally pay—from his connexion with ship-building, would, in the long run, do better for his family, and consequently for the public, by devoting the whole of his labour to the clearing and cultivation of his farm.[2]

In the 'sixties the situation became worse. In these peak years, besides James Yeo, his son James, his son John and William

Richards, Lemuel Cambridge Owen and William Welsh, Henry and George Longworth, Angus MacMillan, John Lefurgey, James, George and Ralph Peake, James Duncan, the McLure brothers, John Gillan, Frederick Hyndman, James College Pope and others were building ships and selling them through agents in Britain empowered to sell for suitable sums. Some elderly people in the Island still remember hearing in their childhood of this era as the time of 'two fiddles and no plow', when the farms were uncultivated and allowed to go to ruin while the men made quick ready credit with the store keeper/merchant/shipbuilder by flocking to the woods and shipbuilding places. When credit was plentiful 'it was all the shipyard or the woods, and for the rest to play the old tunes and drink and be as merry and irresponsible as the happy circumstances allowed'. The habits imposed by the distractions of ready credit gained for the intermittent work away from the farms did not make for the growth either of a stable society or a prosperous agriculture. Nor did this concentration of labour and capital make for diversified industry, ready to take the shock when, in the later 'seventies, the world market for wooden ships began to contract very rapidly.

James Yeo's shipbuilding business began to assume large proportions in 1846, when, greatly helped by his almost limitless supply of cheap timber and with William firmly established in Appledore, he built in financial partnership with him at least six vessels, all of which were sold in Britain. Building continued on this scale, with up to nine ships a year, until 1863, but larger and larger ships began to appear among the smaller craft. The *Louisa*, nearly 150 feet long, built in 1851 under the supervision of William Ellis, was probably the largest ship launched in the Island to that date. The *Lady Seymour* next year was bigger, and the *Princess Royal*, the last and greatest of all the dozens of ships built under William Ellis' supervision, was bigger still. In 1856 the *James Yeo*, nearly 200 feet long, shared with the *Palmyra*, built by James Yeo Junior on Campbell Creek in 1869, the distinction of being the second largest ship the family ever built, but the *William Yeo*, also built on Campbell Creek, and the

Isabella Saunders, which were both launched in 1862, were not much smaller.

In the early 1860s a sudden change took place. The causes are complex. The cyclical pattern of business activity had been in a downswing in the late 'fifties, and the 'sixties began with the inevitable recovery. But much more important were the effects of the Civil War in the United States, which significantly reduced American competition in the world carrying trade and at the same time had a generally stimulating effect on world commerce. In 1863 the Yeo family built thirteen ships; one was kept, twelve sold in Britain for not less than £27,600, nearly a quarter in value of all the ships built in the Island in that year. In 1865 eighteen ships were built and they were all sold in Britain for £43,000 or more. This was the peak year of James Yeo's achievement, when this one part of his business activities and those of his family contributed nearly as much to the Colony's economy as the whole shipbuilding industry had contributed in 1848. These sales alone were equal in value to between a fifth and a sixth of all the recorded exports of the Island in 1865 and, even allowing for the extent to which it was financed from Britain, the total contribution of the shipbuilding industry must have been as great as that of the official exports. After the death of James Yeo in 1868, there was a falling off, in consequence, no doubt, of the loss of his drive and financial genius and the regular contraction of world trade. But in 1874 James and John Yeo and William Richards exported at least £50,000 worth of ships and the next year £34,000 worth. These were the last prosperous days of the wooden sailing ship, and although the largest of all the Yeo ships, the *Flora*, was built at New Bideford in 1877, from then on the decline was rapid.

A study of the minimum prices asked for the ships reveals interesting facts. In the 'sixties the highest prices per ton were asked for small vessels, brigantines and schooners of 100 to 200 tons. There is of course a direct relation between the Class given to a ship by Lloyd's surveyor and the price asked for her. Prices in 1863 were high, £9 to £11 per ton, and it was probably this which gave rise to the great output of 1865 when in fact prices were generally lower. The eighteen Yeo ships of that year were perhaps products of an over-extended industry. They were not in the highest class of the family's shipping and they averaged from £6 10s to £9. Next year prices rose and the ships were better. By the late 'seventies the market had changed. The ships of 1874 and 1875 were on the average larger than their predecessors and they were more sophisticated. They made from £9 10s to £12 per ton. The highest recorded price ever asked for a Yeo ship seems to have been that demanded for the brig *Annie* of 1869 at £12 10s per ton.

In the same year the *Cutty Sark*, a vessel of first-class construction built partly of iron, not very much larger than the *William Yeo* and the *Isabella Saunders* and, like them, equipped with the very expensive rigging and sails of the full-rigged ship, square-rigged on all three masts, cost £21 per ton to build in Scotland—and drove her builders out of business at the price. Her quality of construction is shown by the fact that, having escaped disaster at sea, she still exists on display in a dry dock at Greenwich in England. She gives the visitor some impression of what James Yeo's own big ships were like. They were slightly smaller than the *Cutty Sark*, rounder in the hull form, and most of them had square transom counters instead of her graceful semi-eliptical counter. They were not so well finished as she is, and they were built, at least in part, of relatively less durable soft-wood. A good impression of the general appearance of the smaller square-rigged ships built in the Island can be gained (if proper allowances are made for her very specialised trade) from the whaler *Charles W. Morgan*, also a full-rigged ship, built in 1854 at New Bedford, Massachusetts, and preserved at the Mystic Seaport, Connecticut.

The *Cutty Sark*'s quality of construction reflects perhaps a measure of over-investment. The Island ships were built for the specific purpose of earning enough money to give a reasonable return on capital after depreciation spread over a relatively short period. In fact many of them continued to earn money long after the initial investment had been recovered. James Yeo's *Louisa* of 1851 was still afloat in 1905. The polacca brigantine *Nugget*, which carried the horses to Charlottetown in 1852, earned a bare living for her owner-master carrying cargoes of coal to Fremington near Bideford until well into the present century, and she was afloat after the first world war. The *William Yeo* was still sailing for Norwegian owners in the 1890s. The Richards' brigantine *Aneroid* built in 1874 at West Point by David Ramsay was still sailing from Bideford in the 1920s and was the last merchant brigantine to be owned in an English port. Another Richards-financed ship, the *Raymond*, built at Summerside by John Lefurgey in 1876 was still afloat during the second world war and was the last survivor of all the ships built as a consequence of Thomas Burnard's venture of 1818.

Survivors of the crews lasted longer than the ships they sailed. In the mid 1960s Mr Jewell of Bideford could remember his experiences sailing in the *Nugget* seventy years before. Mr Jewell said, 'Fancy going over to the westward in a craft like the *Nugget* with horses! They kept them alive because they never let them lie down.' Speaking of the ship herself he said that she was slow but very safe, 'She might starve 'ee, but she'd never drown 'ee!' She would sail without ballast, a tremendous advantage in the coasting trade, for as soon as her cargo was discharged she was ready for sea. She was very handy and stiff so that, 'she'd never tell 'ee when to take in sail, old *Nugget* wouldn't, the mast would come down first'.

Some of the ships built for William Richards were employed in the business of carrying copper-ore in bulk from the west coast of South America to the Bristol Channel. The history of this fragment of British industry still awaits the detailed study it greatly merits, but Joseph Conrad had something to say about it in *The Mirror of the Sea*. Speaking of one of his former masters he wrote :

> It appeared he had 'served his time' in the copper-ore trade, the famous copper-ore trade of old days between Swansea and the Chilian coast, coal out and ore in, deep-loaded both ways, as if in want on defiance of the great Cape Horn seas—a work, this, for staunch ships, and a great school of staunchness of West-Country seamen. A whole fleet of copper-bottomed barques, as strong in rib and planking, as well-found in gear,

as ever was sent upon the seas, manned by hardy crews and commanded by young masters, was engaged in that now long-defunct trade.[3]

The strains of the trade came partly from the double rounding of Cape Horn each voyage entailed but more especially from the heavy ore, stowed in a trunk built into the hold, which racked and tore at the ships as they rolled and pitched in the great seas. Into this trade went the three-masted schooners *Bride* and *Bridegroom* and probably the *Bridesmaid* and the bark *Ingomar* and the barkentines *Clansman* and *Antagonist*. Three of these ships were built at New Bideford and three by David Ramsay at Summerside.

That these ships should be big three-masted schooners (the *Bridesmaid*, nearly 160 feet long, was one of the largest ships to be given that rig) and barkentines is indicative of a characteristic readiness to exploit new ideas and techniques. The three-masted schooner came into existence in the eighteenth century, and a ship built in Newfoundland in 1783, the *Jenny*, was described in registration documents as a three-masted schooner when in 1792, now owned in Bristol, she visited the Pacific coast of North America. In the early 1830s several towns in Maine were building three-masted schooners (and later claiming to have originated the rig) and in 1854 William Heard launched the *Choice* into Charlottetown Harbour, the first three-masted schooner to be built in the Island. Between 1849 and 1860, 125 three-masters were built in the United States and many of these sailed across the Atlantic, but despite its age and these early developments there were technical, economic, social and even superstitious reasons why the three-masted schooner was not built in really large numbers until the boom in the United States coasting trade after the Civil War. From then on it became more and more popular and big American three-masted schooners made many overseas voyages in the 1870s. It was one of the most efficient rigs for a moderate-sized ship, but conservative British shipowners, wedded to the square rig of their forefathers, were slow to take up this kind of vessel for general trade and William Richards and his Swansea associates showed much enterprise.

The Island ships, like those of British North America generally, rapidly adopted American developments in sailing-ship equipment and tended to be more efficiently equipped than their British-built contemporaries. Easy-running patent blocks were used, and rigging was designed for easy working and a good all-round performance for the vessel. According to a historian of Canadian sailing ships, Frederick Wallace, the important technical devices of double topsails and double topgallant sails were adopted long before they came into general use in ships built in Britain. There are several contemporary reports of the arrival of ships at Bideford from Prince Edward Island the rigging of which incorporated an unspecified 'New principle'.

More evidence of the enterprise of William Richards and John Yeo came at the very end of the sailing ship era. Between 1888 and 1892 the last five ships were built at New Bideford, the *Rita*, the *Bonita*, the *Ramona*, the *Genesta* and the *Meteor*, all barkentines (or three-masted brigantines as he called them) for Richards. Over the same period and in 1893 Yeo had five barkentines built, the *Thetis*, the *Kathleen*, the *Sidonian*, the *Cosmo* and the *Daisy*.

These last ten ships were medium-sized ocean-going sailing vessels. Those built at New Bideford, and some at least of those built for John Yeo, were of a very special design. They represented a last successful attempt to build wooden sailing ships to compete in general world trade in the conditions of the late nineteenth century. They had two special peculiarities. To make the stowing of cargo easier they had no hold beams except the cabin beams at the ends of the vessel and two beams in the way of each mast. To compensate for the lack of these strengthening timbers the inside planking and the outside planking of the sheer strakes were bolted together edge to edge and there were other additional fastenings. These ships were expensive to build, but, although constructed almost entirely of spruce, they proved themselves to be very strong.

John Yeo planned one more ship after the *Daisy*, to celebrate his appointment as a Senator of Canada in 1898. Her name boards were cut out with *Stentor* chiselled into the softwood.

But she was never built and the boards still lie in a barn at Port Hill.

The best evidence of the merits and defects of Island ship-building is found in the detailed reports of Lloyd's surveyors on ships built after arrangements were made in 1856 to survey ships under construction in Island shipyards. They show the gradual changes in the woods used as the timber resources of the Island became exhausted. In the 'fifties the *James Yeo* was built of birch, juniper (the very durable red cedar), oak and yellow pine. The *Sara Jane* of the same period had birch, beech, ash and maple in her framing and white pine in her planking, but she too was predominantly made of red cedar, and in the 'fifties some ships were built almost entirely of this timber. Eighteen years later the *Bridegroom*, like nearly all her successors, was constructed almost entirely of spruce. The reports show a gradual improve-ment in building standards. In technical terms Island ships, when they could be classed at all, varied in class between 4A and 12A, with the latter classification predominating in later years. James Yeo's ships of the 'fifties can be summed up in the frequently used phrase (which might have been applied to James himself) 'rough but strong'. In the 'sixties quality improves, though some vessels, including Yeo's *Bellona* of 1863, are rejected altogether or have their classification deferred pending improvements. In the 'seventies and 'eighties, despite their spruce construction, the brief description of the later ships is almost always in the same terms 'a very strong and superior Vessel'.

When the hull had been built and tarred against the ship-worm, which was very prevalent at New Bideford, and perhaps if she were a small schooner launched over snow and ice with the help of up to 200 horses, the ship had to be rigged and finished. Much of the latter work was done in the Richmond Dry Dock at Appledore or in dry dock at Swansea, though there were men at Port Hill capable of the finest work, even the making of figureheads. The rigging was done by the crews who came out to the Island from Britain. They brought the sails and rigging materials, anchors and chains, with them, but Strongman, the sailmaker who lived in Thomas Chanter's fine house on Port

Hill farm could make any necessary adaptations. Crews could certainly not be found in the Colony for ninety ships a year and, though many Islanders took to the sea and many masters and seamen from Britain settled in the Island, the bulk of the crews in the 'forties, 'fifties and 'sixties came from Britain to take the ships away. The shortage of seamen in the Island brought about a crisis in 1846, when many new ships were prevented from sailing through lack of men. William Heard suffered particularly from difficulty in getting crews, and on at least one occasion his father shanghaied an Appledore man from his boat on the way out to the bar and took him to Charlottetown. The crews of five of James Yeo's six new vessels of 1846 arrived at Richmond Bay on May 31 in the current *British Lady*, together with the sails and the gear for rigging, and whatever happened to his rivals Yeo's ships were not delayed for lack of men to sail them. Next year the *British Lady* brought the 'rigging for 3 barques and 1 brigantine, 40 sailors and 12 passengers'.

John Yeo and William Richards made their own vessels pay dividends from the freight on other people's cargoes even into the twentieth century. But it is said at Port Hill that shortly before he died in 1872 William Yeo wrote to his brother James in the Island urging on him the importance of diversification, because the days when fortunes could be made with the building of wooden ships for sale were coming to an end. Though there was to be half a decade more of prosperity, he was right. The world was changing rapidly. The farms in the Island were no longer to be abandoned for the shipbuilding places and the farmers had to put up the second fiddle and, with what they had earned at work on the vessels, go out and buy a plow.

CHAPTER ELEVEN

THE DRIVER OF THE GOVERNMENT

'THOMAS ADAMS! Thomas Adams! be 'ee going to lie abed all day?' So, at four in the morning, Damaris Yeo would shout from the bottom of the stairs to the clerk in the little room he shared with John Yeo. The Yeo family believed in the gospel of work. The accumulation of money was less an object than the activity which was part of the process. The menfolk went about their business while the women, except Damaris, worked in the three stores which served the expanding population. Even Susannah Richards worked, though the New Bideford shipyard was booming and the homes of the workers were being built all round the waterfront where once there had been the little clearings of the *Peter & Sarah*'s pioneers. The small robber baron was still always on the move, though as the years went by he took to driving a four-wheeler rather than riding in the saddle. He changed neither his tastes nor his way of life. The Island was his home and he did not seek to leave it. To the end of his days he retained his peasant suspicion of a wider world he did not know. It was perhaps this more than anything else that stopped him founding a millionaire's dynasty with the acquired tastes and habits of an aristocracy. He kept his family around him in the square house at the crossroads. Each Sunday midday everybody, including Thomas Adams, was assembled for dinner. Each Sunday afternoon there were Bible reading and prayers in the drawing-room. William Richards and James Yeo junior, with their wives and children, each had their rooms. On the rare occasions when he was thwarted or crossed James Yeo would sometimes go on a solitary drinking bout on board a small schooner—until 1857 the old *Mary Ann*, his first ship—which was kept moored in one of the creeks.

Gradually they left home. John was sent to England to school and spent his holidays at Appledore with his half-brother William, whom he greatly admired. James set up his own shipyard at the head of Campbell Creek. He built a fine house and stores and called the place Green Park. Here between 1856 and 1886 he launched at least twenty-three ships, including some of the largest and finest the family ever built. Nancy, who had been born of the first marriage near Kilkhampton, married a settler from her birthplace and henceforth called herself Ann. Caroline Alice, the youngest child, married another local settler, John Maynard of Port Hill. Isabella went to England to stay with brother William and there became engaged to J. R. Saunders, a Gloucester timber merchant who had dealings with her father.

In Britain the great house of the Yeos provided the background for the social activities of the new squire. When Isabella was wed the whole town of Appledore was decked out with flags, the guns roared and the bride wore a dress of 'rich, white moiré antique, on her head was a wreath of white roses from which hung a superb veil of Brussels lace. The bridesmaids of whom there were eight, were attired in white muslin, double skirts, four trimmed with pink and four with blue, with wreaths and tulle veils to correspond. The avenue leading to the church was carpeted for the occasion. . . .'[1]

A few years later the banners were out again, the church bells rang all day and in the evening the streets were lit by the smoky flare of burning tar barrels. William Yeo had a son and heir.

His daughters could act their part as ladies bountiful when the occasion arose. In a hard winter they would walk around the town distributing cash or tickets with which the poor could collect free coal. They dressed appropriately for these public parades and any girl of the drangs who took pride in her appearance was liable to be dubbed 'Miss Yeo' by the lads of the village. They were particularly adept at launching ships. They had plenty of practice. Fanny launched two in one day in 1863. When she was married in 1870 the celebrations completely eclipsed those provided for her aunt fourteen years before. Triumphal arches of flowers were put up all over the town, the streets and shipping were literally covered with bunting and the flags of all nations. So many guns were fired that a rumour began to spread in Barnstaple that the French and the Prussians, who were then at war, had had a naval engagement in Bideford Bay. Nearly five thousand people swarmed into the churchyard. In the summer of 1864 thirteen hundred people were fed at one garden party at Richmond House and the toasts were to Her Majesty and to the Yeo family. But four years later Appledore was in deep mourning. William Yeo's only son had died in childhood and although some of his great-great grandchildren live in England today James Yeo's family in Britain was doomed to 'daughter out'.

There is evidence that William Yeo regarded himself as a Colonial rather than a native Devonian. Certainly his lavish entertainment must have been looked upon by the conservative squirearchy as a North American manifestation. So too was his energy and enterprise. In the 1860s he invested extensively in land in Devon and Somerset. In the course of these purchases most of the west bank of the Torridge from Cleave Houses to Appledore and much of the land behind passed into his possession. The shallow water off the river beaches was filled with the Yeo timber booms until the Torridge looked like a New Brunswick river. A second dry dock was built below Chanter's signal tower by filling in a bay with rubble from the growing quarry. As Benson's Quay had been new a century before, so this in its turn succeeded to the title and became the New Quay Dry Dock. In numerous schemes for development, for floating docks at Instow, for a rail-link from Bideford to Appledore, for a steam-tug service, William Yeo took the leading part. Like his father he was a man who was everywhere from six o'clock in the morning; wearing a grey top hat and mounted on a pony or seated in a two-wheeled gig he was at the docks, the shipbuilding yards, the foundry, the quarry which he now controlled, the farms or the timber booms. The ships he shared with his father were bound for India, South America, the cotton ports of the Southern States, the Islands of the Persian Gulf, as well as constantly backwards and forwards over the North Atlantic.

In all these activities William Yeo came frequently into contact with the ageing Thomas Chanter who lived on until 1874. Isabella had died in 1847, soon after he had made his fortune, leaving him several children. In the 1850s he gradually dropped his business interests, becoming more and more a public figure, a Justice of the Peace, an Alderman of Bideford, enjoying the rights of the Lord of the Manor of Northam, founder and for thirty years secretary of the organisation which ran the local lifeboats, agent for Lloyd's, honorary consul for the United States and several other countries, director of railway companies, secretary and mainspring of the company which extended the railway from Fremington, near Barnstaple, to Bideford. Like William Yeo, but with less financial backing, he was in the forefront of every scheme for development and improvement in the area. His daughters married well. One of the sons who spent his fortune for him married Mary Frances Wilson, an American-born great grand-daughter of Mrs Siddons. As Mrs Scott Siddons, she played Juliet to Kendall's Romeo at the Haymarket Theatre in London for a few years in the 1860s. Robert Campbell Chanter followed in his father's footsteps and settled in the Island at Mount Stewart Bridge.

For most of the time the banks of the Torridge were busier than they had ever been in history before. Ships were being built on the river for owners in London, Greenock, Liverpool, Bristol and Swansea and on the south coast. Cheap labour, readily available imported timber which could be rafted to the shipyards on the flood tide of the Torridge, and good natural facilities gave the river a growing reputation in the shipping world. The trade of Appledore was steadily increasing. In 1865 nearly 2,500 ships were recorded as entering this creek of the port of Bideford, the overwhelming majority of them with cargo. A year earlier an observer had watched fifty ships go in and out on one tide. It was 'a pretty sight on a fine clear morning—so many vessels crossing and re-crossing each other on the bar in working out, their white sails glistening in the sun, whilst with a fine breeze they were bravely speeding through the water, with foaming billows at their bows'.[2]

Prosperous by its own standards as Appledore now was, it was still a rough and lawless place. Assaults were frequent and the women of the town had a particularly bad reputation for the violence with which they conducted disputes among themselves and occasionally attacked strangers. The town's two policemen were quite incapable of controlling them. There were sixteen taverns each brewing its own beer. The streets and drangs were cobbled or unpaved and there was virtually no drainage. Not surprisingly there were occasional outbreaks of cholera and typhoid. Communications were slow. Most goods from Bideford came by boat, though there was a daily carrier. The mail came across from Instow by boat and was carried round the town by a postwoman with a market basket. She would deliver letters to the accompaniment of a commentary on the following lines: 'Well, m'dear, yers a letter for 'ee today—from yer man [who was probably away at sea]'. Pause, then 'Whats'n say? Ows'n gettin' on? If 'ee can't read'n, I'll read'n for 'ee.' Although by 1865 the American trade had grown so much that extra customs officers had to be sent from Bristol to Appledore, smuggling of tobacco in the American ships, Continental specialities in the Mediterranean traders and Irish whisky in the coasters was a thriving part-time occupation.

Such a community lent itself peculiarly well to William Yeo's methods of rule. He may have lacked legitimate male offspring, but the nickname the town gave him, 'the Black Ram', had its own significance. Those who crossed him, if they were working men found employment denied them and became 'black Leicesters'; if they were shipowners or merchants the facilities of the port were suddenly not available to them, and their efforts were impeded in all sorts of ways. At the Devon Lent Assizes in 1868 the revealing case of Tatem vs. Yeo was heard. The *Georgina*, a ship belonging to James Tatem of Appledore, was on her way to the Mediterranean with mixed cargo from Liverpool when she sustained weather damage in the Irish Sea and put into Appledore for repairs. William Yeo answered a request to put her into Richmond Dock with the reply that he was too busy to accommodate her and so Tatem, with whom he was described as being at daggers drawn, put his ship alongside the end of the quay near the mouth of the dock in a place still called the Parlour from its sheltered position just inside what had once been the bay at East Appledore. As soon as she arrived Yeo put the *Orient*, a laid-up ship of his own, outside her and moored her with chains crossing the *Georgina* at bows and stern so that the *Georgina* could not be moved. To make quite sure, the chains were padlocked. There the two ships stayed for three and a half months, all work attempted on the *Georgina* being impeded and mysteriously undone again. Yeo claimed the right to the foreshore which gave access to the dry dock. Tatem contested this claim. But the case was really a challenge to Yeo's authority to run Appledore the way he wanted it. There was evidence that acts of violence had taken place. Yeo's men were alleged to have cut a vessel in the Parlour adrift altogether, and to have threatened murder with a sledge hammer. Tatem attacked one of Yeo's men with a cutlass. Yeo lost the case but there was a series of appeals. He was a son of whom his father might be proud.

*   *   *

Evidence before another court, the Commission of Enquiry into Land Tenure in Prince Edward Island, in 1860, revealed something of James Yeo's methods in the Island. The reports of the hearings in the Press and the manuscript notes made during them by one of the Commissioners, Joseph Howe, a distinguished Nova Scotian, are liberally sprinkled with references to Yeo. One of his devices, it appears, was to obtain, or to claim to possess, a general permit to cut timber over land leased to other people and settled by them. In some cases this right was said to be written into leases which tenants had not seen or could not understand, in others no written agreement existed. Sometimes tenants became aware of Mr Yeo's 'right' only when they saw the timber being hauled away. It was alleged that in one way or another he had got himself general cutting licences for all the lots, that he sold these licences off to other shipbuilders and that under them the purchasers claimed the right to go into any tenant's unfenced land. But the tenants themselves, it was said,

Rivermen poling squared timber into position for loading at Quebec

1862, William Yeo, of Charlottetown, 786 tons, a full-rigged ship built by James Yeo junior on Campbell Creek, Lot 13, and owned by William Yeo, James Yeo and James Yeo junior. This photograph shows her late in life under a foreign flag rigged as a bark and equipped with a conspicuous wind-driven pump

1874, Victoria, *of Charlottetown, 748 tons, a bark built at New Bideford by William Richards and owned by him for 16 years*

The two-tiered temporary double bunks of an emigrant ship

found they could never get permits to cut timber. He was said to take advantage of the common situation in which the title to land was not clear. He left tenants for years with only promises which he had no real authority to fulfil. They had no security of tenure and the land was not really Yeo's at all.

James Warburton claimed in evidence before the Commission that years ago, when they were members of the same political group, Yeo had shown him after one election no less than thirty-two writs he was issuing against those who had voted against him. Another witness claimed Yeo used leases to 'deter people from voting and to compel them to vote'. It was alleged that he attended a meeting in Prince County to dissuade tenants from giving evidence before the Commission and that numerous tenants over the whole Colony, and particularly from Lot 13, did not give evidence because they were afraid. It was said more than once that people were terrified of him.

In his own evidence Yeo told the Court that the tenants on part of one of his lots held their land 'by their pitchforks'. They would never let him or his men near enough to them to take any rent. He claimed that he had served writs on only two tenants. His philosophy was still what it had been twenty years before : 'those that pay rent live well and do well. Those that pay nothing are worth nothing'. He had immediate reason to feel strongly. Only a few months before, tenants on Lot 61 had greeted the Sheriff coming to take proceedings for arrears of rent with a volley of shots which had killed his horse. The Sheriff afterwards had found it quite impossible to raise a posse to take the offenders.

In the course of his evidence before the Commission, Warburton referred to Yeo as 'the Driver of the Government'. It was a play on his past as a carrier, but it was apt, for by 1860 he had moved into a very special position in the administration. It was a kind of personal perfection of the system of the family compact.

The Government which had been elected in 1858, with James and John Yeo and James Warburton all representing Prince County, did not last long. The liberal majority was only two and one of these was disqualified. A new election was held in March

1859. The conservatives, brilliantly led and with all the power of Yeo's and lesser ledgers behind them, stirred up the Colony on the question of the compulsory use of the Bible in schools and were returned with a majority of four. All six members from Prince County were Conservatives. Three of them were James and John Yeo and their colleague David Ramsay. Warburton was soundly defeated. Next month Yeo became a member of the Lieutenant Governor's Executive Council, John Ings became the Government Printer with the right to publish the official *Royal Gazette* from *The Islander*'s office, and Lawrence Yeo, James's half-brother and bailiff, was appointed a Commissioner of Highways for Prince County. Soon John Yeo and David Ramsay were Justices of the Peace for the County.

Nancy Yeo had been widowed and re-married to Charles Green, a settler from the growing town of Summerside and a member of one of the oldest and best-established families in the the Colony. Charles Green, once he was Yeo's son-in-law, soon blossomed out as a prominent shipbuilder. The post of Collector of Customs and Excise at Bedeque became vacant and part of the responsibilities of the holder of this office was the overseeing of Customs work at Port Hill. Green was duly appointed. As the *Examiner* put it, James Yeo being, 'the principal importer in the County . . . there was very little difference between allowing him to make out his own entries in such manner as suited his own purposes, and allowing his son-in-law to make them for him'.[3] Soon more jobs began to come the way of Yeo's friends and relations. Another connection, Mr. Hopgood, was made Postmaster of Port Hill. James Yeo, junior, was made Collector of Land Tax and one of Yeo's old employees was Postmaster on Warburton's Lot 11.

The secret of success lay in the Government's majority of four and in Yeo's control of three votes in the Assembly, his own, his son John's and David Ramsay's. Switch those three votes and the Government fell. Yeo was in a position to pull the reins; the Government went the way he wanted it to go. The *Examiner*'s imaginative editorial reconstruction of the scene when the Executive Council discussed Charles Green's appointment was probably not too far from the mark. After a speech from a member discreetly deploring the proposal, James Yeo is depicted as intervening :

> 'Gen-l-men', said Mr Yeo, rising with offended dignity, and seizing his hat; 'I don't care that'—(snapping his fingers in his colleagues' faces) 'whether you appoint Mr Green or not—he can take care of himself without the office; and as my advice won't be taken, I see no use for me to be here whatever, and I wish you good morning, Gen-l-men.'
>
> The honorable Councillor was on the point of rushing out the door when he was prevailed upon to resume his seat, and assured that the Council would give the most favourable consideration to his advice, the upshot of which was, that Mr Green was ordered to be *Gazetted* as Collector of Customs and Excise for Bedeque.[4]

The Executive Council was now constituted entirely of Members of the Assembly, but the departments of Government passed back into the hands of a family compact. The voters had brought it upon themselves, but there were limits. The *Examiner* published a letter alleged to have been written to an elector in the course of the campaign of 1858 which looks like a genuine example of James Yeo's style :

> Port Hill, 8 June 1858—Mr John McLean; Sir—I am credit-ably informed your are supporting of W. Grigg in the Election, and he maketh promise to be adverse to the proprietors. I will advise all Tenants of Lot 9 to be carefull what the are doing, as if any tennents vote for Mr Grigg they had better be prepared to pay their rent; if not, then the must expect Trouble Imeditly. I might say you saw plenty of this kind of work in the year's of 1845, 1846 and 1847, but some are generaly bent for mischef to injure themselves as well as their neighbours.
>
> I am, JAMES YEO.[5]

In the ensuing acrimonious correspondence, Yeo expressed himself characteristically :

> . . . The country may judge of the position which Mr Warburton holds in his own neighbourhood, where he has been, I may say, proprietor for upwards of twenty years—in a District of upwards of 500 electors, he only polled 196 votes.

I might say a great deal more if I had time, but my business keeps me fully employed. Last year I paid from twelve to thirteen hundred pounds into the Revenue. I do not suppose Mr Warburton paid as many farthings![6]

Now was the time for James Yeo to parade his wealth occasionally in the sort of local splendours and acts of charity William was using to advertise his position in North Devon. Next time a Lieutenant Governor came to Port Hill he was very properly received. He was George Dundas, last Lieutenant Governor to rule the Island as a separate Colony for his whole tour of duty in Charlottetown. His big party included John Ings and T. H. Haviland. They were met by Yeo, a band, a coach and four covered with flags and most of the people from miles around. They visited Lennox Island 'Mr Yeo having previously provided comfortable and well-manned boats, this excursion proved a very pleasant one'.[7] On the way over the boats passed a splendid full-rigged ship of over 1,000 tons, launched a few days previously, which Yeo was able to tell the Lieutenant Governor's lady he had named for her the *May Dundas*. The party, much intrigued by the Indians, returned to dine at Port Hill.

Despite the evidence before the Land Commission many stories began to circulate of acts to help unfortunate settlers. He was now wealthy enough to be concerned more with the general social effect of his acts than their immediate advantage to him. He gave long-term credit at low interest where to do so would be to offer hope of reviving a poor district or saving an active man gone on the rocks. The true extent of the fortune he had built up is impossible to estimate. In 1864 *The Islander* asserted, not only that he was the richest man in Prince Edward Island, but that his pay roll and credit advances to employees alone far exceeded the whole revenue of the Government. Such figures as are available suggest that in 1865, the peak year of his commercial activity, the property and investments of the Yeo family may have had a value in modern terms of between ten and twenty million dollars. Accused by George Coles of failing to support the tenants, he told the Assembly :

Talk about my doing nothing for the tenantry, I have done almost everything that lies in my power to favor the country. Last summer, when the Government could not get money to send home to pay for the land, I gave them a £1000 stg. bill, though it was considerably to my disadvantage. I have also frequently taken persons out of jail who were put in for debt; but some hon. members come here, and set up a jabbering, that would never do anything of the kind.[8]

A few weeks later he reminded the House that he had helped a Government without adequate funds on another occasion : 'the bank could not give the sum required, which I did. Of this I do not boast as it is nothing to the purpose. I did it for the benefit of the country and to enable the Government to affect a purchase'.[9] The records of the House of Assembly are full of accounts of numerous petitions presented by settlers and supported by Yeo, whose policy, so correct in terms of modern economic theory, that a prosperous society was one which would serve his interests best, led him to exert his influence and tireless energy towards the building of bridges, the improvement of roads, the development of harbours and shipping facilities, and the increasing of the salaries of local officials, even when they were not his relatives.

But all these activities and the power of the ledger did not prevent his one single political defeat. At the election of 1863 John Yeo and David Ramsay were successful, as was James Warburton, but James Yeo was defeated by fifty votes. The Conservative administration had foreseen some danger of this and arranged that the poll for the Legislative Council, now an elected body, would take place a month after that for the Assembly. At this he was successful and within a month he had been re-appointed to the Executive Council. The election for the Assembly had been a bitter one. The Conservatives as a matter of policy had stirred up the anti-Roman Catholic feelings of the majority. James Yeo ran considerable risk by standing in a predominantly Catholic area, and *The Islander* chose to interpret the defeat of 'unquestionably the most wealthy man in the Colony' as the work of a 'Romanish bishop' who could threaten even greater evils than could the Giant with his Ledger. As the newspaper put it, James Yeo, if he wished, could change the face of the country in the electoral district that had rejected him, but he would be magnanimous and not blame a poor priest-ridden people.

These were years of unprecedented prosperity in the Island. The harvest of 1863 was an excellent one. The American Civil War created an exceptional demand for oats, which were by now the Colony's staple agricultural product. It also stimulated commercial activity throughout the Western world. The demand for ships rose steadily; a hundred were launched in 1863, more than ever before in the Island's history. In the fall the wharves of Charlottetown were crammed with ships of all sizes, some fitting out for the transatlantic voyage, others loading Island produce for the United States, the West Indies, South Africa, New Zealand, Bermuda and for all the neighbouring British North American colonies. All the outports were similarly busy. Port Hill was teeming with activity, with ships coming and going, schooners in the Colonial trade, barks, brigs and full-rigged ships loading for Britain. In Charlottetown the goods advertised in William Heard's stores became steadily more sophisticated and varied. He was President of a new marine insurance company and of a fire insurance company, both formed during the previous year with the support of some of the Colony's most influential inhabitants. There were plans to open an hotel, the side-walks of Charlottetown's streets, hitherto in a deplorable condition, were repaired and the open spaces of the squares fenced in and shade trees planted. A new and much more powerful steamship, the *Princess of Wales* was commissioned by a local steam navigation company (in which James Yeo, James Pope, William Richards and many others held shares) to run a quicker and more regular service from Pictou to Charlottetown in the ice-free months (though the ordeal by ice boat was still the only method of communication with the mainland in the winter and was to remain so for another generation). The Island was on the eve of its most important historical event, the meeting of the delegates of Nova Scotia, New Brunswick, Canada and the Island in Charlottetown in 1864 which led to the Canadian Confederation of 1867 and to the Island's union with it in 1873. Though the initial conference was held in Charlottetown, the Island as a whole did not want Confederation and many of her politicians were opposed to it. An attitude in Canada is summed up in an anecdote of one of the architects of Union, D'Arcy McGee, who told the Islanders, 'Now don't you be too boastful about your little Island, don't let us hear so much about it, or we will send down a little tug-boat and draw you up into one of our lakes, where we will leave you to take care of yourselves'. The division over Confederation cut across party lines. James Yeo and his friends were opposed to it and they played no part at all in the historic discussions.

But thanks to the shipbuilding industry the Island was prosperous, and well might *The Islander* comment that the Colony had 'comparatively few who are in actual want; in truth, all who have strength and the will to work are able to live without having recourse to charity'.

*   *   *

There was one more Election to win. In 1866 James Warburton was put to total route by James Yeo at the Legislative Council hustings. But it was to be a short-lived victory. In March next year a new Council was sworn in and James Yeo was a sick man. He did not stand for election again. A year later Damaris died of pneumonia. Almost her last act was to summon Thomas Adams and charge him 'You'll look after things, Thomas Adams, won't you?' In a few months James Yeo was dead from the same cause.

In the longest and most complete obituary ever printed in the history of the Colony to that date, *The Islander* and the new *Summerside Progress* felt their way towards an appraisal of 'this extraordinary man'. In one passage the anonymous writer conveyed something of the impact Yeo made on the community in which he had spent nearly fifty years :

> . . . In everything he was rigidly a matter of fact man. What he spoke on the floor of the House of Assembly, however was but an iota compared with the information he otherwise

afforded his fellow members. It was in private conferences and consultations that he communicated most of his knowledge respecting the wants and other affairs of the people. No man ever appeared in P.E. Island who made himself so extensively acquainted with the general circumstances and affairs of the Colony. His large and widely extended business transactions alone, independent of other considerations, would lead him to this. These called him frequently to all parts of the Island, and into contact with the inhabitants. . . .

As already stated, his business led him into all parts of the Island—into every harbor, every bay, and every river. His vessels might be seen round all parts of the Island during the whole of the navigable season of the year—if we be allowed the phrase. Others were being built or launched for him in many parts, and at wonderfully short intervals after one another during the same season. In superintending these and other affairs, which we have no time to mention, he was incessantly travelling from place to place, by night and by day; in the extremes of heat and of cold; in wet weather and in dry; through good roads, but often through roads almost impassable to every one else; across bad bridges and over still more dangerous ferries and as a matter of necessity, all this time he was learning more and more of the real circumstances and wants of the country. Few constitutions could endure unbroken the incessant toils and hardship he underwent. . . .[10]

That the stumpy, rigid figure would be seen no more, arriving to a sudden silence in places where he was least expected, confounding with his incredible and embarrassing memory other people's detailed recollections of their own private affairs, calculating and concluding business while others fumbled for a pencil, was at first hard to believe. People talked about him under their breath for years afterwards as if there were a danger that he might hear what they were saying. A mythology grew up around him and an American traveller who visited Charlottetown when Yeo had been dead seventeen years found many anecdotes of him still in day-to-day circulation. Nearly a century after his death we found this British Westcountryman still the subject of a living tradition in a Canadian province.

He was in many ways the personification of an age in British North American history. He was a man for his times. When he died a period of great change had already begun. Confederation was in the air. The shipbuilding industry, the economic miracle to which he had made such a fundamental contribution, had passed its peak, the forests were becoming exhausted. The railroad was coming to the Island and the old isolations were to be broken down. The land question was being settled by Government purchase from the proprietors and sale to the settlers, and the raw edge was going out of local politics. With the end of proprietorship, shipbuilding and lumbering, the merchants and agents lost their grip on the Island. The ledger ceased to be the book of power. The settler was soon no longer the illiterate victim of circumstances, but a man demanding a standard of living which compared with what he could earn for himself elsewhere in the North American Continent. The years of the maritime frontier were over and there would be no more robber barons in Prince Edward Island. James Yeo's death must have seemed to mark the end of an era. In many ways it did.

EPILOGUE

'It was the task of the theorists to interpret this phase of imperialism, but not to create it. That part was the work of the men and women who sailed in the emigrant ships and step by step cut their way through the dark forest to safety and security. The virtue of the British colonial system in the first half of the nineteenth century was that it produced a few men who could see what lay beneath the early crudities of colonial life : "the conquering energy of a host of nameless men and women driven out into exile by the fiery sword of economic pressure, to eat their bread in strange places in the sweat of their faces, and to bear their children in sorrow that through them the men of the future may subdue nature and inherit the earth".'

Helen I. Cowan, 'British Emigration to British North America' (quotation from Bell and Morrell, *Select Documents on British Colonial Policy, xlix*).

EPILOGUE

WHEN William Yeo died in 1872 he was only fifty-nine years old. Seven-years-old Annie Abigail Harding, later Annie Slade, daughter of the impoverished master of a small trading sloop, ventured into the drive of Richmond House a few months later and hid behind the high wall to escape her escorting family. Town children who entered the grounds of Richmond House did so at their own peril and it is not surprising that Annie turned round to see William Yeo on his grey horse towering above her. The horse lunged at her with its head, and then horse and rider slowly sank backwards into the ground. Annie screamed and fainted. Ninety years later the experience was still very real to her.

His death threw Appledore into a depression which lasted for ten years. The dry docks were empty, the town starved and the people drifted away until skilled men could not be found for such little work as there was to be done. A surviving correspondence book of John Yeo shows that for a few years William Pickard, a carpenter from Abbotsham who turned seaman, shipmaster and eventually shipowner and merchant and who knew the Island, acted as agent for John Yeo and his brother James. But gradually the business moved to the Richards family in Swansea and for a while the connection between Northam and North America was broken. There was a slight revival of work on Island ships when the dry docks were re-opened in the 1880s, and the connection was not finally severed until the wooden sailing ship ceased to be a tool of international commerce.

Though the premature death of William Yeo without male heir meant the sudden, almost violent, end for Devon of the great transatlantic business which James Yeo had built out of Thomas Burnard's venture, the effects of his enterprise echo down to the present day. The great dry dock has kept Appledore ever since.

For 110 years, even through the great depression of the early 1930s, except for the few years after William Yeo's death it has been the centre of continuous shipping activity, and today it is at the heart of a prosperous modern shipyard which has swamped old Benson's New Quay and filled in the last of Appledore's sheltered bay. The great house of the Yeos, now a block of apartments, still looks boldly across at an unspoiled Tapeleigh.

The amenities provided by the shipyard James and William Yeo had built, the money accumulated by the small local capitalists who fattened on the droppings from their tables, the presence of scores of skilled seamen they had employed and who knew no better life and had no other legacy for their sons; these necessary factors made Appledore into the last seaport in Britain to be the base of a fleet of merchant sailing ships and it retained much of its mid-Victorian character, its maritime sail and oar culture and its archaic and individual dialect until the second world war. Almost incredibly, the last of the small sailing ships earned a living at sea until 1960. Three years earlier Tommy Chanter's signal tower, long dubbed Chanter's Folly and dangerously riven by lightning in 1937, had been demolished. Today there is only one memorial to this great Devonian. The road which leads from his house to the place at Cleave Houses where Richard Chapman built the *Peter & Sarah*, still the site of a shipyard, is called Chanter's Lane.

John Yeo was a sentimental man at heart; a bachelor, he lived on in the square house at Port Hill crossroads for thirty years. Thomas Adams, deaf from the hardships and tensions of his service to John Yeo's terrible father, had married in late middle age but he carried out the assignment Damaris had given him and continued to manage John Yeo's affairs for the rest of his working life. The four-wheeler James Yeo had used in his later years was left in the barn, whip in position. Damaris's clothes stayed hung in the closets. They were still there when the house was pulled down after the first world war. It was as if people were afraid to disturb anything that James Yeo had left for fear he might be resentful.

John Yeo, a merchant, farmer, banker, shipbuilder and ship-owner was also an active politician all his adult life. When he was first elected to the Island Assembly in 1858 he was twenty-four. He served continuously in that Assembly, its speaker at the time the Island entered the Canadian Confederation, until he was elected to the Canadian House of Commons in Ottawa in 1891. He refused the offer of the Lieutenant Governorship of Prince Edward Island and was appointed a Senator of Canada in 1898. He died, a revered elder statesman, in 1924. His sixty-six years in Parliament, Colonial, Provincial and Federal, almost certainly represent the longest record of unbroken service as an elected representative of the people in the history of the British Commonwealth.

James Yeo junior, 'hunchback Jemmy' as he was known (from the results of being thrown from a horse on which a maidservant had incautiously placed him in infancy) was also a politician. When Prince Edward Island entered Confederation he was elected to the Federal Parliament and served in it until 1891.

Though the robber baron's keep has long gone and Thomas Chanter's house on Port Hill farm was pulled down in the 1930s, hunchback Jemmy's fine house, Green Park, still stands at the head of Campbell Creek, in external appearance exactly as it was more than a century ago. It now belongs to the Provincial Government and it would be a natural place for a maritime museum of Prince Edward Island to tell the story of the great seafaring epoch in the Province's history.

Down below the house, on the shores of Campbell Creek, wild raspberries grow in the sawpits and the spruce forest has grown thick to the water's edge in the eighty years since the last ship was launched here. Across the creek the ruin of Chanter's wharf juts out from old Port Hill farm and the remains of the Devon limekiln stand at the edge of the forest. Port Hill farm is as park-like and well-kept as even Thomas Chanter could have wished. Old anchors and chains and other pieces of sailing ships' equipment can still be found around the farm. For miles around the country of Lot 13 has a settled and well-cultivated air, as of land farmed for many years and once very prosperous, a country where things have happened. The site of Port Hill is beautiful, at the edge of the great bay. It is open to the sun and the sea air. In the evenings the luminous white farmhouses stand like buildings in a Wyeth painting, washed in light of a peculiar clarity. People live long lives here.

Port Hill, Charlottetown, Ottawa,
New York, Warwick, Bideford, London.
1961-1966.

1884, Auriga, of Charlottetown, 886 tons, the last bark to be built at New Bideford. She was owned by the Richards family for 16 years. Here she is shown in the Avon Gorge on her way to the City Docks at Bristol. Her jibboom is being rigged in so that she will take up less space at the quayside

1893, Daisy, of Charlottetown, 430 tons. This barkentine shown lying in Cumberland Basin, Bristol, built at Shipyard Creek, Grand River, Lot 14, for Senator John Yeo was the last ship to be built in consequence of the venture that started with the voyage of the Peter & Sarah. She remained afloat until well into the twentieth century

William Heard

James Warburton
Portrait by Robert Harris

William Yeo, 1813-1872

James Yeo, 1788-1868. Portrait by Robert Harris

APPENDIX 1

Key to the Quotations

CHAPTER ONE

1. The Poor Rate Books of the Parish of Northam, Devon, England.

CHAPTER TWO

1. Report of the Select Committee on Foreign Trade, 9 March 1821, The evidence of John Hill.
2. Parliamentary Papers (House of Commons) 1839, xxxii, pp. 204-5, quoted in Clark, *Three Centuries and the Island*, p. 51.
3. Seymour of Ragley, CR114A/561-572, County Record Office, Warwick, England.
4. Prince Edward Island, Land Records, Charlottetown, Liber 13, f. 363.
5-9. Public Archives of Canada, Microfilm, A. 499, Customs, Plantation Papers Vol. 6605.

CHAPTER THREE

1. The Port Hill Papers.
2. Seymour of Ragley, letter of J. B. Palmer to the Hon Capt G. F. Seymour, R.N., of 12 August 1816.
3. P.A.C., MSS Group 11, Prince Edward Island, A. 37.
4. P.A.C., MSS Group 11, Prince Edward Island, A. 38.
5. *The Western Luminary*, Exeter, England, 30 April 1822.
6. *The Western Luminary*, 28 October 1823.

CHAPTER FOUR

1. *The Prince Edward Island Register*, Charlottetown, 13 November 1824.
2. *The Prince Edward Island Register*, 29 December 1824.
3. Prince Edward Island, Land Records, Charlottetown, Liber 31, f. 259.
4. Seymour of Ragley, letter of T. H. Haviland to Hon Capt G. F. Seymour, RN, of 7 August 1824.
5. Society for the Propagation of the Gospel, London, letter from Rev L. C. Jenkins to Rev A. Hamilton, reproduced in *S.P.G. Journal*, Vol. 36, pp. 59-62.
6. *Prince Edward Island Register*, 27 May 1825.
7. Prince Edward Island, Land Records, Charlottetown, Liber 33, f. 267.
8. The Port Hill Papers.
9. *Prince Edward Island Register*, 7 August 1826.
10. *Prince Edward Island Register*, 19 September 1826.
11. The Port Hill Papers.
12. *North Devon Journal*, Barnstaple, England, 14 March 1844.

CHAPTER FIVE

1. *A Walk through some of the Western Counties of England*, by the Rev Richard Warner, Bath, England, 1800.
2. *The Rural Economy of the West of England* by William Marshall, quoted in *The Secret People* by E. W. Martin, London, 1954.
3. *North Devon Journal*, 25 July 1872.
4. Folksong quoted in *The Epic of America*, by James Trueslow Adams, New York, 1931.

CHAPTER SIX

1. Uncatalogued Legal Documents, Legislative Assembly Building, Charlottetown.
2. The Port Hill Papers, letter from Thomas Chanter to William Ellis, undated, 1830.
3. The Port Hill Papers.
4. *North Devon Journal*, 23 January 1828.
5. *North Devon Journal*, 16 October 1828.
6. *North Devon Journal*, 24 June 1830.
7. *Royal Gazette*, Charlottetown, 1 June 1830.
8. *North Devon Journal*, 14 April 1831.
9. *North Devon Journal*, 31 March 1836.
10. *Prince Edward Island*, Land Records, Charlottetown, Liber 43, f. 297.
11. *Royal Gazette*, 5 March 1833, letter from George Beer.
12. The Port Hill Papers, letter from Thomas Chanter to William Ellis, undated, 1830.
13-18. The Port Hill Papers.
19. Survey Report on the ship *Atalanta*, Bideford 1836, original in the National Maritime Museum, Greenwich, England.
20. *North Devon Journal*, 29 December 1842.
21. *North Devon Journal*, 26 January 1843.

CHAPTER SEVEN

1. *Larry Gorman, The Man who Wrote the Songs*, by Edward D. Ives, Indiana University Press, 1964.
2. Seymour of Ragley, letter of James Yeo to Francis H. Seymour, 18 May 1846.
3. P.A.C., C.O.226, 1840, 544-546, Memoire by Sir G. Seymour.
4. Seymour of Ragley, Notes on a crossing of Prince Edward Island.
5. P.A.C., C.O.226, Vol. 64, f. 261, Seymour to Stanley, October 1842.
6. Quoted in *Historical Notes on the Parish of Port Hill*, by Thos R. Millman, 1941, General Synod Archives of the Anglican Church of Canada.
7. Journal of Legislative Assembly.
8. P.A.C., C.O.226, Lt. Governor Fitzroy, 5 May 1841.

CHAPTER EIGHT

1. *Royal Gazette*, 14 March 1843.
2. *Royal Gazette*, 12 April 1844.
3. *Royal Gazette*, 1 January 1844.

4. *Royal Gazette*, 5 March 1844.
5. *Royal Gazette*, 28 August 1846.
6. *Dishing the Reformers*, by D. C. Harvey, Ottawa, 1931.
7. *The Government of Prince Edward Island*, by Frank MacKinnon, Toronto, 1951.
8. *Journal of the House of Assembly*, Charlottetown, 22 February 1849.
9. P.A.C., C.O.226, Campbell to Grey, 12 June 1848.
10. *The Islander*, Charlottetown, 2 March 1848.
11. Seymour of Ragley, Letter of T. H. Haviland to Seymour, 23 March 1846.
12. Seymour of Ragley, Letter from Yeo to Seymour, 18 May 1846.
13. Seymour of Ragley, Letter from Yeo to Seymour, 9 October 1846.
14. Seymour of Ragley, Yeo to Seymour, 9 October 1846.
15. Seymour of Ragley, Yeo to Seymour, 20 March 1848.
16. P.A.C., C.O.226, Vol. 69 f. 353, Bannerman to Colonial Office, 15 November 1951.
17. *North Devon Journal*, 24 July 1856.

CHAPTER NINE

1. *The Rise of the English Shipping Industry*, by Ralph Davies, London, 1962. Quoted by courtesy of Messrs MacMillan, London and the MacMillan Company of Canada.
2. *Royal Gazette*, 5 March 1833.
3. Commonplace Book of Mary Jane Yeo, original in possession of Group Capt Stewart, Ottawa.
4. *North Devon Journal*, April 1849.
5. *North Devon Journal*, 16 April 1857.
6. *Illustrated London News*, 1855 (undated).
7. *North Devon Journal*, 13 June 1854.
8. *North Devon Journal*, 16 April 1857.
9. *North Devon Journal*, 5 April 1849.
10. *North Devon Journal*, 31 March 1853.
11. The Port Hill Papers.
12. The Port Hill Papers.
13. P.A.C., Imperial Blue Books on Affairs Relating to Canada, Volumes on Emigration.
14. *North Devon Journal*, 14 April 1853.
15. *North Devon Journal*, 13 February 1851.
16. *Bideford Journal*, 26 May 1853.
17. *Wooden Ships & Iron Men*, by Frederick William Wallace, published by Hodder & Stoughton, London, England, No date.
18. *In the Wake of the Windships*, by Frederick William Wallace, Toronto, 1927.
19. *In the Wake of the Windships*, by Frederick William Wallace, Toronto, 1927.

CHAPTER TEN

1. *The Islander*, 27 April 1849.
2. *The Islander*, 26 April 1850.
3. *The Mirror of the Sea*, by Joseph Conrad, London, England, 1906. Quoted by courtesy of J. N. Dent & Sons and the Trustees of the Joseph Conrad Estate.

CHAPTER ELEVEN

1. *North Devon Journal*, 22 October 1857.
2. *North Devon Journal*, 15 December 1864.
3. *The Examiner*, 30 May 1859.
4. *The Examiner*, 30 May 1859.
5. *The Examiner*, 11 April 1859.
6. *The Islander*, 2 September 1859.
7. *The Islander*, 30 September 1859.
8. *The Islander*, 15 March 1861.
9. *The Islander*, 29 March 1861.
10. *The Islander*, 11 September 1868.

The quotation which prefixes Part I is to be found in Sloan MSS 2497 (British Museum). It was quoted by Rowse in *Sir Richard Grenville of the Revenge*, London, 1937. The first quotation before Part II is from *The Robber Barons* by Matthew Josephson, New York, 1934.

APPENDIX 2

The Writing and the Sources

Westcountrymen in Prince Edward's Isle began in the fall of 1961 when the authors fell into conversation at a reception in Ottawa with the Hon J. Angus MacLean, then Fisheries Minister in the Canadian Government. One of us remembered oral traditions extant among old people in Appledore thirty years ago about a connection between the town and Prince Edward Island in the person of a Mr Yeo who was said to have built Richmond House. Angus MacLean is an Islander and he knew something of the Island traditions of what had happened on Lot 13. It was his idea that the story might repay research and he gave us great and very practical encouragement.

The key to successful research into this essentially maritime fragment comprised the names of the ships owned by the various merchants involved. This key was provided by Grahame Farr's examination of the Bideford registrations of the ships of the Burnards, Thomas Chanter, the Chappells, Hows, Lowthers, Heards, Williams and Yeos and the Bristol registrations of the Yeos and Cambridges in the period from 1786 to 1850, which resulted in a list of several hundred vessels. It is not too much to say that this book could not have been written without this and other help from Grahame Farr. Our own examination of the Yeo registrations in the Charlottetown books in the Public Archives of Canada for the years from 1833 to 1893 produced some three hundred and fifty ships. Equipped with these tools it became possible to relate the evidence provided by documents to the actual movements of ships and people and to begin to reconstruct the outline of events. There began a study which had all the fascination of historical detection and which had to be conducted on both sides of the Atlantic.

We were aided greatly by a number of fortunate happenings. The first of our visits to the Island followed very closely on the discovery on Lot 13 of the Port Hill Papers, a series of letters, accounts, IOUs and other material which comprised fragments of the business papers left behind in the Island by Thomas Chanter and some of the papers of William Ellis. They were made available to us by their discoverer, Mr R. Grindlay, who introduced us to Lot 13 and from whom we received much kindness, help and encouragement. A fall when exploring the site of the shipbuilding yard on Campbell Creek where the *William Yeo* and numerous other vessels were built made medical attention necessary and this resulted in aquaintance with Dr Henry Moyse of Summerside whose family papers cast light on the part played by Richard Moys in the early stages of the story. A chance encounter in the Students' Room of the Public Archives of Canada in Ottawa led to a prolonged correspondence with Mrs Nina Ross of Kamloops in British Columbia, born on Lot 13, whose knowledge of the local history of the Lot is without parallel. Her help with suggestions of source material and clarifications of detail, with ideas in the interpretation of the evidence we discovered was invaluable.

Mr Grindlay introduced us to the late Mr Collingwood Yeo, James Yeo's last surviving grandson, whose remarkable memory at a great age proved accurate at every point at which it could be checked. Collingwood Yeo patiently endured many hours of interrogation and his help was fundamental to the interpretation of much evidence from primary sources.

In addition to those already mentioned we should like to express our acknowledgment and gratitude to the following men and women who helped in various ways in the preparation of this book:

PRINCE EDWARD ISLAND
Mr Walter Shaw, former Premier of Prince Edward Island, Senator Orville Phillips of Summerside, Senator Mrs Inman.

Lot 13
Mr and Mrs Claude Yeo, Miss Daisy Adams, the Reverend Delmonte Yeo, Mr Richard England, Mr and Mrs Edwin Yeo, Mr William Dennis of Port Hill Farm, Mr Strongman.

Lot 14
Loman and Isobel MacLean, the late Mrs MacLean, Mr John MacDonald.

Lot 16
Mr James MacLean.

Charlottetown
Dr Frank MacKinnon, Mr Kenneth Richards, Mr Douglas R. Boylan, Mr G. D. Dennis, Mr J. F. MacAleer, Miss Dorothy Cullen, Miss Frances B. Vinnicombe, Mr Craswell.

NEW BRUNSWICK
Dr George MacBeath, St John, Mrs Louise Manny, Newcastle.

OTTAWA
Dr W. K. Lamb and the staff of the Public Archives of Canada, Group Captain H. R. Stewart, RCAF, Dr Needler, Permanent Under-Secretary Ministry of Fisheries, Mr Eric Spicer and the staff of the Parliamentary Library, Dr Andrews, Mrs Joan Young for invaluable and most efficient secretarial help, Mr J. A. Warburton.

TORONTO
The Reverend H. R. Millman, Mr W. H. Graham.

USA
Captain W. J. Lewis Parker, USCG, for much advice and for his trans-script from the New York Maritime Registers, the staffs of the Peabody Museum of Salem, the Mariners' Museum of Newport News and the Shelburne Museum, Burlington, Vermont, for their help in searching for illustration material.

BRITAIN
Devon
We are greatly indebted to Michael Bouquet of Bampton for a very great deal of assistance with suggestions for source material, transcriptions, and ideas on the interpretations of evidence. Captain William Harris of Apple-dore spent long hours helping to reconstruct the changes in the town's waterfront which took place during the nineteenth century. The Beara brothers were most generous with material and the Reverend Michael Lucas allowed us to make prolonged studies of the Parish Records of Northam. Captain William Lamey of Appledore was the first man ever to mention to us the traditions of the Yeo story in Britain. Mr Percy Harris put material on the origins of the Richmond Dry Dock at our disposal. We should also like to thank Mrs Vernon Boyle, Mr Robert Harper, the staff of the Bideford Public Library, Captain Thomas Jewell, the Reverend Ronald Watts of Kilkhampton, Mrs Cecil Oliver and Mr Galliford of Bideford, Mr N. S. E. Pugsley of Exeter, Miss Lancaster of Exeter, Miss Valerie Dyble, Assistant Archivist, Devon Record Office, and the Librarian of the North Devon Athenaeum, Barnstaple. Captain W. J. Slade was our constant and most helpful companion during three months of field work in North Devon. His mother, the late Mrs Annie Slade, vividly portrayed Appledore ninety years ago.

London
Mr R. C. Jarvis, formerly Librarian of the Custom House, gave us valuable advice, Mr Michael Robinson of the National Maritime Museum helped in the search for illustrations, Mr G. Plant, the Registrar General of Shipping and Seamen, could not have given more generous and un-stinting help from his vast archives, as did also Miss Belle Pridmore,

Archivist for the Society for the Propagation of the Gospel. Mr Colin Denniss advised on the interpretation of legal documents and Dr Ronnie Williams on the probable significance of James Yeo's medical symptoms. The staff of the British Museum Newspaper Library, Colindale, were most helpful. Mr Richard Cox searched among the records of Somerset House.

Bristol
We thank the Director of the Bristol Museum for help with illustration material.

Warwick
We thank the Marquis of Hertford for allowing us to use the Seymour of Ragley series and the staff of the County Record Office, Warwick, for their help.

GENERAL
Miss Frances Halpenny of the Toronto University Press gave us continuous encouragement during the research and writing of this book. John Chadwick, Harold Smedley and Sydney Giffard all read the text in draft versions and we acted on their very useful comments.

The principal documentary sources we have used are as follows:

CANADA
The Public Archives of Canada
  (1) C.O.226, transcripts and microfilm of the correspondence between the Administration in Prince Edward Island and the British Government over the period 1785-1870.
  (2) Manuscript Groups 9, 11, 21 and 24, Papers Concerning Prince Edward Island.
  (3) Plantation Papers, Customs, microfilm of the correspondence between Customs Officers in Charlottetown and the Commissioners of Her Majesty's Customs in London.
  (4) Imperial Blue Books on Affairs Relating to Canada—Material relating to Emigration.
  (5) The Howe Papers, volume 65, Commission of Enquiry into Land Tenure in Prince Edward Island, 1860.
  (6) The documents of Registration of Shipping at Charlottetown Custom House, 1833-1893. These are in Record Group 12, A1.
  (7) Minutes of the Executive Council of Prince Edward Island, volumes 13-19 on microfilm.
  (8) Files, in original or on microfilm, of the *Prince Edward Island Gazette, Prince Edward Island Register, Royal Gazette, The Islander,* the *Examiner* and others over the period 1814-1868.
  (9) Lloyd's Surveyors' Reports on British North American Shipping, on microfilm.

PRINCE EDWARD ISLAND
  (1) The records of the Registrar of Deeds, of the Estates Division of the Supreme Court, and of the Provincial Treasurer, Charlottetown.
  (2) The Port Hill Papers.
  (3) The records of the old Richmond Bay congregation.
  (4) Numerous uncatalogued legal documents stored in the attics of the Provincial Assembly Building in Charlottetown.

USA
   The files of the New York Maritime Register, New York Public Library.

BRITAIN
   (1)   The Parish Records of Northam, Bideford, Clovelly, Chumleigh, Monkleigh, Great Torrington and Westleigh in Devon and Kilkhampton in Cornwall.
   (2)   The Archives of the Western Region of British Railways.
   (3)   Files in original of the *Western Luminary*, the *North Devon Journal*, the *Bideford Gazette* and *Lloyd's List* over the period 1816-1870 in the British Museum Newspaper Library at Colindale.
   (4)   The Seymour of Ragley papers in the County Record Office at Warwick.
   (5)   Crew lists, Registration documents, correspondence, etc. in the care of the Registrar General of Shipping and Seamen, Cardiff.
   (6)   Correspondence concerning Prince Edward Island in the Archives for the Society of the Propagation of the Gospel, London.
   (7)   Notes on Bideford by W. H. Rogers, typescript in Bideford Public Library.
   (8)   'Port of Bideford. Daily Account of Ships and Vessels Arrived and Sailed 10th June 1805-10th June 1813.' Bideford Borough Council Office.
   (9)   Lloyd's Surveyors' Reports on Bideford Shipping, National Maritime Museum, Greenwich.
   (10) The wills of Thomas Burnard, William Yeo and Thomas Chanter, Somerset House.
   (11) The letter books of the Port of Barnstaple.
   (12) The documents of Registration of Shipping at Bideford Custom House 1786-1850.

Numerous published works have been consulted, either to provide background information or for specific matters of detail. Among them are the following:

Three Centuries in the Island by A. H. Clark, Toronto, 1959.

The French Régime in Prince Edward Island by D. C. Harvey, Yale, 1926.

The Loyal Electors by D. C. Harvey, Transactions of the Royal Society of Canada, 1930.

Dishing the Reformers by D. C. Harvey, Transactions of the Royal Society of Canada, 1931.

Responsible Government in Prince Edward Island by W. Ross Livingstone, Iowa, 1931.

The Government of Prince Edward Island by Frank MacKinnon, Toronto, 1951.

Historical Notes re the Parish of Port Hill by T. R. Millman, Toronto, 1941.

The Parish of New London by T. R. Millman, Toronto, 1959.

Journeys to the Island of St John by D. C. Harvey, Toronto, 1955.

The Nightingale Scandal by Stanley Thomas, Bideford, 1959.

Cradled in the Waves by J. T. Croteau, Toronto, 1951.

Life and Labour in Newfoundland by C. R. Fay, Toronto, 1956.

Sailing Directions for the Bristol Channel published by James Imray, London, 1850.

The Great Migration by Edwin C. Guillet, Toronto, 1963.

The Atlantic Migration by Marcus Lee Hansen, New York, 1940.

The Developing Canadian Community by S. D. Clark, Toronto, 1962.

The Cod Fisheries by Harold A. Innis, Toronto, 1954.

The Place Names of Prince Edward Island by R. Douglas, Ottawa, 1925.

Historic Bedeque by George A. Leard, Bedeque, 1948.

Ships of Miramichi by Louise Manny, St John, N.B., 1960.

Ships of Kent County by Louise Manny, Sackville, N.B., 1949.

The Erie Canal by Walter D. Edmonds, The Munson-Williams-Proctor Institute, Utica, N.Y. State, 1960.

Architecture in Early New England by Abbott Lowell Cummings, Stourbridge, Mass, 1958.

The Country Stores of Early New England by Gerald Carson, Stourbridge, Mass, 1963.

The Living Sands by David M. Baird, Ottawa, 1962.

Some Pages from an Artist's Life, Charlottetown, 1919.

Shediac by John Clarence Webster, St John, N.B., 1953.

North Devon Pottery and its Export to America in the Seventeenth Century by C. Malcolm Watkins, Smithsonian Institution, Washington, 1960.

Wooden Ships and Iron Men by Frederick William Wallace, London, undated.

Forests and Sea Power by Robert Greenhalgh Albion, Cambridge, Mass, 1926.

Sails of the Maritimes by John Parker, North Sydney, N.S., 1961.

Catalogue of the National Watercraft Collection by Howard I. Chapelle, Smithsonian Institution, Washington, 1960.

The Charm and History of Instow by Alfred E. Blackwell, Instow, 1948.

An Essay towards a History of the County of Devon by John Watkins, Exeter, 1792.

The Rise of the English Shipping Industry by Ralph Davis, London, 1962.

English Merchant Shipping 1460-1540 by Dorothy Burwash, Toronto, 1947.

The Cruise of the Schooner Argus by Alan Villiers, New York, 1952.

Sir Richard Grenville of the Revenge by A. L. Rowse, London, 1937.

The Roanoke Voyages 1584-1590 edited by D. B. Quinn, London, 1955.

Devonians and New England Settlement before 1650 by R. D. Browne, Transactions of the Devonshire Association, Vol. XCV, Torquay, 1963.

The West Country Ports and the Struggle for the Newfoundland Fisheries in the Seventeenth Century by W. B. Stephens, Transactions of the Devonshire Association, Vol. LXXXVIII, Torquay, 1956.

Register of Blundell's School by Arthur Fisher, Exeter, 1864.

History of Northern New Brunswick by Robert Cooney, Halifax, N.S., 1832.

Various articles in the *Prince Edward Island Magazine, circa* 1900.

History of Prince Edward Island by Duncan Campbell, Charlottetown, 1875.

British Emigration to British North America by Helen I. Cowan, Toronto, 1961.

The Oldest Diary in Prince Edward Island by Ada MacLeod, The Dalhousie Review, undated.

An Account of Prince Edward Island by John Stewart, London, 1808.

Past and Present of Prince Edward Island by MacKinnon and Warburton, Charlottetown, *circa* 1906.

Devon by W. G. Hoskins, London, 1954.

The Epic of America by James Adams, New York, 1931.
Ships of the North Shore by Phyllis R. Blakeley and John R. Stevens, Halifax, N.S., 1963.
The Great Coal Schooners of New England by Captain W. J. L. Parker, USCG, Mystic, Conn, 1948.
From the Log Book of Memory by F. C. Hendry, Edinburgh, 1950.
Land and Sea by F. C. Hendry, Edinburgh, 1948.
The Industries of North Devon by Strang, Barnstaple, 1881.
On the Stowage of Ships and Their Cargoes by Robert White Stevens, Plymouth, 1869.
History of Bideford by Rev Roger Granville, M.A., Bideford, 1883.
The Vicar of Morwenstow by S. Baring-Gould, M.A., London, 1876.
A History of the United States by R. B. Nye and J. E. Morpurgo, London, 1955.
American Political and Social History by H. U. Faulkner, New York, 1937.
The Buildings of North Devon by Nicholas Pevsner, London, 1952.
Directory of Devonshire by William White, Sheffield, 1850.
White Men came to the St Lawrence by Morris Bishop, Montreal, 1961.
The Atlantic Provinces by W. S. MacNutt, Toronto, 1965.
History of the Ellis Family by Preston Ellis, Summerside, 1950 (from which the source material listed in this Appendix has led us respectfully to differ at many points).

ACKNOWLEDGMENTS

Plate 1: Mrs Cecil Oliver, Northam; *Plate 2:* Ashmolean Museum, Oxford; *Plates 3, 10, 20:* Basil Greenhill; *Plate 4:* Hutchings, Appledore; *Plates 5, 6, 24:* National Maritime Museum, Greenwich; *Plate 7:* Michael Bouquet collection; *Plate 8:* R. L. Knight Ltd., Barnstaple; *Plates 9 and 23:* Bideford Museum; *Plates 12, 14, 15, 26, 27, 30, 33:* The Public Archives of Canada; *Plate 16:* Shelburne Museum, Vermont; *Plates 11, 13, 17, 18, 19:* Meachams Illustrated Atlas & Public Archives of Canada; *Plate 21:* Gillis collection; *Plate 22:* Parkhouse, Appledore; *Plate 25:* Kenneth Richards, Charlottetown; *Plate 28:* The Mariners Museum, Newport News; *Plates 29, 31:* The Peabody Museum of Salem; *Plate 32:* Bristol Museum & Art Gallery; *Plate 34:* Warburton, Hull, Province of Quebec; *Plate 35:* Collingwood Yeo, Lot 13; *Plate 36:* Trustees of the Robert Harris Memorial Gallery, Charlottetown.

INDEX

Illustration pages are indicated by italics

243